"This is an important book and should be rea
understanding post-2011 Singapore. The authors, Donald Low and Sudhir
Vadaketh, are two of our most original thinkers."
—Tommy Koh, Ambassador-at-Large, Ministry of Foreign
Affairs, Singapore

"These wide-ranging, diverse, and richly stimulating essays deserve to be read
by anyone seriously interested in Singapore's future. The arguments against
presumed vulnerability and chaotic populism as reasons for elitist illiberal
rule will be contested. The book's own title predicts as much. But if they are,
so much the better; especially if their public airing serves to hasten salutary
reforms."
—Donald K. Emmerson, Director, Southeast Asia Forum,
Stanford University

"This is a thoughtful collection of essays on recent political developments in
Singapore that raises penetrating questions and offers plausible answers. The
authors brilliantly pull together a variety of seemingly unrelated developments to highlight systemic patterns that deserve attention and response. It is
a must-read for anyone interested in politics and public policy in Singapore."
—M Ramesh, Professor, Lee Kuan Yew School of Public Policy,
National University of Singapore

# Hard Choices: Challenging the Singapore Consensus

# HARD CHOICES

Challenging the Singapore Consensus

Donald Low and Sudhir Thomas Vadaketh
with contributions from
Linda Lim and Thum Ping Tjin

NUS PRESS
SINGAPORE

© Donald Low and Sudhir Thomas Vadaketh

Published by: NUS Press
National University of Singapore
AS3-01-02, 3 Arts Link
Singapore 117569
Fax: (65) 6774-0652
E-mail: nusbooks@nus.edu.sg
Website: http://www.nus.edu.sg/nuspress

ISBN: 978-9971-69-816-4 (Paper)

First edition 2014
Reprint 2015

National Library Board, Singapore Cataloguing-in-Publication Data

Low, Donald.

Hard choices : challenging the Singapore consensus / Donald Low and Sudhir Thomas Vadaketh, with contributions from Linda Lim and Thum Ping Tjin. – Singapore : NUS Press, 2014.

pages cm

ISBN : 978-9971-69-816-4 (paperback)

1. Political planning – Singapore.  2.  Singapore – Politics and government.  I. Vadaketh, Sudhir Thomas.  II. Lim, Linda.  III. Thum, Ping Tjin.  IV. Title.

JQ1063

320.95957  – dc23                                    OCN 871013072

Cover image: Chun Kai Feng, "It Seemed Like A Good Idea at the Time" (2012).

Image courtesy of: FOST Gallery, Singapore.

Cover design by: Nelani Jinadasa

Typeset by: PressBooks.com

Printed by: Markono Print Media Pte Ltd

# CONTENTS

# PREFACE

Singapore's economic success masks some uncomfortable truths about life in this city-state. While per capita GDP has risen astronomically (by some estimates, it is the highest in the world today), Singapore is also one of the most unequal societies among developed economies. Incomes at the bottom are relatively low by rich country standards. Meanwhile for many Singaporeans, the country's impressive material achievements have not necessarily translated into higher levels of happiness. In various surveys, Singaporeans are found to work some of the longest hours in the developed world, are described as one of the world's least happy peoples, and more than half indicate they would emigrate if given the chance.

And perhaps for the first time in the country's history, citizens have given political expression to their dissatisfaction. Singapore's general and presidential elections in 2011 mark a significant turning point in the country's political history. For many, it heralded the end of dominance by the only party—the People's Action Party (PAP) —that Singaporeans have elected into office since the country gained self-government in 1959. Although it is still by far the largest party in parliament, the decade-long erosion of popular support for the PAP (it won 75.3 per cent of the vote in the 2001 general election compared with just 60.1 per cent in the 2011 election) suggests that the era of mostly unchallenged political dominance is over. The presidential election of August 2011, in which the PAP's preferred candidate secured a plurality of just 35.2 per cent of the popular vote in a four-man contest, is further evidence of the party's weakening grip on the Singapore polity.

The by-election defeats in 2012 (Hougang) and 2013 (Punggol East) cemented perceptions of the PAP losing ground ineluctably. More importantly, a number of highly contentious issues, both new and old, have emerged since the 2011 elections. Events in 2013 have provided establishment critics in Singapore with plenty of fodder: the widespread unhappiness over the government's Population White Paper in January 2013, the adverse reactions to the government's new rules on online news sites, questions about the sustainability of the country's growth model and its high reliance on foreign labour, continuing frustration with the public transport system and its frequent breakdowns, and concerns over the government's tendency to resort to hard-ball measures to deal with political opponents and dissenters. As this book was going to press, a riot on 8 December 2013 reportedly involving 400 foreign workers from South Asia shocked Singaporeans (and foreign observers) and raised deeper questions about the prosperous city-state's relationship with its large contingent of foreign workers.

The PAP has sought to respond to these societal, economic, and political changes. It has mounted a serious effort to change, reform, and even abandon policies that are viewed as a source of public unhappiness. New social spending measures targeted at lower- and middle-income Singaporeans have been emphasised in the government's recent budget statements. A year-long public consultation exercise ("Our Singapore Conversation") resulted in a raft of measures in the areas of housing, education, and healthcare announced by the Prime Minister at the National Day Rally in August 2013. These measures, the government contends, mark an important shift in the way the Singapore state shares risks with citizens, and how the government builds an inclusive society.

At the same time, the reforms announced since the 2011 elections are noteworthy for what they do *not* include. Commentators have pointed to the dearth of reforms that would expand the democratic space in Singapore. Some, including contributors to this book, have also argued that the PAP's old verities of vulnerability, meritocracy, elite governance, economic growth, and technocratic rationalism have remained mostly intact. That the changes announced so far have been entirely in the policy realm also suggests that the PAP remains much more concerned with shoring up its performance legitimacy than with expanding the state's basis of legitimacy to include the liberal ideas of voice and representation, transparency, and political freedoms. It has probably assessed that Singaporeans care more about the material benefits of its rule, and that its hold on power still relies on the production of economic benefits for the majority of Singaporeans.

While the PAP's strategy of focussing on material benefits may well be sufficient in slowing or even reversing the electoral slide in the near-term, we believe that it is ultimately a limited strategy because it underestimates how diverse, heterogeneous, and politically contested the Singaporean polity has become. The policy changes the government pursues will invariably produce winners and losers. Without a wider debate over the kind of society and economy Singapore should become in the future—and without an acceptance of the unavoidable contests of political values and ideologies that will increasingly characterise Singapore's political future—a strategy of appeasing Singaporeans' angst over bread-and-butter issues will always be a self-limiting one.

Perhaps the clearest expression of how the Singaporean polity has changed is the erosion of the largely unquestioned trust that the PAP government enjoyed in decades past. The mostly benign political context allowed a technocratic government to think beyond the next election and craft policies that may have been unpopular in the short-term, but today it is confronted with a more rambunctious political landscape. In this political "new normal", the government finds it much harder to set the terms of the debate, especially when many of its underlying beliefs and principles are no longer automatically accepted by the electorate. Whereas dissent and criticism were quite muted for much of Singapore's history after the mid-1960s, a new generation of Singaporeans—empowered by the internet and social media—has emerged in the last decade to openly question many of the PAP's long-held assumptions and beliefs.

At the heart of these political changes is a deeper and more profound shift. The debates in Singapore do not simply reflect technical disagreements over different policies and policy approaches. Rather, they also occur over the assumptions, values, beliefs, and ultimate goals that underpin policies. These debates suggest that the "Singapore consensus" that the PAP government constructed and maintained in the last five decades is fraying, partly because many perceive it to be outdated. The assumptions of Singapore exceptionalism—the argument that the country's situation is so uniquely vulnerable that it has limited policy and political options, that good governance demands a degree of political consensus that ordinary democratic arrangements cannot produce, and that sustaining the country's success requires a competitive meritocracy accompanied by relatively little income or wealth redistribution—are far more challenged and contested today.

These contests of ideas and ideologies will become increasingly important and, we believe, necessary as Singaporeans move beyond the old beliefs of vulnerability and exceptionalism. While a single collection of essays cannot provide all the policy and institutional answers (or even ask all the right questions) necessary for a far more contested Singapore, we hope it provides a sufficient range of alternatives. We argue that more than ever, Singapore's success depends on the competition of policy and political ideas. Success can no longer come from a tiny, enlightened group of elites—if it ever did. Instead, it has to be grounded in the distributed intelligence of Singaporeans, and honed by the practices of democratic debate and deliberation. Historically, this has also been the experience of other small, developed countries. One thinks of Switzerland, the Nordic countries such as Denmark, Finland, and Sweden, and Israel as countries that over time have developed deeply democratic practices and institutions in spite of their challenging contexts. Consensus in these countries is usually the result of debate and compromise, mediated through the democratic process, rather than imposed from above by an all-powerful state.

That a democracy can become dysfunctional, get captured by interest groups, be corrupted by money, or degenerate into demagoguery and populism is neither surprising nor unusual. But in Singapore's context, we believe that a more fruitful line of inquiry would be to ask how we can create the conditions for Singapore to become a healthy, thriving democracy that protects—institutionally—the contest of ideas and ideologies. In this spirit, the essays in this book do not just address the substance of government (i.e., policy alternatives), but also the *system of governance* (i.e., how the government makes decisions, encourages a wider range of ideas, and allows debate and dissent to flourish).

Many of the essays in this volume have been published on other publicly available platforms, either in the print media or online, in the last few years. Some readers may find the difference in styles across the essays jarring. We made a deliberate decision to retain the authors' original styles and to edit the essays as lightly as possible. We felt that such an editorial approach would allow us to be true to the authors' original intents and convey the crux of the arguments they made at the time the original essays were written. But we were also cognisant of the fact that the fast-changing policy and political context in Singapore might render some of their arguments less salient or relevant now than when the essays were first written. Hence, we have provided the dates and references of the original essays in the endnotes of each chapter.

We hope that a diverse collection of essays on the policy and political reforms Singapore needs, framed as alternatives to the Singapore consensus and the dominant beliefs of the PAP government, will provoke fresh insights and questions. At the heart of this is our belief that anyone invested in this country's future should question the Singapore consensus—not only as a means of delivering progress, but also the very ends it seeks and the values it represents. Above all, we hope that this collection gives readers a deeper appreciation of the challenges that confront Singapore and of the real alternatives we should consider.

Donald Low and Sudhir Thomas Vadaketh
23 December 2013

# ACKNOWLEDGMENTS

This book would not have been possible without a great deal of help from many people. Most importantly, we would like to thank Linda Lim and Thum Ping Tjin for their contributions. Their essays add immeasurably to the diversity of this book and expanded significantly the range of expert opinion represented here. Peter Schoppert, the Director of NUS Press, provided invaluable advice throughout the entire process—from how the book should be positioned to how the arguments in each of the chapters could be refined and enhanced. We are grateful for his expert guidance.

Below are the individual authors' own words of appreciation:

**Donald Low:** I am indebted to my colleagues at the Lee Kuan Yew School of Public Policy for allowing me the space and time to work on this book, and for being a source of good advice. I am especially grateful to Kishore Mahbubani, Kanti Prasad Bajpai, Kenneth Paul Tan, M Ramesh, Dodo Thampapillai, Hui Weng Tat, Wu Xun, Norman and Susan Fainstein, Eduardo Araral and Peggy Kek. My comrades at the Economic Society of Singapore—Manu Bhaskaran, Yeoh Lam Keong, and Tan Kim Song—provided me intellectual comradeship; David Skilling can always be counted on to offer honest counsel; and my students at the LKY School continually inspire me with their curiosity and energy. I am also thankful for the advice given by Jeremy Lim and Devadas Krishnadas—like me, former civil servants who have written about public policy and governance in Singapore. Many of my former colleagues in the Singapore government continue to engage me; they would prefer not to be named here, but I am very grateful for their encouragement.

**Sudhir Thomas Vadaketh:** I am grateful to the following people for providing comments and suggestions that helped with the essays in this volume: Farah Cheah, Sharon Siddique, Laurel West, Andrew Loh, Simon Long, Sumana Rajarethnam, and Justin Wood. For sharing broader insights into Singapore that have helped shape my understanding of the issues discussed here, I would like to thank Chia Soo Hui, Jen Wei Ting, Phua Mei Pin, Karishma Vaswani, Prem Anand, Manu Bhaskaran, Andre Cheah, Richard Cockett, Farouk Khan, Ler Kuang Yuan, Lien We King, Ron Luhur, Harveen Narulla, Quek Yong Hai, Allanjit Singh, Terry Smagh, and Tan Kane Juan. Most importantly, for their undying moral support of my writing career, I must thank my wife and mum.

There are many other people who provided commentary, feedback and quotes for my pieces, but for various reasons prefer to remain anonymous. I am indebted to all of you. Finally, at a larger level, I would like to thank all the Singaporeans—activists, artists, business-people, citizens, journalists and politicians—who have, through their own actions, resisted the tyranny of national groupthink, and consistently encouraged Donald and I to complete this book. It is, we can only hope, another small step in a long journey towards a more diverse civil and political society.

# CONTRIBUTORS

**Donald Low** is Associate Dean for executive education and research at the Lee Kuan Yew School of Public Policy, National University of Singapore. Prior to joining the School in 2012, Donald served for more than 14 years in various parts of the Singapore government. He was the director for fiscal policy in the Ministry of Finance in 2004–05 and the director of the Strategic Policy Office at the Public Service Division in 2006–07. In 2008, he established the Centre for Public Economics at the Civil Service College of Singapore to advance economics thinking in the Singapore government, and headed the centre for its first three years, putting in place its training and research programmes.

At the Lee Kuan Yew School, Donald's research interests include inequality and social spending, behavioural economics, economics in public policy, public finance, and governance and politics in Singapore. He is also the co-author and editor of *Behavioural Economics and Policy Design: Examples from Singapore* (2011), which describes how the Singapore government has applied ideas from behavioural economics in the design of public policies.

Donald holds a double first in Politics, Philosophy and Economics from Oxford University, and a Masters in International Public Policy from Johns Hopkins University's School of Advanced International Studies. He is also a Vice President at the Economics Society of Singapore.

**Sudhir Thomas Vadaketh** is an author whose first book is *Floating on a Malayan Breeze: Travels in Malaysia and Singapore* (2012), a socioeconomic narrative of the two countries. His literary and research interests are about the way political and socio-economic systems influence ordinary people's lives, their worldviews, and their interactions with each other.

From 2006 to 2013, Sudhir worked for The Economist Group in Singapore. As associate director of the Economist Corporate Network, he analysed the macroeconomic, political, and business environments of Asian economies, with a particular focus on Southeast Asia. Later, as senior editor of Industry and Management Research, he oversaw the analysis and writing of numerous global research projects, including the global city competitiveness index and an international ranking of preschool environments.

Sudhir has a BA (Geography), BA (South and Southeast Asian studies) and a BSc (Business Administration) from the University of California at Berkeley; and a Masters in Public Policy from the Harvard Kennedy School. He has written for a variety of publications, including *The Economist, The Economist Intelligence Unit (EIU), The Straits Times* and *Yahoo! News.*

**Dr Linda Lim** is Professor of Strategy at the Stephen M. Ross School of Business at the University of Michigan, where she also served as director of the 53-year-old Center for Southeast Asian Studies. With economics degrees from the universities of Cambridge (BA), Yale (MA) and Michigan (PhD), Linda has been studying and writing about Singapore's economy for 37 years, with academic articles ranging from "Singapore's Success: The Myth of the Free Market Economy" (*Asian Survey,* 1983) to "Singapore's Success: After the Miracle" (*Routledge Handbook of Emerging Economies,* 2013). A specialist on Asian economies and business, she has consulted for multinational companies with Asian investments and for international agencies such as the United Nations and The Organisation for Economic Co-Operation and Development (OECD), particularly in the areas of trade, investment, and government industrial and labour market policy. In addition to teaching MBA students about the world economy and business in Asia, she has trained business executives and government officials. A Trustee Emeritus of The Asia Society, a New York-based nonprofit, she has served for 15 years (sequentially) as an independent director of two US public companies with technology manufacturing and regional headquarter operations in China and Singapore.

**Dr Thum Ping Tjin** is Research Fellow at the Asia Research Institute, National University of Singapore; co-ordinator of Project Southeast Asia, University of Oxford; and a visiting fellow at the Centre of Global History, University of Oxford. He works on the history of decolonisation in Southeast Asia and its continuing impact on contemporary Southeast Asian politics, society, and culture, with particular emphasis on plural societies from the vernacular and subaltern perspective.

His recent publications include "Chinese newspapers in Singapore, 1945–63: Mediators of elite and popular tastes in culture and politics", in the *Journal of the Malaysian Branch of the Royal Asiatic Society* 83, part 1 (June 2010); "'Living Buddha': Chinese perspectives on David Marshall and his government, 1955–56," *Indonesia and the Malay World* 38, no. 113 (July 2011); two chapters in *Studying Singapore's Past: CM Turnbull and the History of Modern Singapore* (NUS Press, 2012); and "Flesh and Bone Reunite as One Body: Singapore's Chinese Speaking and their Perspectives on Merger," *Chinese Southern Diaspora Studies* 5 (2011–12): 29–56.

# INTRODUCTION

*Reframing Policy and Political Debates in Singapore*

*Donald Low and Sudhir Thomas Vadaketh*

Singapore is in the midst of a profound economic and sociopolitical transition. This began around the turn of the century and accelerated after the 2011 General Election (GE 2011). A number of global and domestic forces are converging to create a different political and policy landscape in Singapore—a "new normal" in the words of Dr Tony Tan, Singapore's president, just before his election in August 2011. These forces are changing the nature of governance and policymaking in Singapore in unpredictable ways, making it harder for the People's Action Party (PAP) government to sustain good governance based on its current assumptions, beliefs, and worldviews.

In the last 20 years or so, globalisation and the rise of neoliberal market ideologies around the world have shaped and influenced policy making in Singapore far more so than in countries that are less open to global trade, ideas and immigration. The emergence of a number of large, newly liberalising economies in Asia has also heightened the sense of competition in Singapore, raising questions about how the city-state will stay relevant in a world likely to be dominated by economic giants. The primacy of growth, long embraced as government dogma, gained renewed urgency and saliency in the 2000s in the context of fast-growing emerging economies in Asia, more frequent macroeconomic shocks, and constant reminders of a global war for talent and investments.

Recent economic developments seem to bear out policymakers' fear that unless Singapore maintains its long-standing emphasis on economic growth, it risks losing relevance in a more competitive, uncertain and volatile world. In the last 15 years, the economy experienced more externally induced shocks and slowdowns than in the 30 years prior. Much of this is due to Singapore's increasing connectedness with the global economy, to volatile and fickle capital flows, and to rapid technological changes that shorten business cycles.

On the political front, the digital and telecommunication revolution of the last 30 years—particularly the near universal access Singaporeans now have to mobile telephony, the internet, and social media—has dramatically altered state-society relations in Singapore. It has challenged the long-standing notion that establishment elites in the country know best, and has provided highly accessible (and widely accessed) platforms on which citizens can question, scrutinise and criticise those in power. Government-controlled media channels have seen their influence wane in the face of a mushrooming blogosphere. Citizens' views are spread and amplified through the densely connected networks of social media, producing information cascades and shaping mass perceptions far more quickly than traditional media channels can.

In this environment, it is hardly surprising that the authorities in Singapore sometimes bemoan the passing of an era when they were largely insulated from the criticisms on a wide range of issues they are subject to today. They warn also about the dangers of polarisation and populism, and raise the spectre of paralysis in government if Singaporeans cannot forge a consensus on the critical challenges confronting the country.

These political trends have interacted with socioeconomic forces—the ageing population, rising inequality, stagnating wages, decreasing social mobility, and a growing foreign population—to create stresses on social cohesion and Singapore's political consensus; greater demands for democratic accountability, representation, and participation; and higher expectations for a more redistributive state.

In the new normal created by these forces and the elections of the last three years, the Singapore government's space for manoeuvre has narrowed considerably. Its widely admired solutions in a number of areas—housing, education, healthcare, social security, transport and infrastructure—have come under greater public scrutiny and criticism in recent years. These have also become vastly more contested compared with just a decade ago.

Meanwhile, Singaporeans' trust in the government's ability to deliver can no longer be assumed. The hithero pristine "policy lab" that Singapore's policymakers used to operate in is today being monitored by a more critical and sceptical public, and by a more diverse polity with potentially competing and conflicting interests.[1] Increasingly, Singapore's policymakers have to make *hard choices*—where there are winners and losers—and not just remind themselves of the hard truths that have enabled independent Singapore to succeed in its first 40 years. Indeed, as the essays in this book try to show, there is a wide range of credible policy and political alternatives that could and should be considered.

Maintaining good governance in this new normal is not impossible, but it will require significant institutional, democratic, and policy reforms on the part of the government. These reforms will be critical as Singaporeans debate and renegotiate the principles of governance that have, until recently, been largely taken for granted.

## Principles of Governance Revisited

Many of the policy debates in Singapore in recent years reflect deeper, more fundamental disagreements over the normative beliefs, principles and desired outcomes that underpin Singapore's public policies. The disagreements, say, over economic restructuring, social spending or population policy, are not just over *how* government should achieve its outcomes but the outcomes themselves. The principles and beliefs that public policies are founded on, as well as the meanings attached to those principles, are also increasingly being questioned and challenged.

Consider meritocracy, perhaps the most crucial principle of governance, so vital and fundamental that it was one of the reasons Singapore separated from Malaysia. For the PAP government, meritocracy has an egalitarian streak: it gives everyone a fair shot at success and ensures that a person's position in life will not be determined by his or her race, parentage or lineage, and social connections. Yet, in the context of rising inequality and concerns over declining social mobility, many Singaporeans now perceive the meritocratic system as being less fair and just than before. Rightly or wrongly, they view meritocracy as thinly-veiled justification for elitism, and the reason for the state's indifference towards equality and redistribution.

Part of this dissatisfaction with meritocracy is a reaction to growing inequalities of income and more conspicuous displays of wealth in Singapore. But it is also driven by the government's constant harping on how the talented should not be held back by policies, or shackled by onerous regulations, how they are the ones who create jobs and prosperity for the rest, and how if their taxes were raised, they would leave Singapore to the detriment of the greater good. With rising inequality and the perception that elitism is sanctioned by the state, it is hardly surprising that a defence of meritocracy on the grounds of trickle-down economics will grate on the nerves of many Singaporeans, including some who have benefited from the very meritocratic system they decry.

Or consider the critique of a second deeply-held principle of governance: vulnerability and elite governance. The political establishment in Singapore has largely defined the Singapore condition as one of inherent, permanent, and immutable vulnerability. Given Singapore's vulnerabilities of size, geography, its neighbourhood, the country's lack of natural resources and its ethnic make-up, it is commonly argued that the country's survival depends on a strong, exceptional government composed of the best and brightest in the country (they are compensated at levels comparable to the highest incomes in the country). The vulnerabilities that Singapore is saddled with have also been used to justify a wide range of restraints on the democratic freedoms one normally finds in countries at similar levels of development and with similarly large middle classes.

One can, of course, question the correctness and validity of this vulnerability narrative. At a public lecture he delivered at the Lee Kuan Yew School of Public Policy in 2011, Thomas Friedman, a columnist at *The New York Times*, was asked what he thought were Singapore's key strengths. His reply: that it is small (and so can be very agile and flexible, and can forge political consensus more easily), and that it has no natural resources (and so will never suffer from the complacency or the resource curse that has blighted many resource-rich countries). Vulnerability is not necessarily an objective fact; it is just as much a matter of perspective, and may even be a social construct created by those in power.

Nonetheless, Singaporeans have largely accepted this vulnerability story for decades. They have also bought into the basic trade-off offered by the PAP government: if they want growth and rising living standards, they have to forgo some of their democratic rights and freedoms. Being exceptional in the Singapore government's view does not simply mean achieving excellence or good governance. It also means accepting that Singapore is not normal, that citizens cannot enjoy the same rights and freedoms enjoyed by the citizens of normal democracies, or have the same levels of social protection. The term "new normal" should be contrasted not with the "old normal", but with the "old *abnormal*". For many decades, Singaporeans' acceptance of the old abnormal reflected their grudging acceptance of a national ideology emphasising Singapore's inherent vulnerabilities, and the constraints this imposed on democracy, civil liberties, and social protection.

In the post-2011 new normal, the previously unquestioned logic of vulnerability and exceptionalism is increasingly being challenged. At one level, what this means is that there is no longer the presumption that "the government knows best" or that trust in the government should be given by default or unquestioningly. Part of the growing disillusionment with the government is due to the policy failings of the last decade (in immigration and foreign worker policies, housing, transport etc.), but perhaps a larger part is the consequence of citizens' greater global exposure, in turn made possible by rising educational attainment, the digital revolution, and the democratisation of information.

If this is correct, it suggests that the Singaporeans who are least likely to accept the ruling elite's basic ideologies are also the most educated, the most globalised, and the most mobile of its citizens—indeed, the ones who have benefitted most from successful governance in Singapore. This is perhaps the main paradox of the new normal in Singapore: upper- and middle-class liberals who have benefitted the most from the PAP's long hold on power are also the segment of society most likely to challenge and question its stories and ideologies.

A third long-cherished principle of governance that has come under greater scrutiny and criticism in recent years is the state's reliance on economic incentives as the primary instrument of governance. A common gripe in Singapore is how everything the government does is framed and justified in narrow monetary terms. This is a government that takes the economist's policy prescriptions —of getting incentives right, of using cost-benefit analysis—seriously.

There are various objections to the extensive reliance on incentives as a policy lever, but two are commonly highlighted. The first is it reduces citizens' relations with the state to a purely monetary transaction. Rather than foster citizenship, commonality and identity, the relationship between state and citizens breeds a "what-the-state-owes-me" mentality. It reinforces the impression that the role of government in Singapore is to dispense patronage and secure people's compliance through economic incentives.

The second objection is that the current approach is highly individualised rather than universal. Singapore's social spending has become more narrowly targeted at lower-income citizens through means-testing. An individual's income and socioeconomic status matter a great deal in determining the benefits he or she gets from the state. In contrast to the more universal approaches taken by the Singapore government in the past—in public housing, public healthcare and education, recent policy changes have tended to stress *targeting*, surgically directing financial aid to those who need it most.

While this approach makes sense from a fiscal and efficiency perspective, it also breeds a calculative, zero-sum, "your-gain-is-my-loss" mentality. It makes the Singapore system of taxes and transfers a potentially divisive and exclusionary one, rather than one that builds trust, solidarity, and a sense that "we're all in this together". When society was already becoming more unequal in the 2000s, the fiscal system increasingly emphasised individual entitlement, differentiation and targeting, instead of social protection and risk pooling, universalism, and solidarity.

## The Resilience Imperative[2]

So how should a government respond to an operating environment in which many of its long-standing assumptions and beliefs are being challenged, often in unexpected and disruptive ways? In such a context, perhaps the most valuable asset a government can have is resilience. Resilience is the capacity of a system to bounce back, not necessarily to its original form, but to a state that allows the system to maintain its core purpose and integrity and to continue performing its key functions.

Resilience—whether of an ecological system, an organisation, the internet, or a species—is a function of two things. First, a resilient system is one that has been exposed to a *variety* of shocks. Each of these shocks is not large enough to destroy the system but over time force the system to adapt and develop diverse capabilities to respond to a wider range of shocks and stimuli. Conversely, systems that are fragile are those that have been insulated from external shocks or protected from competition for long periods. This is why, for example, the Galapagos Islands are so fragile ecologically, even if they are highly stable as long as they remain undisturbed in their current pristine state.

The US financial crisis of 2007–09 is another example of how a lack of diversity creates a fragile economic system. The health of banks became increasingly tied to the availability of cheap credit, rising house prices, and the willingness of home owners to continually refinance their mortgages. Financial institutions mostly pursued a strategy of originating and then securitising sub-prime mortgages. The result was too much mimicry and insufficient variety in the financial system. Such monoculture systems can exhibit long periods of stability but are also extremely vulnerable to specific shocks, no matter how slight. The collapse of Lehman Brothers had such far-reaching consequences, not because it was a particularly large investment bank, but because of its connectivity within the financial system. And because many other institutions were doing the same thing, there was a great deal of "interlocking fragility;"[3] such that when Lehman collapsed, the entire banking system became highly vulnerable.

The second essential ingredient of a resilient system is *selection*. Resilient systems all have some mechanism for "choosing" between competing, alternative strategies or designs. We normally think of the selection process as being undertaken by individuals or leaders. But selection by distributed, decentralised, and impersonal forces such as market competition is likely to be more reliable in the long run. Markets are resilient because they encourage variety and diversity, and because they provide strong signals for firms to select "fit" strategies or designs, and then replicate and scale them up. This is why the economist William Baumol describes markets as "innovation machines."[4]

It is extremely tempting for the human mind to respond to uncertainty and complexity with a greater desire for control, harmony, and stability. But the reality is that the complete avoidance of shocks and failures is a utopian dream. More problematically, insulation from competition and shocks weakens the signals for the system to adapt, and breeds strategic brittleness and fragility. In the long run, such insulation leads to instability and the system's eventual collapse.

This resilience perspective can also be applied to the study of governance. If we agree that what governments need most in the context of rapid and disruptive change is resilience, then we would also agree that they need to ensure sufficient diversity and variety, and develop selection processes that are not reliant on a few individuals making the right calls. A political system can also suffer from too much mimicry, and have too little diversity to allow for the experimentation and adaptation that is needed for long-term survival. Without sufficient diversity, a political system can become trapped by groupthink and ideological rigidity.

Amid rapid global and domestic transformations, this resilience perspective ought to replace the vulnerability and elite governance perspective that Singapore's government and society at large have traditionally relied on. Rather than emphasise our vulnerability and how it imposes constraints on what Singapore can do or be, and why we need to rely on elites, resilience thinking broadens our discussion on governance. It invites us to think about what policy alternatives are available to us, what institutional shock absorbers we need in a more volatile world, and how we can achieve a better and more equitable allocation of risks between the state and citizens. It also encourages the government to explore how it can tap on the distributed intelligence of citizens, and how democratic practices and institutions can bolster Singaporeans' trust in the government and their confidence in the country's future.

## A Greater Diversity of Ideas

The resilience perspective to governance and public policy is at the heart of this compilation of essays that aims to do two things. The first is to put together, in a single volume, a wide array of practical alternatives that have emerged in the country's political discourse since GE 2011. As Singapore's operating context becomes more complex and unpredictable, the *variety* of policy and institutional options that the government should consider has to increase correspondingly. A more complex, plural and heterogeneous polity demands a commensurate increase in the range, sophistication, and diversity of ideas that the country considers. Indeed, not only should there be a greater variety of ideas in the substantive sense, this diversity should also apply to the *sources* of ideas that the government draws from and the *processes* it relies on to generate options and alternatives.

The essays here are not intended to be exhaustive or comprehensive. Neither do they cover the entire range of contentious issues that have emerged in the post-2011 landscape. Instead, the essays were chosen to provide a broad sample of the alternatives that are widely discussed and debated outside establishment circles. They are intended to provide policymakers, analysts, students of the Singapore government, and the general public an understanding of the range of policy and institutional alternatives that are available *if* we are prepared to broaden our minds.

In so doing, we question the implicit but widely-held belief that Singapore has very few choices when it comes to politics, governance, and public policy. While the authors of the essays in this volume do not agree on every issue, one of the things they do agree on is that Singapore has many more viable and workable alternatives than the PAP government has presented; rather than the TINA ("there is no alternative"), we firmly believe in TARA ("there are real alternatives").

## Reframing our Debates

The second aim of this compilation of essays is to *reframe* policy, governance, and political debates in Singapore. More often than not, these debates in Singapore have been framed in ways designed to justify the status quo and discourage a deeper, more robust discussion of the possible alternatives. As cognitive psychologists have long observed, how an issue is framed to an audience—whether it is presented as a loss or a gain, whether it appeals to people's tendency to focus narrowly on memorable or recent events, or whether it "anchors" people on the status quo and so increases the fear of regret and aversion to change—can be extremely consequential in determining how one responds.

One of the main contentions of this book is that policy and political debates in Singapore are stunted and held back by the government's often narrow, stark, and binary framing of issues. Take for instance the notion that Singapore should not be a welfare state. The government typically frames the welfare state as a system that encourages collective sloth and dependence on the state, undermines the work ethic and individual and familial responsibility, and erodes national vigour and economic competitiveness. But a careful study of welfare states around the world does not support such a stark conclusion. There is little evidence to show that a country's economic growth prospects or its competitiveness are influenced by the size of the welfare state or levels of social spending. Neither is there much evidence to suggest that innovation or productivity levels are lower in developed countries with higher welfare spending.

Much of the discourse surrounding "welfare" in Singapore reflects the PAP's ideology rather than a comprehensive study of its adverse economic impacts in other countries. This is not to say that welfare systems *cannot* have any serious disincentive effects, only to point out that welfare states have often adapted and found ways of designing incentive-compatible policies that do not produce the perverse, undesired consequences commonly cited by the PAP government.

One way of reframing the debates is to embrace the resilience perspective discussed earlier in this introduction, and consciously ask ourselves what this might mean for public policies and institutions in Singapore. For instance, it is commonly asserted that given the country's size, its limited talent pool and its inherent vulnerabilities, Singapore needs leaders of great ability and high integrity, individuals who will do what is right, not what is popular. While most Singaporeans probably accept these statements unquestioningly, applying a resilience frame—as opposed to just a vulnerability frame—changes the nature of the discussion. While Singaporeans might still say that good leadership matters, we are also now more likely to agree that good and durable institutions matter too, and probably matter more in the long run. This is partly because while leadership is highly context-dependent, good institutions work in a variety of contexts.

Just as importantly, the singular emphasis on good leadership goes against the grain of the earlier argument that what determines resilience is not a single wise man or a small group of knowledgeable elites. Rather, it is by ensuring sufficient variety and diversity in the system that a society or economy becomes more resilient. In the long run, we are better off relying on a system of distributed intelligence—with a diversity of competing ideas and options—than one that is critically dependent on a small group of people, no matter how intelligent they may be.

Government leaders have, in the recent past, often expressed concern about how increasing political polarisation might paralyse the government. The authors of the essays here are more worried about how the desire for control, order, and stability might weaken the already weak incentives in Singapore's governance system to allow competing ideas to surface, and to subject these ideas to careful consideration and serious analysis. We are less worried about the risks of polarisation than we are about the effects of incumbency, the inertia of the status quo, and the tyranny of old ideas and unquestioned, unchallenged ideologies.

## The Essays

This compilation has three parts. The first, "The Limits of Singapore Exceptionalism", contains essays that question and interrogate many of the PAP government's long-standing beliefs: Singapore's inherent vulnerability, meritocracy, the primacy of growth, the indifference towards inequality, and the reflexive aversion to welfare. These beliefs are at the heart of what makes governance in Singapore exceptional; they also underpin many of Singapore's public policies. We also argue that these beliefs are increasingly at odds with the PAP government's own ambitions for the country and how Singapore society and its economy are changing.

For instance, the government's aspirations for Singapore to be an entrepreneurial and innovation-driven economy collide with the institutions, policies, and practices in government that inhibit risk-taking, experimentation, collaboration, and the cultivation of egalitarian social norms—all of which are critical for a creative economy. The state's prioritisation of growth over distribution and its aversion to welfare are also ill-suited for an ageing population, slower economic growth, rising income inequality and wage stagnation. Its global city ambitions bump up against an emerging Singaporean identity. Many of the beliefs that made Singapore's governance exceptional—although mostly useful in the first 40 years since Independence— are increasingly out of sync with current and future realities and with the aspirations of Singaporeans.

The second part, "Policy Alternatives for Post-Consensus Singapore", examines a wide range of policies that should be rethought and reformulated *if* one accepts the argument that the contradictions and limits of Singapore exceptionalism are holding the country back. In this section, we ask how policies in a few policy domains—specifically population, housing, and social security—should be reformed. Much of the government's discourse after 2011 has centred on how its (essentially) sound policies need to be better communicated and explained to the populace. The essays in this section question the premise that these policies are still sound in light of changing economic, social, and political realities. These essays also try to reframe Singapore's policy choices by examining many of the assumptions and ideologies that underpin current policies. Such a reframing suggests that Singapore has many more viable policy options than the PAP government has tended to present.

The third section, "Governance and Democracy: Past, Present, Future," explores the historical narratives, ideological blinkers, and cognitive biases of the ruling party, and how these have narrowed the range of alternatives the government considers and shrunk the space for policy debates in Singapore. We conclude with thoughts on how the Singapore state might evolve in light of the significant economic and sociopolitical changes it is going through. We also present a liberal agenda for the Singapore state, and speculate how democratic change might occur in Singapore.

## Notes

1. Singapore's Prime Minister once described the country's civil servants as "practis[ing] public administration in laboratory conditions," referring to the environment that supports "Singapore's ability to take a longer view, pursue rational policies, put in place the

fundamentals which the country needs, and systematically change policies that are outdated or obsolete. Speech by Prime Minister Lee Hsien Loong at 2005 Admin Service Dinner, 24 Mar. 2005, http://app.psd.gov.sg/data/SpeechatAdminServiceDinner2005final.pdf.

2. Many of our thoughts on complexity, change and resilience draw on the work of complexity scientists. For more in this field, we highly recommend Eric Beinhocker, *The Origin of Wealth: Evolution, Complexity and the Radical Remaking of Economics* (Cambridge: Harvard Business School Press, 2006); Duncan Watts, *Six Degrees: The Science of a Connected Age* (New York: W. W. Norton & Company, 2004); and Andrew Zolli and Ann Marie Healy, *Resilience: Why Things Bounce Back* (New York: Free Press, 2012).

3. In *The Black Swan: The Impact of the Highly Improbable* (New York: Random House, 2007), Nassem Nicholas Taleb argues that "[g]lobalization creates interlocking fragility, while reducing volatility and giving the appearance of stability. In other words it creates devastating Black Swans. We have never lived before under the threat of a global collapse. Financial institutions have been merging into a smaller number of very large banks. Almost all banks are interrelated. So the financial ecology is swelling into gigantic, incestuous, bureaucratic banks—when one fails, they all fall. The increased concentration among banks seems to have the effect of making financial crisis less likely, but when they happen they are more global in scale and hit us very hard. We have moved from a diversified ecology of small banks, with varied lending policies, to a more homogeneous framework of firms that all resemble one another. True, we now have fewer failures, but when they occur … I shiver at the thought."

4. William Baumol, *The Free Market Innovation Machine: Analyzing the Growth Miracle of Capitalism* (Princeton: Princeton University Press, 2002).

PART 1

# THE LIMITS OF SINGAPORE EXCEPTIONALISM

# 1

# THE FOUR MYTHS OF INEQUALITY IN SINGAPORE

*Donald Low*

Whether measured by the Gini coefficient, or by the ratio of incomes between the top and bottom quintiles, the evidence points to an incontrovertible fact: income inequality in Singapore has risen significantly in the last ten years or so. While this fact is beyond dispute, there is little agreement in the government on whether it represents a problem that merits serious policy action.[1]

The Singapore government's approach to inequality is grounded in a number of implicit, but strongly-held, assumptions about the objectives of economic policy and the relationship between economic growth and social equity. These assumptions have attained an almost mythical status in Singapore, both among policy circles and among

Singaporeans at large. They are reflexively applied in any debate on inequality, and form a common point of reference—an internally consistent paradigm—against which alternative ideas for organising the social security system are evaluated.

The purpose of this essay is to articulate these mythical assumptions and subject them to a closer examination. Like all myths, they contain an element of truth. But it behooves the policymaker to question and assess the validity of these myths in light of economic theory and evidence. Only then can they approach the problem of inequality in a pragmatic way devoid of dogma and ideology.

## Myth #1: Inequality is a necessary counterpart of economic dynamism and competitiveness

### What the Myth Says

The first myth is the belief that rising inequality is an inevitable conse-quence of rapid economic growth, or put more strongly, a necessary condition for economic competitiveness. Since unequal rewards spur individual effort and enterprise, it has been argued that policies that reduce inequality invariably reduce incentives for people to work and strive.

Governments that try to mitigate the unequal consequences of globalisation—through more progressive taxation, more redistributive spending, and a stronger social safety net—will raise costs for busi-nesses and capital owners, who are now far more mobile than before. In doing so, they kill the goose that lays the golden eggs. They sacrifice economic dynamism. There is an inescapable trade-off between economic growth and social equity. This is the "Golden Straightjacket" that Thomas Friedman famously expounds in *The Lexus and the Olive Tree* (1999): when countries join the globalisation system, they find that their economy grows and their politics shrinks.[2] If they want their economies to grow, governments have no choice but to slash income taxes, cut spending on social protection programmes, and roll back state provision.

Prime Minister Lee Hsien Loong also alluded to this trade-off between economic performance and social equity in his speech at the ComCare appreciation lunch in 2010:

"If you look at America and Europe, they have different models. In America, somewhat less welfare and greater emphasis on self-reliance. In many countries in Western Europe, a very comprehensive welfare state. You can see the result of these different approaches and the way the two societies and two economies feel. America has a more dynamic and competitive economy with fiercer competition. Europe has more generous benefits, more solidarity, not so strong competitiveness but the Europeans believe that they have made a rational choice, a rational trade-off. In return for less growth, they enjoy more welfare, more solidarity and they felt that they were the happier for their circumstances. But it was not entirely as happy as that. In fact, Europe was living beyond its means. It took some time for the problems to show up but I think Judgment Day has been brought forward by the financial crisis. After the huge hole in their budgets because of the rescue of the banks over the last couple of years, the Western Europeans have woken up to a very serious problem and they have been forced to make very tough choices."[3]

## What the Evidence Says

At first glance, this myth seems consistent with international evidence and economic theory. Income inequality in almost all the rich countries has risen in the last 20 to 30 years. The reasons for this are fairly well-known though they remain subjects of academic debate. Rapid technological advances have pushed up the wages of highly educated, highly skilled workers (paying them what economists call the "skill-biased premium"), while globalisation and the entry of large numbers of low wage workers from China, India, and other developing economies have held down the wages of the less-skilled in rich countries.

Other policy and institutional factors have also contributed to the rise of inequality in rich countries. The collapse of unions in the US, for instance, has reduced the bargaining power of labour relative to capital-owners. Immigration in some rich countries has brought low wage competition to the non-tradable sectors of the economy. Meanwhile, reductions in corporate and personal income tax rates in many countries—partly in response to increasing global competition—have reduced the progressiveness of tax systems and accentuated inequality within countries.

But does the relationship between inequality and economic growth stand up to closer scrutiny? It appears not. Despite its intuitive logic, there is little evidence to show that more unequal countries do better economically, or that more equal ones pay a large economic price in terms of competitiveness.

Developed countries that spend less on social welfare—such as the US—are not necessarily richer than those that spend more. What about the claim that Europe's social security systems are unsustainable? True, many of them need to be reformed for their ageing populations and be put on a stronger fiscal footing. But the countries that are facing the most severe fiscal problems—Greece, Italy, Portugal and Spain—are hardly known for their generous welfare systems. The ones with the most generous social provisions are the northern European countries: Germany, Netherlands, Denmark, Sweden, Finland, and Norway. These are export-oriented, surplus economies with sound fiscal balances and strong social safety nets. The claim that Europe's fiscal mess is the result of overly generous social welfare systems simply cannot be substantiated.

More importantly, we should question whether the economic performance of countries should be measured only in terms of income (or per capita GDP). Surely, what citizens care about is not some abstract notion of aggregate production that does not take into account how that "national income" or GDP is distributed or how society values the stuff that is produced. Various economists have therefore suggested that governments, in measuring economic progress, should also take into account other indicators of well-being. These include consumption, health and longevity, leisure time, and yes, how fairly incomes are distributed. By these measures, Singapore does not do as well as its per capita GDP suggests.[4]

The conclusion that inequality neither contributes to economic growth nor is its necessary consequence should not be surprising at all. Economic growth is a complex process involving a number of technological, policy, and institutional factors. It is not apparent that a country's income inequality has a statistically significant correlation with economic growth or competitiveness. Even if it does—to the extent that citizens care about the distribution of income and other indicators of well-being, and not just the level of per capita income—nothing in economics says that countries should pursue only per capita GDP growth at the expense of the broader indicators of well-being. That some countries do is a consequence of their own values and politics, not of economic logic.

## Myth #2: The best way to help the poor is to help the rich

### What the Myth Says

A common refrain that one hears in the Singapore government is that we first have to grow the economic pie before we can share it. Like it or not, it is the rich and talented who invest, spot, and exploit economic opportunities, and create jobs for the rest. Depriving them of their just rewards by levying high income or wealth taxes on the rich simply reduces the incentive for them to create wealth, thereby hurting the poor and the rest of society. In the long run, the best way to help the poor is to help the rich grow the pie. Societies can afford more generous redistribution when the economy is doing well and governments can afford to increase social spending. "Equity needs growth" is the common refrain from the PAP government.

### What the Evidence Says

Have pro-rich policies led to faster economic growth, which then raised the incomes at the bottom? The evidence on this is mixed at best. Among rich countries over the last 60 years, the evidence in fact suggests the opposite: countries tended to grow faster in the years they were doing more for the poor than in the years they were trimming social safety nets and cutting taxes for the rich. Following the Second World War, there was rapid growth in progressive taxation and welfare spending in most of the rich capitalist countries. Despite this (or perhaps, partly because of this), the period between 1950 and 1973 saw the highest-ever growth rates in these countries. Since then, rich countries have never managed to grow faster than that.

When growth slowed in the mid-1970s onwards, the diagnosis in many developed economies was that the reduction in the share of income going to capital owners was the reason for the slowdown. Across the rich world, and especially in the US and Britain, policies that reduced the redistributive role of the state were introduced. There were tax cuts for the rich (top income tax rates were brought down) even as social welfare spending was reduced. Financial deregulation created huge opportunities for speculative gains as well as astronomical pay cheques for top executives and financiers. Unions were weakened, making it easier for employers to sack their workers. And trade barriers were dismantled, putting downward pressure on low-end wages in the rich world.

During this period, income inequality is the US, already the highest in the rich world, rose to a level comparable to that of some Latin American countries. Much of this was driven by the rise of the super-rich in the US. Between 1979 and 2001, the top 5 per cent in the US saw their share of national income increase from 15.5 per cent to 21 per cent. This was mainly because of the astronomical increase in executive pay, which in the aftermath of the 2007–09 financial crisis appears both unjust and unjustified.

Trickle-down economics may be justified if the benefits of growth do in fact trickle down. Again, the evidence from highly unequal countries such as the US suggests that this does not occur if simply left to market forces. In contrast, countries with a strong welfare state find it much easier to spread the benefits of economic growth. Through more redistributive fiscal systems, northern European countries have much more equal income distributions than the US even though their income distributions before taxes and transfers are not all that different from the US's.

To sum up, there is no reason to presume that trickle-down policies will accelerate growth or benefit the poor. Even when there is more growth, the trickle-down that occurs through the market mechanism is very limited.

What about Singapore's experience? Has trickle-down worked? It is less clear whether the increase in income inequality in Singapore over the last decade has been accompanied by a similarly perverse distribution of income to the super-rich as experienced in the US. Nevertheless, there are some reasons for concern. To begin with, the state may have become less redistributive at a time when its redistribution functions are needed most. Government policies over the decade may have accentuated the rising income inequality wrought by market forces. For instance, the tax system has become less progressive. Corporate and personal income taxes have been reduced significantly while the Goods and Services Tax (GST), a regressive tax, has more than doubled. More liberal foreign worker policies might also have worsened income inequality in Singapore.

If these tax and labour policies had in fact generated more growth, and if the government had been aggressively redistributing the fruits of growth to large segments of the population affected by wage stagnation, trickle-down economics may not be all bad. But while the Singapore government has increased spending on lower income segments of the population, through Workfare and discretionary fiscal transfers, its redistribution has simply not been aggressive enough. This is demonstrated by fact that the income inequality after taxes and transfers has worsened at about the same rate as the income inequality before government redistribution. Indeed, income inequality today, after taking into account government taxes and transfers, is worse than it was a decade ago *before* accounting for government redistribution. This implies that the growth that Singapore has enjoyed in the last decade or so has not translated into proportionate gains for those at the lower end of the income distribution, and that growth has not reduced inequality.

## Myth#3: Inequality is not really a problem as long as there isn't extreme poverty and incomes are rising across-the-board

### What the Myth Says

The third myth says that policymakers should not worry about inequality per se. As long as there are opportunities for all to a good education, high social mobility will dampen people's demands for a fairer distribution of income. Furthermore, as long as everyone's incomes are rising, the fact that incomes at the top are rising much faster than those at the bottom is not a cause for concern. An analogy would be that as long as the rising tide lifts all boats, the fact that some boats (the yachts for instance) are being lifted up much faster than the rest should not matter. Meanwhile, extreme poverty can be addressed with targeted measures such as social assistance. These limited welfare programmes for the indigent and those who cannot work and have no other means of financial support are affordable so long as they are strictly means-tested. There is no need for measures that redistribute incomes significantly since the problem—poverty—is a relatively limited one that can be surgically addressed.

The underlying assumption behind this myth is that people care only about their absolute, and not relative, levels of income. So long as my income is rising, I should be happy and should not begrudge my neighbour's income rising at a faster rate. To do so is irrational, and governments should not pander to my irrationality or green-eyed envy by redistributing income from my neighbour to me. Parents should also teach their children to be satisfied with what they have and not compare themselves with those who have more.

## What the Evidence Says

To begin with, conventional economics does not prescribe that distributional concerns should be subordinate to growth objectives. Even if one takes a purely utilitarian view, there is a case to be made for redistribution. Since an additional dollar is worth more to the poor person than it is to the rich person, a utilitarian perspective says that any growth in incomes should accrue to the poor and that this should continue until everybody's marginal utility is the same. Furthermore, to the extent that increasing inequality reduces society's well-being, it hurts the rich as much as it does the poor, and redistribution would enhance overall welfare. For instance, inequality has been shown to increase crime, which hurts the interests of everyone, not just the poor.

People's general psychology also provides additional reasons for redistribution. Behavioural experiments have suggested that people care just as much about fairness and relative income as they do about absolute gains. In the ultimatum game, for instance, people routinely reject offers that they consider too low even though they are better off accepting whatever offer that is made to them. This suggests that people believe that windfall gains should be shared with others in society.

We should also try to understand the effects of inequality and why people care about them. One line of argument emphasises the role of positional goods (i.e., goods in which people's utility depends on how much they own relative to others). The point about positional goods—and of fashions and brands in general—is their relative attractiveness. Owning a better car or the latest branded fashion item gives me more utility when others do not have it, much like how buildings are valuable because of their location. With such goods, the rising tide does not lift all boats. I yearn to be not merely richer, but richer than my neighbours. The more important brands, fashion, houses, cars and other positional goods are in a society, the more relative income and inequality matter.

Rising inequality causes people to be more conscious of their status and to channel more of their spending to positional goods. Because the incomes of the rich are rising faster than everyone else's when inequality is increasing, they can afford to spend more on such goods. Their spending causes "expenditure cascades" that induce others lower on the income ladder to also spend more just to keep up. But in an era of rising inequality, the incomes of the middle class and the lower income groups are not rising as fast; they can only spend more on positional goods by diverting resources from non-positional goods (such as leisure time, or having babies) or by taking on more debt.

What about the claim that equality of opportunity ensures social mobility and so governments need not worry about rising income or wealth inequality? Again, while this has some intuitive appeal, it is not borne out by empirical evidence. Countries that are more unequal, such as the US, also tend to be less mobile (as measured by how much of a person's income is predicted by his parents' income) than countries that are more equal, such as Canada or the welfare states of northern Europe. Why should this be? It turns out that equality of opportunity cannot be easily separated from equality of outcomes. Unequal resources easily translate into unequal access to opportunities, say to quality education. Families with more resources have greater means to ensure that their children have a better education. A more unequal society therefore finds it harder to achieve genuine equality of opportunity and social mobility than a more equal one.

To sum up, there are sufficient reasons—both theoretical and empirical—for policymakers to start taking inequality seriously even when incomes across-the-board are rising. They should also reject the glib and empirically false dichotomy between equal opportunities and equal outcomes. Being an opportunity society requires active government redistribution of incomes if market forces are producing more unequal outcomes.

## Myth #4: Since pay is tied to ability, rising inequality is simply the result of increasing differences in people's ability

### What the Myth Says

In a market economy, people are paid according to their marginal productivity. If the worker in the top 20th percentile earns ten times more than the worker in the bottom 20th percentile, it is simply because the former is ten times more productive than the latter. While this outcome may be difficult to accept, it is nevertheless the case that there are wide differentials in people's ability and that these are reflected in wide income disparities. Attempts to reduce these pay differences—say by introducing minimum wage legislation—lead only to inefficient and rigid labour markets. Consequently, it follows that the best way to increase the incomes of middle and low wage Singaporeans is to increase their productivity. That their wages have been growing slowly in the last decade is the result of their stagnant productivity levels.

### What the Evidence Says

As with the first three myths, this one also contains a kernel of truth. There is some evidence to suggest that Singapore's workers in the service industries are less productive than their counterparts in other rich countries. Cleaners, service staff, and construction workers are probably more productive in, say, Sweden than they are in Singapore.

But the question still remains: why has inequality increased at a time when quality education in Singapore has become widely available? The democratisation of education suggests that differentials in productivity should have narrowed, which in turn suggests that wage differentials should also have been reduced. Singapore prides itself in having one of the world's most successful education systems that not only enables bright children to do well, but also everyone else. If so, why should a lower-wage Singaporean worker, who has benefitted from the state education system, be less well-paid than his Swedish or Swiss counterpart doing a similar job? Is it possible that something else other than individual productivity determines our wages?

In reality, wages are not just a function of one's productivity levels.

The other important determinant of market wages in rich countries is immigration. Low-skilled workers in many European countries earn more because of tight immigration controls. If these countries were to import large numbers of low-skilled workers from poor countries, it is hardly conceivable that their low-skilled workers can continue to earn the wages they do now, their relatively higher productivity levels notwithstanding. A Swedish bus driver, for instance, probably earns 30 times what his Indian counterpart does. If Sweden were to allow Indians and other immigrants from poorer countries to enter its labour market, simple economics tells us that the wages of bus drivers in Sweden will be immediately depressed.

If the above analysis is correct, it suggests that to raise the wages of our low-skilled workers, the emphasis should *not* be on raising their productivity, but on reducing our intake of low-skilled foreign workers. All societies have limited capabilities to absorb immigrants. How open a society wants to be to immigrants is not just an economic choice, but also a political choice with social and economic consequences. Too rapid an inflow leads not only to more competition for jobs and reduced wages, but also stretches the country's physical and social infrastructures.

What about the high incomes of top-earners in Singapore? Aren't their high incomes the result of their higher ability and productivity? Yes, but only to a point. It is not only, or even mainly, because they are more clever and better-educated that the rich in Singapore earn many more times what their counterparts in poor countries do. They achieve this because they live in an economy that has better technologies, better infrastructure, better organised firms, better institutions, and better government—all things in large part products of collective actions taken over generations. As Warren Buffet said in a television interview in 1995:

> "I personally think that society is responsible for a very significant percentage of what I've earned. If you stick me down in the middle of Bangladesh or Peru or someplace, you'll find out how much this talent is going to produce in the wrong kind of soil. I will be struggling 30 years later. I work in a market system that happens to reward what I do very well—disproportionately well."

## Why These Myths Matter

The myths matter for public policy because they shroud almost every discussion of inequality and of how our social security system should be organised in a thick and unquestioned set of assumptions. They act as an ideological blinker, and cause the policymaker to respond reflexively to any suggestion to redistribute incomes and reduce inequality with the argument that doing so will compromise the efficient working of markets. The myths matter because they reduce the ability of the Singapore government to pursue pragmatic and creative solutions to the challenge of inequality. And like many other myths and ideologies, they prevent a comprehensive and objective assessment of the policy alternatives successfully pursued by governments elsewhere.

As cognitive psychologists have found, having a strong predisposition to a particular worldview deeply influences our assessment of the evidence. People—including policymakers—suffer from confirmation biases. This means that we seek and pay more attention to evidence that supports our existing worldviews rather than revise our worldviews constantly in light of new evidence. When confronted with contrarian evidence, or evidence that goes against our worldviews, the result is cognitive dissonance. This is uncomfortable and so we react by denying the evidence altogether (e.g., "the northern European countries are not as successful as they are made out to be") or by discounting the veracity and credibility of the evidence (e.g., "your data is suspect", or "your methodology is flawed"). That policymakers also suffer from such cognitive biases is well-documented.

Questioning these myths opens up a number of possibilities for public policy in Singapore. At the broadest level, it throws up the question of whether the object of economic policy should be to maximise growth or per capita GDP regardless of its distributional consequences. Even if we assume that there is a trade-off between economic growth and social equity, the implication is not that societies should maximise the former at the expense of the latter. A trade-off means that governments should try to find the right balance of economic growth and social equity that reflects society's preferences.

In Singapore's context, given that per capita GDP is by some measures already the highest in the world, the marginal gains in society's well-being from further increases in income at the expense of social equity are likely to be very small. Put another way, Singaporeans are likely to be happier with a more equitable distribution of income (at the margin) than with further increases in per capita GDP that are not equitably distributed. The old adage of concentrating on growing the economic pie before worrying about how it is distributed—which may have been valid and relevant when Singapore was relatively poor—is no longer adequate as a guide for policymaking today.

Another implication is that policymakers should try to decipher the apparent mysteries around the more successful European economies. Once these myths are jettisoned, policymakers will be liberated to ask: Why have these countries been able to combine high levels of economic performance and productivity with high levels of equality? What economic and social policies have enabled them to achieve this? Why do their citizens appear willing to accept the high rates of taxation that are necessary to finance their generous social provisions? How do they deal with the problems created by moral hazard and free riders? What lessons can we draw from them in designing our own social safety nets?

My study of the issue suggests that what matters more for economic growth and competitiveness is not how generous a country's social protection system is, but how it is designed. It is not the level of social welfare spending that determines whether a country is on the efficiency-equity frontier but the way its social welfare programmes are organised and the incentive effects they create. Good design means paying attention to individual incentives, structuring the programmes in a way that encourages work, and redistributing incomes without reducing the incentive for investments. In short, the question governments should be asking themselves is not whether they can improve social equity without reducing growth but how they can achieve this.

Governments, including Singapore's, have more choices than they think. They can expand the range of choices they have by first discarding these myths about inequality.

## *Notes*

1. I wrote this essay in March 2011. It has been slightly modified for this collection.

2. Thomas Friedman, *The Lexus and the Olive Tree* (New York: Harper Collins Publishers, 1999).

3. Speech by Prime Minister Lee Hsien Loong at the Comcare Appreciation Lunch, 2 Dec. 2010, http://www.pmo.gov.sg/content/pmosite/mediacentre/speechesninterviews/primeminister/2010/December/speech_by_prime_ministerleehsienloongatcomcareappreciationlunch2.html

4. Jones and Klenow for instance show that while Singapore's per capita GDP in 2000 was 83 per cent of the US's, Singaporeans' well-being (measured by consumption adjusted for factors such as leisure, longevity, and income inequality) was only 44 per cent of the US's level. Charles I. Jones and Peter J. Klenow, "Beyond GDP? Welfare Across Countries and Time", NBER Working Paper No. 16352 (2010), http://www.nber.org/papers/w16352

# 2

# HOW LAND AND PEOPLE FIT TOGETHER IN SINGAPORE'S ECONOMY

*Linda Lim*

The ongoing debate about Singapore's population policy provides a timely opportunity to reconsider how different pieces of our economic growth model fit—or do not fit—together.[1]

GDP (output) growth in any country comes from increases in inputs (primarily land, labour, and capital) and/or increases in the productivity of those inputs. As noted by various economists, Singapore's GDP growth has depended more on input than productivity increases, as reflected in the high dependence on foreign labour.

This has had the unintended but predictable consequence of

discouraging increased labour productivity. Employers can increase output more readily and cheaply by recruiting foreign workers, particularly from lower income countries, than by investing in capital-labour substitution and upgrading the skills of the domestic labour force. This was and is an entirely rational decision for profit-maximising private enterprises. But increasing output by increasing inputs eventually runs into the problem of diminishing marginal returns. In Singapore's case, this is because the addition of more and more people to an essentially fixed and extremely scarce complementary resource, land, inevitably raises other costs. These include rising residential housing and commercial rental costs, and congestion costs especially in transportation.

Furthermore, both higher housing costs and lengthening commute times effectively lower the real wage of workers (e.g., because it now takes them 10 or 11 hours to earn an 8-hour daily wage). In a closed labour market, the rising cost of living eventually translates into higher nominal wages. But in an open labour market like Singapore's, wage increases held down by the increased supply of foreign labour discourages the substitution of capital, higher technology, and sophisticated management processes, for labour. This is why the policy of tightening foreign labour supply and increasing labour productivity is necessary.

## Economic and Social Implications

One way by which the chronic excess demand for labour that Singapore has long suffered (despite or because of a liberal immigration policy) might be reduced is by some businesses moving out of the country. This is a normal process of adjustment to shifting comparative and competitive advantage. What is important here—to smooth such adjustments and minimise the costs to both employers and workers—is commitment to a clear long-term labour market policy that will not vary according to short-term business or electoral cycles. But the application of such a policy should not be blunt (i.e., applied with immediate and equal force across all sectors) but nuanced and gradual, according to the circumstances of individual sectors and businesses.

Economic planning agencies need to be involved in calibrating the demand side of the labour market. For example, they should not provide incentives to businesses that have highly specific manpower needs, rely heavily on imported labour and talent, provide few jobs for native Singaporeans, or are highly land-intensive. Choices and trade-offs must be made—not just between growth and foreign labour dependence, but also between the different sectors that contribute differentially to growth.

Given Singapore's extreme land scarcity, the continuation of heavy (even if reduced) reliance on foreign labour and immigration has more unintended consequences. It contributes marginally to the low fertility rate and emigration of native Singaporeans, and to labour force participation rates that are lower than they might be for certain demographics. These are, for example, mothers of young children, and professionals and skilled workers over 50 years of age who in other developed countries would be at the pinnacle of their careers, but in Singapore are too often side-lined in favour of cheaper or more globally accomplished imported talent in Singapore.

High housing costs reduce fertility by delaying the age of marriage, since both parties in a young couple need to work for quite some time to before they can afford their own home. This is especially so in the unsubsidised private market where they must compete with large numbers of foreign buyers. Meanwhile, long commutes on congested public transportation reduce time for social interaction and family formation, and make it difficult to transport children for childcare and schooling.

The cost of child-raising in Singapore is also high, including for some the need for mostly foreign maids and nannies so that both parents can work. This again increases population density, manifested most directly in the ever-shrinking space at home. Competition with foreigners in school and the job market also increases the stress and expense of child-raising.

Emigration to more land-abundant countries thus becomes more attractive to young Singaporeans who do not foresee themselves being able to replicate or approach their parents' standard of living if they stayed in Singapore; they are faced with the ever-increasing costs of living, declining quality of life, increasing job market competition and a growing perception of discrimination vis-à-vis foreign talent and immigrants. The feeling of being treated as a "second-class citizen in my own home", and being crowded out by foreigners, combines with the loss of physical markers of "home" (buildings, land, green and wild areas, which in every country constitute part of the native's national patrimony and identity) in discouraging the sojourner's return to be a "stranger in a strange land".

The over-representation of foreigners or immigrants in the leadership and even middle ranks of many organisations also suggests that a "glass ceiling" exists for the locally-born, such that upward career mobility may be more limited than in other, larger countries.

From a purely GDP input perspective, it may not matter if emigrating or low reproducing native Singaporeans are readily replaced in the labour market by immigrants and new citizens. But at the high end of the skill ladder, among the globally-mobile talent that the country wishes to attract, many of the same "push factors" operate to discourage a permanent stay in Singapore—from the cost of living to quality of life—reinforced by lack of the bond of a shared collective national identity. For the foreigners who do stay, sheer numbers encourage "clustering among their own" rather than integrating into native Singapore society. Their birth rates will also fall over time for the same reasons as native Singaporeans'.

## Some Policy Solutions

The prevailing discourse about how Singapore's changing population profile will interact with the economy seems to assume that fewer foreign workers and lower immigration levels will hurt economic growth and businesses—and ultimately, Singaporeans as well. But other affluent economies with low fertility, ageing demographics, and small populations have managed to achieve continued, if modest, improvements in living standards without importing large numbers of foreign labour and talent. There is no reason why Singapore cannot do the same by borrowing the technological and business process innovations that have already been implemented elsewhere. Higher productivity (more output per worker) can substitute for more workers in achieving a particular GDP growth rate.

Lower aggregate growth is inevitable for a mature economy, given diminishing marginal returns to added inputs of labour and capital. It may also be desirable, when real income (discounting for inflation) and total well-being (reduced congestion, environmental degradation, income inequality, social unease) are considered. Below are some possible solutions that policymakers could consider.

## Locals Fuel the Economy

Economically sustainable activities that may generate lower growth but employ a higher ratio of Singaporeans will also contribute to higher wage and domestic shares of GDP (Singapore's is currently among the lowest in the world). Simply put, a higher proportion of a given dollar of GDP will accrue to Singaporeans, so local living standards can be maintained or increased more slowly.

Policy instruments to achieve this could include investment incentives tied to the hiring and training of Singaporeans, and awarding work permits and employment passes only after a process ascertaining that there are no qualified Singaporeans for the jobs—standard practice in the US.

Higher wages would encourage firms to improve productivity and attract more Singaporeans into particular jobs, giving both employers and employees an incentive to invest in upgraded skills (since there will be a higher income payoff). Businesses that cannot afford the higher wages would exit, releasing manpower for the businesses that remain. A reduction in demand would alleviate any labour shortage. Fewer foreign workers would also ease pressures on the housing market and on commercial rents, so businesses may benefit from more moderate rent hikes even as they pay out higher wages. Reduced foreign capital inflows to purchase property, and other investments, would mitigate asset inflation and appreciation of the Singapore dollar, thus helping to maintain cost competitiveness.

Higher wages with higher productivity together with moderating rents do not necessarily mean higher costs. But if they do, these are costs Singapore's consumers will have to pay. As consumers are also workers, their real incomes may increase with higher salaries, lower rents, and mortgage payments. If those enjoying higher wages are Singaporeans (rather than foreigners, who typically have higher savings rates and remittance outflows), the multiplier impact of their local spending will be greater—their higher costs are other Singaporeans' higher income, most of which is spent in Singapore.

## Better Productivity, Different Mindsets

Many high income economies have trodden this path of increasing productivity before Singapore. However, emulating their market-derived solutions requires mindset and values shifts among Singaporeans. Consider three sectors in Singapore that are labour-intensive, and are usually considered low-wage, low-skilled, and low-productivity jobs that Singaporeans "don't want to do".

First is the construction industry. In no other high income country is this associated almost exclusively with foreign labour from neighbouring countries. In the US, this is a high-wage, high-skill, capital-intensive industry that employs mostly unionised native workers, complies with high safety standards, and utilises sophisticated equipment and processes. Construction workers earn at least twice the median national wage in the US state I live in (Michigan); their hourly wage is probably three times higher. Some Singaporeans would be willing to work in this sector if adequately compensated, while construction firms would employ them at high wages if productivity were sufficiently high.

Second is the food and beverage (F&B) industry. In even high-immigrant big cities and on the coasts of the US, most restaurant workers are locals. They include students or mature individuals (mothers, retirees) working part-time for extra income or social interaction, as well as seasoned professionals pursuing a full-time, long-term career. Conversation skills, customer relations, and knowledge of the menu and wine list are required and rewarded, with tips that average 20 per cent of the bill and above. There is a strong monetary incentive to develop skills and even a personal brand; at high-end, brand name restaurants, aspiring job candidates often queue for months and even bid (pay) for the privilege of waiting tables. In the kitchen, much food preparation has been automated and outsourced to specialist food services such as Sysco.

In Singapore, the use of temporary foreign workers and the standardised service charge has kept wages and upward mobility low, thus discouraging the participation of Singaporeans in this sector.

Third is the domestic service industry of household help, care for children, the elderly and disabled. This is a heterogeneous sector, but nowhere in the rich world (with the possible exception of Hong Kong) is the dominant mode of operation that of the individual maid bound to a single individual or household. Rather, professional services of house maintenance, cleaning, food preparation and delivery, child and elder care and transport are the norm, compensated at hourly rates many times the minimum wage. Many self-employed workers in this sector serve multiple clients simultaneously, some for many years at a stretch, or work part-time, while private enterprises employing such workers provide a range of customised services.

Many individuals offering child and eldercare services are personally dedicated to helping others, or are training for careers in teaching or nursing. Foreign workers in both this and the F&B sector are usually new long-term immigrants, not temporary guest workers, so integration into the majority society is only a matter of time.

## Improving Wages and Status

In all three sectors discussed above, much higher wages would both attract more workers and encourage investments in higher productivity methods. But there is also a mindset shift required, with regards to the social status and value collectively ascribed to such occupations.

In the US, social barriers are highly permeable and there is respect for hard work, enterprise, and professionalism even in "blue collar" or manual service occupations. This is helped by the fact that they may pay better than many "white collar" jobs.

A socially egalitarian ethic in Europe and national group solidarity in Japan, both regions with much lower income inequality, perform the same function. More money alone cannot compensate for lack of respect, which in Singapore is inordinately directed towards those with academically based credentials and professional achievement. This can be extended to many other occupations such as highly compensated "skilled trades", and personal services (such as the beauty and wellness industry), which are particularly attractive to self-employed entrepreneurs.

Many solutions are possible but businesses will be motivated to innovate only if the easy alternative of importing low-wage, low-skilled foreign labour is restricted. Innovations can be accelerated by temporary public subsidies that would not cost more than the investments in the housing and transport infrastructure required to accommodate a larger population.

## Slower Growth, Stronger Nation

The situation at the higher end of the labour market is more complex, given the global or regional role many companies fulfil from their Singapore base and the geographically mobile talent that they may require.

Employment passes should be flexibly awarded according to each company's needs and value to the nation. Businesses should professionalise human resource practices to maximise recruitment of Singaporeans, for example through school or university partnerships and campus recruitment efforts.

The bottom line is that Singapore can survive economically, and even prosper, without further large increases in foreign labour and immigration. A reduction in both will also deliver compensating benefits, such as lower housing costs, higher domestic consumption, lower income inequality and a less congested, more environmentally friendly city whose residents may then be more willing to have children.

In short, businesses and people can adjust to slower labour growth as they do in other countries. The nation—which is more than its GDP—will be the stronger for it.

## Land and People

Territorial land is the essence and foundation of a nation. In Singapore, the wisdom of using retirement savings to fund home ownership, including in subsidised public sector housing, has been premised on the assumption of constant asset appreciation. Large-scale immigration contributes to asset appreciation, and thus to the profits of REITs (real estate investment trusts) and both private and government-linked property developers. But asset appreciations based on increased land scarcity are essentially rents that transfer income from buyers to sellers, thus contributing also to rising inequality. From a long-term growth perspective, they distort incentives to work, save and invest in value-creating activities in favour of rentier wealth or income from property "investments" (or speculation).

Asset inflation also hurts growth by raising the cost of doing business and discouraging entrepreneurship especially by SMEs (small and medium enterprises) and local businesses that cannot afford to compete with global multinationals for commercial and retail space. We should not forget that a major factor in the downfall of the medieval Italian city-state of Venice was the diversion of entrepreneurial capital and energy into property as the small land-area drove rising rentals and land prices, leaving the city with beautiful buildings that today are but a shell for visiting spectators to admire.

Beyond these economic considerations, an increase to the already absolutely and proportionately large numbers of temporary foreign workers and new immigrants has resulted in social pressures and political tensions that threaten to make Singapore less liveable and less attractive to foreigners turned off by the perceived hostility of natives, as well as natives who feel their livelihood, lifestyle and national identity undermined by the overwhelming presence of foreigners.

Land and people together constitute a nation. All of us, new and old Singaporeans and temporary residents, will be better off if our population policy takes a more comprehensive view of both economic growth and social integration in this small but precious piece of land.

## Notes

1. This essay combines two of my articles on the Singapore population and the economy. The first, titled "How Land and People Fit in Singapore's Economy," was published in *Yahoo! News Singapore* on 21 Feb. 2013 (http://sg.news.yahoo.com/blogs/singaporescene/land-people-fit-singapore-economy-025020996.html); the second, "Can Slower Growth Lead to a Stronger Nation?", was published by *Straits Times* on 22 Feb. 2013.

# 3

# ECONOMIC MYTHS IN THE GREAT POPULATION DEBATE

*Donald Low, Yeoh Lam Keong, Tan Kim Song, and Manu Bhaskaran*

> Practical men, who believe themselves to be quite exempt from any
> intellectual influences, are usually the slaves of some defunct
> economist.
> —John Maynard Keynes

The debate on the Population White Paper has surfaced a number of myths and fallacies that seems to dominate the current discussion on Singapore's population policies. Economics provides us with a very useful set of analytical tools to clarify thinking and to develop sensible, evidence-based policies. The purpose of this essay is to examine some of the ways these myths have inadvertently, or even subconsciously, been used to justify inaccurate thinking about policies.[1]

## Myth #1: GDP growth, no matter how it is achieved, is an unambiguously good thing

There seems to be an implicit and unspoken assumption that Singapore must continue to grow at a certain rate, and that if the growth does not come from labour productivity increases, then it must come from labour force increases. This is poor economic reasoning. GDP growth *per se* does not improve individual well-being; it only does if it is driven by productivity improvements that raise workers' wages.

If labour productivity is not increasing, it means that whatever GDP growth we "achieve" comes from brute force (i.e., injection of more labour inputs). Not only does this not increase society's well-being, it actually reduces it. If the 3 per cent GDP growth that the government aims for is attained by a 3 per cent labour force increase, Singaporeans are no better off in per capita terms. Meanwhile, they have to contend with negative externalities such as more congestion and competition for public goods, depressed wages, inflation and higher asset prices, and dilution of national identity.

Associated with the growth fetish is a somewhat irrational fear of zero GDP growth. There seems to be an implied belief that high GDP growth driven mainly by labour force injections is superior to slow or zero GDP growth. This is again bad economics. Consider a country whose GDP has stagnated. Its labour force is declining (say because of an ageing population), but it manages to eke out productivity improvements of 1–2 per cent annually. In gross terms, the country is not producing more. But per capita GDP is increasing, and incomes and standards of living are still rising because of productivity growth. This scenario describes Japan's current situation. Obviously, this is an extreme scenario; no one is recommending zero GDP growth for Singapore. But even in this extreme scenario, it is clear that zero GDP growth does *not* spell the end of rising incomes and standards of living. Historically much slower growth rates (of, say, 2 per cent) should not be feared as long as all (or most) of that growth comes from increases in labour productivity.

## Myth #2: If we don't have sufficiently large injections of foreign labour, business costs will rise, some businesses will shut down or move out of Singapore, and Singaporean workers will be laid off

Businesses that rely on cheap foreign labour receive an implicit subsidy from the rest of society. The low cost of labour encourages them to persist with low value-added production and discourages them from upgrading and improving their business processes. Meanwhile, cheap foreign labour discourages automation and holds down wages for citizen workers doing the same job.

If the Singapore government were to tighten foreign worker policies over a sustained period, there is no doubt some businesses would not be able to adapt and would have to move out of Singapore or shut down. Is this necessarily a bad thing? No, in a vibrant capitalist economy, this is exactly what one expects. Businesses that cannot adapt should and will exit the market; the state should not be propping them up with ever more inputs of cheap labour. Their exit also frees up labour and capital resources for the more productive parts of the economy.

Such "creative destruction" is a necessary part of the economic restructuring process. In economic restructuring, there will always be some firms that are disadvantaged. The economically sensible decision is not to protect these firms in their existing labour-intensive state (which imposes high social costs) through easy access to cheap foreign labour. Instead, the government can help lessen the pain in this process. For instance, it can help local SMEs (small and medium enterprises) by ensuring that they have access to the cheap credit, new technologies, and business restructuring expertise needed to adjust and adapt to the new environment.

What about workers who are laid off and who lack the skills to move to other industries? Again, the economically sound answer is not to prop up employment, but for the state to intervene directly to help the workers whose livelihoods are affected—through unemployment protection, higher wage subsidies through the Workforce Income Supplement, skills retraining and upgrading programmes, and one-off social transfers. Public policy should be aimed at helping workers and local firms cope with economic restructuring, not at helping uncompetitive firms that rely on cheap foreign labour stay afloat.

## Myth #3: Economic growth is a zero-sum game

A second fallacy is that with the emergence of fast-growing cities in Asia, Singapore will need to maintain a certain growth rate or it will stagnate and eventually become irrelevant. This is the essence of the "competitiveness" argument. But economists usually use competitiveness to refer to attributes such as comparative advantage, total business environment, innovation, and the quality of a country's policies and institutions. The rate of workforce growth, especially in cheap labour, is not considered a sustainable source of competitiveness.

This myth also has little basis in economics. Growth in a fast-growing and increasingly interdependent region like Asia is not a zero-sum contest. Just because Bangkok, Jakarta, and Shanghai grow at a rate much faster than Singapore does not make Singaporeans any worse off. It is not the case that there is a finite amount of GDP growth for the whole world (or the region) and we must grab as large a share of it as possible. Indeed, the opposite is true. The growth of other cities in our region is more likely to raise our growth rate. The larger markets that their growth generates and the higher incomes their citizens earn should be viewed as economic opportunities for Singapore, not as "competitive" threats.

Similarly, the pursuit of foreign direct investment (FDI) is also not a zero-sum game. It is not necessarily a bad thing that, if as a result of a more modest increase in our workforce, Singapore "loses" some FDI that it would have received had it continued to grow its workforce as rapidly as before. First, the marginal investments that are lost will probably be of the type that requires cheap labour inputs. Such investments do not raise productivity, and therefore per capita GDP by much. Second, such investments in lower-cost locations benefit Singapore via the standard comparative advantage argument. That is, as these lower-cost countries raise their output and incomes, they can better afford the higher value goods and services that Singapore produces. Economic growth, rather than being a zero-sum proposition, is a positive-sum one— all the more so in a fast-growing region where the individual economies are at different (and therefore, complementary) stages of development.

## Myth #4: Denser, larger populations create significant economic benefits for cities

It is true that rich cities with larger populations enjoy something called agglomeration effects (i.e., when skilled workers cluster together, their output increases by more than the increase in the number of workers). Knowledge expands and spreads more quickly in dense cities than they do in sparsely populated ones; innovation tends to thrive in denser, more populous cities. Indeed, the agglomeration effects arising from a greater concentration of highly skilled knowledge workers should have been the main argument the government relied on for increasing the population and density of Singapore.

So why didn't this happen? The reason is that these agglomeration effects apply only in certain industries, namely those that require highly skilled knowledge workers. Industries such as biomedical science research, higher education, and business services like legal and management consulting clearly fall into this category. This line of argument suggests that Singapore needs more, not fewer, immigrants in these parts of the economy. But the benefits of agglomeration do not apply to low-cost, labour-intensive industries like construction, cleaning or security services. In these industries, more workers do not lead to larger increases in output per worker.

In the context of the White Paper, much of the projected increase in our labour force would be to serve our lower-skilled industries. These are exactly the industries that do not benefit from agglomeration effects but contribute to the externalities such as congestion and wage stagnation. Consequently, the argument in favour of a denser city with a larger population because of agglomeration effects does not really apply in this context.

## Myth #5: Spending on healthcare and social services are costs that have to be financed by higher taxes, and are therefore a drain on the economy

The final myth is that some parts of the economy—like healthcare and social services—are a drain on the economy, while others are productive, "value-creating", and generate "exciting jobs". This characterisation of the economy has no basis in economic theory or evidence, although it is true that some sectors of the economy experience persistently lower productivity growth than others.

In the White Paper debate, there seems to be a common perception that healthcare and social services are a drain on the productive parts of the economy. Since they have to be funded by taxpayers, they are a cost that reduces national output. This is again bad economics. Healthcare and social services, like other industries such as manufacturing, financial services or construction, also contribute to national output (or GDP) growth. A person's spending in healthcare is someone else's income and his or her spending, in turn, boosts another person's income. So raising our spending in these healthcare or social services is no different from increasing spending in other parts of the economy. There is no economic basis for the common intuition that some industries are a cost while others are a form of investment.

What about the fact that healthcare and social services have to be financed by taxation? Doesn't that mean they are a drag on the economy? Again, there is little economic basis for that argument. Many other things are financed by taxation too—MRT lines, public housing, law and order, security—but we don't view these as a drag on the economy. Indeed, we may even see these things as productive investments.

But won't taxes have to rise sharply to finance our higher spending on healthcare and social services? Not necessarily. First, Singapore has large fiscal surpluses that can be used to finance a well-planned expansion of such services in a sustainable way. Second, if productivity increases and people's incomes across-the-board rise, we should be able to afford the rising costs of healthcare.

The real issue in healthcare spending is how the risks of incurring high healthcare costs are allocated. Most economists argue that given the low-frequency, high-impact nature of many medical contingencies, the most efficient way of financing healthcare would be through some form of risk-pooling or social insurance. That Singapore lacks a comprehensive and universal health insurance programme, combined with the fact that the bulk of healthcare spending currently comes from out-of-pocket payments, suggests that we can have a more equitable healthcare financing system without compromising on its efficiency.

With an ageing population, won't rising health and social care expenditures hurt our economic dynamism, as it has in Japan and other rapidly ageing societies? Perhaps, but not for the reasons commonly cited. Health and social care services tend to experience slower-than-average productivity growth. This is because they are more dependent on labour, and are much less amenable to automation and other labour-saving technological improvements. But despite productivity growth in healthcare and social services being lower than in other industries (such as manufacturing or information and telecommunications technology, or ICT), wages in these "stagnant" sectors rise just as fast as they do in other sectors because if they did not, workers would leave these sectors. This means costs and prices in healthcare and social services rise faster than they do in other parts of the economy. Over time, healthcare and other social services will take up a larger share of our incomes—both individually and nationally. But this outcome does not spell doom. As long as we sustain labour productivity growth at historical rates of about 2 per cent, we can afford more of everything even as the share of healthcare and social services in our total spending rises.

The real risk of the "cost disease" (a term coined by the economist William Baumol) is *not* that health and social care costs are rising, but that policymakers misdiagnose the problem and deal with it in a knee-jerk way.[2] For instance, they may shift a larger share of the rising costs to citizens. This does not solve the underlying problem and may, in fact, make the problem worse as privatised healthcare is likely to experience faster cost inflation than socialised healthcare.

## Conclusion

These myths exist because they seem to be intuitively correct. They appeal to our everyday experiences, and are consistent with popular accounts of the economy. These include the idea that cities or countries are locked in economic competition with one another, and that jobs must be protected in order for workers to be protected. At the individual level, people's experience of health and social care as costs to be avoided, may explain their intuition that this must also apply at the national level. But these stories, although consistent and coherent, are neither correct nor valid. As cognitive psychologists have found, people tend to rely on explanations that are consistent with their own experiences or with conventional wisdom, rather than on careful deliberation and reasoned analysis.

Economics is not, and should not be, the only lens through which we examine, analyse, and debate our country's population policies. But when we do apply economics analysis, we should try to get it right.

## Notes

1. I wrote this essay with my fellow council members of the Economic Society of Singapore in response to some of the economic fallacies that had surfaced during the Population White Paper debate in February 2013. Most of this essay was published on *IPS Commons*; the original version is available at http://ipscommons.sg/index.php/categories/featured/118-economics-myths-in-the-great-population-debate.

2. William Baumol, *The Cost Disease: Why Computers Get Cheaper and Health Care Doesn't* (New Haven: Yale University Press, 2012).

# 4

# GOOD MERITOCRACY, BAD MERITOCRACY

*Donald Low*

Meritocracy is widely regarded as a core principle of governance in Singapore. Basic disagreement over it was one of the reasons why Singapore separated from Malaysia. The meritocracy principle—equalising opportunities not outcomes and allocating rewards on the basis of an individual's merit, abilities, and achievements—is as close as anything gets to being a national ideology.[1]

In recent years however, there have been growing concerns over meritocracy as it is practised in Singapore: the excessive competition it engenders (particularly in our education system), the stress and anxiety it causes, and the inequality that many see as the result of an unfettered meritocracy.

As other commentators have pointed out, the choice facing Singapore is not a binary one between meritocracy and other ways of distributing rewards.[2] Rather, the critique is over how meritocracy is practised in Singapore: how we translate the meritocratic ideal into practice matters more than the fact that we subscribe to the principle of meritocracy in the abstract.

To help frame the debate, I would like to propose four binaries that can inform the meritocracy debate in Singapore. In particular, I want to argue that there are *varieties* of meritocracy—some desirable, others possibly malignant. The debate should not be over whether we embrace meritocracy or not; rather, it should be over the *kind* of meritocracy we want.

## Absolute Performance versus Relative Position

The first principle that should guide our debate is that some forms of meritocratic competition do not promote our collective well-being. Meritocracy is the system of rewarding people according to their abilities and achievements. But these can be assessed in absolute or relative terms. Meritocracy is unambiguously desirable only if we distribute rewards on the basis of absolute performance.

To give a simple example of how rewards might be distributed on an absolute basis, consider the Individual Physical Proficiency Test (IPPT) cash awards that the Singapore Armed Forces (SAF) gives to servicemen or women who achieve the gold or silver standards in the test.[3] Here, the individual strives to clear the standards set by the SAF. He or she competes with only him or herself and not with others as it does not matter how many other people achieve those standards or do better than him or her.

This form of meritocracy—where rewards are based on absolute performance—clearly enhances society's well-being. Its main advantage is that it is set up as a positive sum game: my attainment of those standards does not prevent someone else from achieving the same or doing better. Meritocracy of this sort has the potential to promote cooperative behaviours. At the same time, those who fail the IPPT cannot blame others for their performance. And as long as the system provides help (as the SAF does) to the laggards who fail to meet the minimum standards, it is and is perceived to be fair.

Now, consider what would happen if the IPPT awards were given on *relative* merit. Rewards and punishments are now dispensed on the basis of how well a serviceman does *against* his or her peers. For instance, the top 10 per cent of servicemen or women in each age cohort earns a large cash prize, the next 10 per cent a smaller sum, the middle groups get nothing, and the bottom 20 per cent suffers penalties. This purer, more competitive form of meritocracy is undesirable for at least three reasons.

First, such a system is wasteful. It changes the game from a positive-sum one to a competitive, zero-sum one over relative position. To increase their chances of winning the cash awards and of avoiding penalties, everyone will divert more resources and time from non-positional goods (e.g., leisure time, family time) to compete for what is now a *positional good*. But while this is individually rational, it is wasteful and sub-optimal for society as a whole. When everyone decides, rationally, to devote more resources for the positional good, relative positions remain unchanged (the very fit will still be at the top and the least fit will still be at the bottom). But everyone now spends more time and resources just to maintain our (unchanged) relative positions. It would be collectively beneficial and more efficient to come to some binding collective agreement to spend less time and resources in this "arms race", an arms limitation treaty to prevent individuals from over-spending to outdo one other.

This kind of "arms race" phenomenon characterises many parts of the meritocratic system practised in Singapore. For instance, it ails our education system where students are graded on a curve, and it explains why parents probably spend much more on private tuition than what is collectively optimal.

Confronted with such a collective action problem, it is not good enough for leaders to beseech parents to "let your children have their childhood."[4] Such advice, no matter how well-intentioned, is as good as pushing on a string. It goes against the grain of individual incentives and the logic of the collective action problem that describes much of our competitive, examinations-oriented education system.

Second, a system that distributes rewards based on relative performance reduces social trust, cooperation, and cohesion. Anyone who has ever been in competition for a promotion where only one person can get the position will understand this dynamic. Since my success now depends on me outperforming the others, I have no incentive to help my colleagues succeed. "Success" in this context is a highly limited resource.

Meritocracy is not a value-free, naturally just or "inert" mechanism for distributing rewards. Instead, it shapes individual behaviours and society's norms. When the form of meritocracy that is practised rations rewards by relative performance, it promotes a selfish, me-first mentality and potentially erodes desirable norms.

Third, a meritocracy based on relative performance may not necessarily raise average performance, but "stretches out" and increases disparities in the group's performance. One might argue that the incentives for individuals to excel are magnified when rewards are distributed on the basis of relative performance. Average performance should also increase. While this is probably true for top performers, its effects on the rest of the group are more unpredictable. For instance, those further down the performance curve might feel so discouraged and demoralised that they ultimately opt out of a system in which they feel they will never have a reasonable chance of success. Stress and (performance) anxiety are also likely to increase across-the-board. And as epidemiologists have argued, higher levels of stress produce cortisol in our bodies; over sustained periods, this increases the risks of illnesses such as hypertension, psychiatric disorders, and cancers. As with the logic of an arms race, everyone suffers when we compete for relative position or status.

The point is not that we should only allocate rewards based on absolute performance and avoid measuring ourselves on relative performance in all contexts. This is simply unrealistic. Sometimes we have no choice but to compete for relative position. Some things are intrinsically scarce, and competition for these things will inevitably be zero-sum and based on how well we do relative to others. One thinks of the university valedictorian, the Olympic champion, limited university places, the CEO appointment, job promotions, and many others. In these contexts, we have no choice but to accept that scarce rewards are allocated according to *relative* merit.

But when we compete for relative gains, let us also recognise that this form of meritocracy imposes potential costs on society. This makes it incumbent on the government (which has a special responsibility to deal with collective action problems) to find ways to temper and ameliorate the harmful effects of competitive "arms races"—especially through fiscal redistribution (I will return to this point later in the essay).

As a society, we also have a degree of autonomy to decide when to use an absolute performance yardstick and when to use one based on relative merit. Neither meritocracy nor common sense prescribes that we always choose the latter. For instance, while it may seem natural to us that admission to secondary schools should be based on relative performance, the reality is that in many other countries with high-performing education systems, examinations graded on a curve are *not* used to determine high school admissions.

Indeed, I would go further to argue that the things that are most consequential for our economic well-being—growth, productivity, innovation, people's sense of security—are *not* positional goods. These things do not have to be framed as zero-sum, competitive games for relative advantage. On the contrary, they are far more likely to be achieved if we structure our systems—economic, education, research, organisations—in collaborative and cooperative ways, rather than in ways that drive people to compete for relative position.

## Type versus Effort

The second question that should guide our reflections on meritocracy is whether it should reward type or effort. The main rationale for a system that rewards people by merit is that it encourages effort. An economist might argue that meritocracy helps society deal with the problem of moral hazard that is likely to arise with other ways of allocating rewards. When rewards are tied to one's abilities and achievements, people are motivated to strive and be the best they can be. However, when rewards are tied to inherited wealth, connections, or race, people's behaviours change in morally hazardous ways: corruption and rent-seeking behaviours increase, and people channel more resources to socially unproductive activities that benefit themselves (and their families) but not society.

But it appears that the meritocracy practised in Singapore is one that rewards type rather than effort. That is, the meritocratic system rewards people who possess the "right" attributes. An economist might describe our system of meritocracy as one that aims to solve the problem of adverse selection—sorting or distinguishing the good from the rest. Adverse selection problems are, for instance, common in insurance markets where the insurer often cannot distinguish between good risks (those he wants to insure) and the bad risks (those he does not want to insure). Consequently, the insurer devises ways to get his potential customers to signal or reveal their riskiness; he also chooses to insure only the right risk types.

Like moral hazard, the problem of adverse selection is also a problem of information asymmetry. Both problems arise because one party is unable to perfectly monitor or observe the behaviour or quality of the other party. But whereas the moral hazard perspective highlights how people's behaviours might change when the rules for allocating rewards are changed, the adverse selection perspective focuses attention on how quality (or merit) is determined.

A meritocracy that is focussed on rewarding type rather than effort suffers from at least three disadvantages. The first is that we may define or measure merit poorly, and go on to assign too much importance to these imperfect measures of merit. Many commentators have pointed out how the Primary School Leaving Examination (PSLE) system—a very precise way of dealing with the sorting problem—is too consequential in that a single examination at the relatively young age of 12 determines so much of a person's subsequent educational outcomes. Given reasonable doubt over whether it is capturing and assessing merit correctly, the great importance that the current education system attaches to PSLE scores is clearly problematic.

Second, when a meritocracy is overly focussed on sorting the best from the rest—with more rewards channelled to the former—the incentive for individuals to gain a competitive edge through non-meritocratic means is accentuated. Starting positions, parental background, and connections begin to matter more; inequality in this generation is more likely to be reproduced in the next. In the context of our education system, the preferential access to schools that the children of alumni enjoy, the higher concentration of good schools in affluent neighbourhoods, and the greater resources that well-to-do families have for preschool, tuition, and enrichment programmes are examples of how our meritocracy might contribute to inequality and lower mobility.

Third, a meritocratic system focussed on rewarding type forces people to compete for relative position or advantage, the problems of which were discussed earlier.

## Wall Street versus Silicon Valley

The third question that should guide our thinking on meritocracy is what rules should govern and constrain the behaviour of those who have done well in the meritocratic system. There is no prima facie reason to believe that those who have succeeded in a meritocracy will channel their energies to socially useful activities. Neither should there be a presumption that our legal and regulatory systems are always able to deter, anticipate, and punish the abuses and wrongdoings of the successful. The risks of regulatory capture and of regulators lacking the information and incentives to do the right thing are all real—even for advanced economies with well-developed institutions.

The 2007–09 global financial crisis that began on Wall Street is a case in point of how an ostensibly meritocratic system can wreak havoc on the rest of society. Wall Street meritocracy—where losses are socialised and gains privatised, and "innovation" results in products that are potentially socially harmful—is toxic for at least three reasons.

The first is moral hazard. Bankers took on enormous risks knowing that their institutions enjoyed implicit guarantees from the state and would be bailed out if their losses ever threatened the banking system. They enjoyed an unlimited upside even as their downside was back-stopped by the state. This system of flawed incentives, combined with the opportunities created by financial innovation and securitisation, explains why Wall Street banks peddled so many subprime mortgages to people who were not credit-worthy, why they sliced and diced these mortgages into securities that were then sold to investors who could not easily monitor their quality, and why they paid themselves large fees for effectively increasing risks in the financial system. When these securities lost their value following the real estate crash, Wall Street banks were shielded from the consequences of their bad decisions because these institutions were deemed "too big to fail".

Second, it is highly doubtful that all the financial innovation on Wall Street was socially useful. While securitisation is potentially a good thing (structured properly, it spreads and diversifies risks), it actually increases systemic fragility when the risks of the individual securities are highly correlated and when the maintenance of their values depends on flawed assumptions (like the assumption that house prices would never fall). The former chairman of the US Federal Reserve, Paul Volcker, went as far as to say that "the only socially useful banking innovation (in recent decades) was the invention of the ATM."

Third, Wall Street meritocracy breeds a pernicious, self-justifying, entitlement narrative. For example, Wall Street bankers justified the decision to pay themselves millions in bonuses from the bailout monies they received from taxpayers on the grounds that a failure to do so would result in talent leaving the financial industry. This kind of Wall Street meritocracy breeds a belief among its beneficiaries that they are entitled to their rewards, that the system is inherently just, and that inequality is a natural consequence of an efficient and normatively desirable system. They view those who have not succeeded in the system as slothful or lacking in talent or merit—and undeserving of state support. This increases the resistance of the rich to the redistributive policies needed to tackle rising inequality. Over time, such a meritocratic system entrenches inequality and immobility; the risks of this society becoming more stratified permanently and divided by class are also much greater.

Contrast the meritocracy of Wall Street with the meritocracy of Silicon Valley. Nobody is bailed out in Silicon Valley: an entrepreneur succeeds or fails based on whether consumers find his or her inventions useful. While Silicon Valley is also prone to speculative booms and busts, the damage it causes society when its bubble bursts is far more limited. It becomes clear that we have two kinds of meritocracy with contrasting outcomes.

Needless to say, the kind of meritocracy practised in Silicon Valley is superior to the meritocracy laced with corporate socialism practised on Wall Street. The former is just and legitimate in the eyes of average citizens because the successful bear the full consequences of their decisions and are not insulated from the risks they take. People are less accepting of inequality and uneven rewards when there is one set of rules for the winners and another for the rest. Wall Street suffers from a severe legitimacy crisis not only because of its sense of entitlement but also because it is widely perceived to have gotten away with all the damage it caused.

The US banking crisis is a powerful reminder that the risks of moral hazard are far greater when the rich and successful are not properly regulated and reined in. Corporate malfeasance imposes a much larger cost on society than the fecklessness of the poor addicted to government welfare.[5]

Another important lesson from the crisis is that not only do markets sometimes fail, but also that the rules and institutions designed to anticipate and correct these market failures can also fail. In a healthy democracy (and meritocracy), the watchman also needs to be watched. This calls for eternal vigilance on the part of citizens and civil society. It means creating strong safeguards against regulatory capture, increasing transparency and public accountability, and ensuring the (political) independence of public institutions.

## Trickle-Down versus Trickle-Up

The fourth question is how we reconcile meritocracy with inequality. While we like meritocracy for rewarding hard work and recognising people's talent and abilities, we dislike the unequal outcomes it produces. Is this an inevitable trade-off? If we want an efficient system that creates strong incentives for people to strive, must we also accept the highly unequal distribution of incomes and wealth that such a system produces?

One way to think about this question is to contrast two worldviews. The first, which might be termed "trickle-down meritocracy", sees the growth of the economy and the progress of society as driven by its elite, its best and brightest. A society organised along the lines of this worldview channels a larger share of resources and opportunities to its high performers and talents. A trickle-down system is not concerned with equality of outcomes, but with ensuring that its talents have the room to achieve and excel, and are not shackled by high taxation and excessive regulations.

In such a society, economic efficiency takes precedence over distributional concerns or considerations of social equity. Indeed, this view contends that the poor are best served by providing the best and the brightest with the maximum opportunities to succeed, as they are the ones who create jobs for the rest. Holding the talented back by having onerous taxes or regulatory restraints on markets undermines growth and hurts the poor—the very people whom the advocates of social justice claim to help. A trickle-down approach also means that government and society should be more concerned with growing the pie (through market-friendly and pro-talent policies), and less with how the pie is distributed.

For the last 20 years, Singapore society has embraced this world-view. Income tax rates have been slashed, wealth taxes reduced (e.g., not only does Singapore not tax capital gains, but the estate duty was also abolished in 2008), and public spending as a share of GDP reduced. The state has also not become more redistributive in the face of rising inequality. Consequently, even after taking into account taxes and transfers, inequality today is higher than it was a decade ago before government redistribution.

A second worldview, which one might term "trickle-up meritoc-racy", sees government redistribution and fair outcomes as necessary corollaries to market-friendly, pro-capital policies and the merito-cratic system. According to this view, meritocracy is legitimate only if it benefits the bulk of society—not just in absolute terms, but also in relative terms. This is because greater inequality reduces subjective well-being, social mobility, and trust. Meritocracy with high and rising inequality sows the seeds of its own demise. If society cares about preserving meritocracy, it is incumbent on its members to limit the rise in inequality.

Trickle-up meritocracy also differs from the trickle-down variant in at least two other ways. First, it contends that ensuring equal opportu-nities is necessary, but not sufficient. Because people start with differ-ences in talent and resources, equalising resources at the start to some extent is justified on the grounds that this is necessary to ensure equal access to opportunities. Such a system is still meritocratic as the equalisation is done at the start of the competitive race and does not diminish incentives for everyone to run as fast as they can. The race is competitive and meritocratic, but the state has intervened to adjust starting positions and given those with fewer resources a head start.

Second, trickle-up meritocracy believes that instead of subsidising and extending tax breaks to the rich in the hope that they will create jobs and prosperity for the rest, fiscal policy should be focused on increasing the human capital of the rest, ensuring they can afford basic needs like housing and good healthcare, assuring them of retirement security and social protection against contingencies like involuntary unemployment, and reducing inequality. In the long run, these measures also benefit corporations and those further up the income ladder by raising incomes and consumption at the bottom.

Spending on these social goods, which is likely to require vigorous fiscal redistribution in the context of today's globalisation and rapid technological change, is necessary to save meritocracy from itself. Indeed, without these redistributive measures, meritocracy rests on increasingly shaky and tenuous foundations.

## Conclusion

In the national debate on meritocracy, let us avoid framing the issue as a false choice: meritocracy or no meritocracy. A constructive and meaningful debate would instead focus on whether ours is a meritocracy that forces people to compete for absolute performance or relative position; whether it rewards effort or type; what rules and institutions we should have to regulate those who have succeeded in the meritocratic system; and how it can maximise "trickle-up" benefits.

## *Notes*

1. This essay was originally written for the Institute for Policy Studies' online platform, *IPS Commons*, in December 2012. It has been slightly modified for this publication. The original can be found at http://www.ipscommons.sg/index.php/categories/featured/104-good-meritocracy-bad-meritocracy.

2. *See* for instance, Lydia Lim, "Striking the right balance in meritocracy", *Singapolitics*, 17 Dec. 2012, http://www.singapolitics.sg/views/striking-right-balance-meritocracy.

3. An annual assessment of fitness that Singaporeans typically begin taking in secondary school.

4. In the 2012 National Day Rally, Prime Minister Lee Hsien Loong urged parents to "let your children have their childhood". Speech at http://www.pmo.gov.sg/content/pmosite/mediacentre/speechesninterviews/primeminister/2012/August/prime_minister_leehsienloongsnationaldayrally2012speechinenglish.m.html.

5. For a longer exposition on the social costs and risks imposed by the rise of the super-rich, *see* Joe Stiglitz's May 2011 article in *Vanity Fair*, http://www.vanityfair.com/society/features/2011/05/top-one-percent-201105.

# 5

# THE END OF
# IDENTITY?

*Sudhir Thomas Vadaketh*

China-born Singapore citizen Feng Tian Wei's Olympic table tennis bronze medal in 2012 sparked an outcry. Many Singaporeans expressed the view that they feel no sense of pride about the country's first individual Olympic medal in four decades. What then does it mean to be a "true" Singaporean?[1]

Yet the issue is not so much that Ms Feng has failed to integrate into Singapore. It is that many people who grew up in Singapore have failed to integrate into Ms Feng's Singapore—the Singapore of the future. They cling to a romantic notion of national identity that is now passé. For better or worse, the era of Singaporean national identity, the one that our founding fathers tried to establish, is fading.

## From Birth, an Artificial Nation

In many countries, national identity develops from a common tribal base, whether stemming from ethnicity, as in Japan, or religion, as in Pakistan. In some other countries, national identity is nurtured through a shared values system, for example, freedom and opportunity in the United States.

On 9 August 1965, Singapore had neither.

"Some countries are born independent. Some achieve independence. Singapore had independence thrust upon it," says Lee Kuan Yew, Singapore's first prime minister, in his memoirs. "How were we to create a nation out of a polyglot collection of migrants from China, India, Malaysia, Indonesia, and several other parts of Asia?" As Mr Lee says, most modern states are the products of a drive to self-determination from a nation of people. Singapore's genesis occurred in reverse: a state was born, and then a nation had to be artificially created.

Singapore hence tried to establish a polyglot tribal base as well as a shared values system. The polyglot Singapore tribe comprises Chinese, Indians, and Malays, who speak English, Mandarin, Malay, and Tamil, and worship at temples, mosques, and churches. Other dialects (e.g., Hindi) and religions (e.g., Zoroastrianism) that might belong to these three main groups in their homelands were occasionally tolerated, but sometimes, as in the case of Chinese dialects, actively suppressed.

Meanwhile, almost every other person from outside this polyglot tribe was welcomed into the new Singapore of 1965, but was stuck with the rather uncharitable, amorphous label of "Others".

When Singaporeans first receive an identity card, which states one's ethnicity, at age 12, we huddle and swap them around with our friends, poking fun at unflattering photographs and pontificating about exactly where young Mr/Ms "Others" is from. The message to "Others" has always been clear: please stay, but do remember that you are different from us.

In other words, in Singapore the notion of a polyglot tribe evolved based on the so-called "CMIO" (Chinese-Malay-India-Others) model. By its very definition, the "C", "M", and "I" are part of the core, and the "O" on the outside.

According to Ang and Stratton, "Singapore invests enormously in the official validation of the three separate reified Chinese, Malaya, and Indian cultures (the "Others" category, often designated as "Eurasian", is generally ignored), as it is through these three "Asian high cultures" that Singapore aims to forge its unique and quintessential multiracial Asianness."[2]

To be clear, the government conceived the CMIO model as an administrative tool of governance, not as a pillar of an idealised Singaporean identity. Indeed, Singapore has always attempted to promote a broad multiculturalism—or "multiracialism", as it has been called. However, given the CMIO classification's sustained adoption in numerous spheres of everyday life, it has become indelibly linked to notions of what it means to be Singaporean. Sociologist Chua Beng Huat has argued, "One can examine any sphere of cultural endeavour, from theatre to television drama to everyday handling of items like food and clothes, and discover the encoding of the CMIO scheme."[3]

## Defining a Singaporean: Poetry, Pragmatism, and Patois

Singapore also ingrained a common set of values in people: hard work, tolerance, the importance of meritocracy, and the belief in pragmatism both in day-to-day behaviour and national policies. These values were born out of the sense of crisis and vulnerability that first emerged during that period, and were seen as appropriate responses to ensure the survival of the nation.

Moreover, the ideals of multiculturalism and meritocracy, in particular, must be viewed in opposition to the pro-Malay position Malaysia was adopting, as this philosophical divergence lay at the heart of Singapore's split from the Federation of Malaysia.

While Singapore's economy grew rapidly, the Singaporean identity always remained in flux. It has not been easy creating an imagined community out of nothing. "What does it mean to be a Singaporean?" has never had an easy, consistent answer. Singaporeanness can range from the trivial ("our food") to the profound ("pragmatism").

Yet even the famed Singaporean pragmatism has no consistent definition. At its meekest, it points simply to the habit of making rational rather than reckless decisions. At its most draconian, Singaporean pragmatism can refer to an austerity of action and thought where every single interaction is pregnant with cold calculation, where every calorie, it seems, must be expended only towards some higher economic purpose.

"Poetry is a luxury we cannot afford," Mr Lee famously told students in 1968 at the then University of Singapore. This brand of Singaporean pragmatism is our brutal riposte to Europe's joie de vivre. Even today, when fans of the fiscally prudent Singapore government thumb their noses at southern Europe's parlous public finances, the crux of their triumphalism is a preference for disciplined pragmatism over the perceived trappings of joie de vivre.

Tensions between Singapore's various cultural narratives have always simmered below the surface. They came to the fore most prominently in the late 1990s, when a segment of Singapore's elite, led by Goh Chok Tong, the then prime minister, fought a misguided battle to dampen the use of Singlish in Singapore, claiming that foreigners may not be able to understand Singaporeans who speak Singlish. Confused Singaporeans lamented the possible loss of one of our few truly unique cultural markers.

## Global or Local?

The Singlish debate was a microcosm of a much greater sociocultural tension that emerged in the early 1990s. On the one hand, the governing elite believed that Singapore's economic success could be guaranteed only by embracing globalisation wholeheartedly; even more than that, Singapore had to become a global city, attracting capital and talent from across the world. On the other hand, there was a concern about whether the nascent, delicate Singaporean culture and identity could crystallise if buffeted by the relentless waves of global culture.

Aaron Koh has said that there is an "irreconcilable tension through the processes of globalisation (celebrated as multiple identities) and localisation (perceived narrowly as national identity)."[4] The tension manifested itself everywhere, from Singlish to architecture. For instance, many Singaporean artists had deep misgivings about the government's decision to plump more than S$600 million into the construction of the Esplanade Theatres on the Bay, largely in a bid to attract top international acts, a thrust that was perceived to come at the expense of local art. According to Koh's analysis, there are three forces prompting this shift away from a narrow national identity: "an accelerated pace of global population movements in our contemporary trans/postnational time," "nationalist discourses and bounded territories that are giving way to what is now known as transnational and diasporic networks," and technological change, which is allowing individuals to practise "long-distance nationalism" but also enabling them to adopt multiple identities more easily.

## A Country for Migrants

While these pressures affect all nation states, Singapore is unique in that it has witnessed radical population change, following a dramatic experiment in mass immigration as a means to counter low birth rates.

In 1990, more than 86 per cent of Singapore's population was made up of citizens. By 2011, this had dropped to below 63 per cent. More telling, given the high number of new citizens from abroad, is the fact that perhaps less than 50 per cent of Singapore's total population was actually born here.[5]

Put another way, Singapore is one of the few countries in the world where there are more migrants—including temporary workers, permanent residents and foreign-born citizens—than native-born people.

The recent furore over "The Sticker Lady" dug up some old debates about vandalism and the nature of art.[6] What was missing was a discussion about her linguistic choice and the market for it. Perhaps the reason Sticker Lady doesn't have more fans in Singapore is because less than half the country even understands the meaning of *kancheong*. Perhaps, to the immense relief of English pedants, the 1990s will one day be remembered as the apex of Singlish.

## Differentiation in the Face of Globalisation

Proponents of high immigration in Singapore point to the demographic make-up of global cities such as London and New York as exemplars. This argument is somewhat defensible from an economic point of view, but it also reveals the fundamental problem with Singaporean identity.

London and New York are global cities that are connected to much larger heartlands. No matter how cosmopolitan they become, there will never be any doubt about what it means to be British or American. The identity of those countries is never in question.

Singapore, largely because of history and politics, is untethered from our most obvious heartland, the Malay Peninsula. Singapore is not a primary city for the Malay-Indo region, or for China, or for India. It has tried to position itself as the Asian jack of all trades, a developed world hodgepodge that is both all of Asia and yet not Asia at all. While this may work economically, from an identity standpoint, contradictions abound.

This combination of globalisation, low birth rates, and high immigration has essentially overturned the very essence of Singaporean identity that our forefathers tried to build. The traditional notion of "tribe"—Chinese, Indian and Malay— has been disrupted.

While diversity must be celebrated, it would be callous to ignore immigration's impact on feelings of identity and belonging. Singaporeans welcomed "Others" when they were a small minority; now that "Others" are flooding in, completely displacing native-born Singaporeans in places such as Marina Bay, the core feels vulnerable.

"My Singaporean Chinese friends used to speak only English to me," says Farouk Khan, a Singaporean who lives in Kuala Lumpur. "Now whenever we meet, they are always trying to litter their conversation with Malay words and phrases. They are trying to show that they are local Chinese, different from the Mainland Chinese."

Some suggest that when Singaporean Chinese try to differentiate themselves from Mainland Chinese—or, for that matter, Singapore Indians from India Indians—it is because of class consciousness, racism, or some other prejudice. While perhaps true in some instances, the most basic instinct that is driving these actions is the loss of identity. Singaporeans are desperately clinging onto any vestiges of Singaporeanness.

The pro-migration camp does not seem to understand these grumblings. The common refrain is that many countries welcome migrants, and so Singapore should be no different. But this harks back to the earlier point about magnitude. While migration does occur globally, few countries have enacted such dramatic demographic change.

The seemingly irrepressible waves of migrants over the past two decades have affected Singaporeans' job opportunities, quality of life and, most importantly, identity.

Moreover, therein lies one of the ironies of the "CMIO" model of tribal identity. Even though new Chinese and Indian migrants should technically be part of the "CMI" core, in the popular imagination, they are, as a result of their cultural differences, effectively part of the "O", Others.

## Failed by Meritocracy

This is true not only in terms of our tribe but also values. Singapore's meritocracy has long promised that as long as individuals work hard, they will enjoy the fruits of their labour, with the best workers rising to the top of the ladder. Here, again, mass immigration has undermined this social contract.

At the top end, the perception is that the global elite has moved here with containers of cash in hunt of lower tax rates, and is creaming off the spoils of Singapore's growth. At the bottom end, a seemingly endless stream of low-cost migrants from neighbouring countries has allowed businesses to keep wages low, squeezing out hardworking Singaporeans who face spiralling living costs.

In the middle, there are many stories about how the infusion of migrants has torpedoed Singapore's meritocracy. One common anecdote relates to India Indians in the financial services sector who prefer to recruit their friends from back home rather than promote well-qualified Singaporeans from within.

Unlike many other countries, including Hong Kong and the US, Singapore does not require employers to look for locals first. For any particular vacancy, companies are free to hire from anywhere in the world (up to their foreign worker quota). They do not even have to advertise the position locally.

As a result, over the past few years, there have been countless accusations of employers giving preference to foreigners over locals—the reasons vary, depending on the sector and seniority. In mid-level service jobs, for instance, employers can generally hire foreigners from less-developed parts of Asia at lower wages.

Singapore's meritocracy was meant to reward people fairly for their efforts; but in the eyes of many locals, it appears to be performing less and less equitably. This, in turn, has threatened the very notion of Singaporean identity.

## Ethnic Integration: Double Standards?

Finally, mass migration has dented Singapore's attempts at inter-ethnic integration. Recall that the entire thrust of Singapore's national identity formation from the 1960s onwards involved a gradual deemphasising of ethnic, clan, and communal identities and sentiments in favour of a higher, common Singaporean identity.

Don't speak Hokkien, Singaporeans were told, because it alienates the non-Hokkien speakers. Don't allow too many Indians or Malays to live in the same area, Singaporeans were told, lest a ghetto forms. The Singaporean, a new glorious pan-Asian breed, was meant to rise from the ashes of ethnic and religious strife, to tower above the clannish impulses that govern lesser beings.

But somebody forgot to tell the new migrants. Ethnic enclaves have now formed, including a rather posh Indian one in the East Coast and a more humble Vietnamese one in Joo Chiat. Foreign languages and dialects are all the rage, echoing through the corridors of high finance down to the back alleys of coffee shops. Ms Feng, to the bewilderment of her fellow citizens, has not bothered to learn English, despite having lived in Singapore for five years.

In terms of identity, it is as if native-born Singaporeans have been marshalled and spanked for years while migrants, including new citizens like Ms Feng, have been given carte blanche to be whoever they want to be.

## Unweaning the Need for State Guidance

There is perhaps also a lesson here about the state's role in identity creation. Singapore has always had a strong state and an active, top-down national identity campaign. But the flipside is that the state might have always come across as overweening, moralising and paternalistic. This may have bred a certain dependence among the population, who seek guidance on all issues—from ethnic relations to whether graffiti should be considered art—that might be important for identity creation.

Most of the institutions, including those in the arts, media, and civil society that might have played a role in organic identity creation, have been co-opted or subdued by the state. In short, Singaporeans know who we are *supposed* to be, but have not been given much of a chance to say who we *want* to be.

Eschewing poetry might have helped focus Singaporeans on technical skills, but it probably also eliminated our identity-creating instincts. How many Singaporeans still know the words to "Di Tanjong Katong"?

There are, no doubt, signs that space has opened up for artists and individuals to have more influence on notions of a Singapore identity. According to Stephen Ortmann, "In Singapore today the most important platform for the negotiation and construction of national identity is the internet."[7]

Personal blogs such as the *mrbrownshow* and online news portals such as *The Online Citizen* are providing channels for popular commentators as well as ordinary people to engage in organic identity creation. Ortmann cites a wide variety of art forms—from the Jack Neo films *I Not Stupid* and *Money No Enough*, which "tend to emphasise Singapore's negative national characteristics," to Alfian Sa'at's poem "Singapore You Are Not My Country"—all of which "contribute to the invention of what constitutes the Singapore nation."

Nevertheless, it is difficult to escape the spectre of the state, particularly when the renegotiation of identity involves a sensitive topic like race. This position was reinforced during the drawn-out saga in 2012–13 over whether to allow the local film *Sex.Violence.FamilyValues*—which pokes fun at Indian stereotypes—to be screened in Singapore. After initially banning it, Singapore's Media Development Authority (MDA) later permitted it with edits and an above 21 rating. In a statement the MDA said that it "is of the view that while it does not condone or promote racism, some of the racial references employed in the film are indeed offensive to the Indian community."[8]

In most democracies, ethnic references—positive or negative—are discussed openly, certainly when presented in comedic films. In Singapore, however, it is clear that certain aspects of identity are open for renegotiation while others are off limits.

## Global Citizens versus National Citizens

With birth rates unlikely to rise rapidly, and immigration likely to continue, albeit at a more moderate clip, it will be interesting to see what happens to this fragile, embryonic Singaporean identity. How can a country construct a national identity when less than half the total population was born there?

Some will argue that a person does not need to be born in a country to really feel at home. Perhaps, but it certainly helps. People will always have one set of feelings for the land where they were born and grew up, and another for their adopted home.

Perhaps the reality is that Singapore cannot build both a national identity and a global city identity. The national identity served the country well in our formative years, but the global city identity is what will carry it forward. In fact, Singapore is already in the midst of a transition from the former to the latter. A global city identity is much more fluid and less rooted than a national identity. People do not take up Singapore citizenship today for the same reasons they take up, for example, American citizenship.

In Singapore, migration is not about ideals or dreams or what the country stands for. In Singapore, the impetus is often purely transactional—including lower tax rates, safer streets, and the ability to invest in property. Migrants, many of whom now have a critical mass in Singapore, tend to live their own lives in their own silos. They interact with others, of course, playing, working, and breaking bread together. But there is no larger, imagined community here that binds all the people in Singapore.

The migrants of today will probably never integrate like the migrants of yesterday. The world is more globalised and cognitive distances are getting shorter. Before the 1990s, it is likely that many migrants arrived in Singapore with the intention of establishing permanent roots here. Since then, however, Singapore has clearly seen an increasing number of so-called transnational migrants, also sometimes referred to as "third culture people" or those with "hyphenated" identities. These are people "happy to move between a variety of local cultures with which they develop a practical, working acquaintance and the bridging third culture which enables them to communicate with like persons from around the world."[9]

Many of these migrants already think of "Singaporeanness" in terms of a global city identity, not a national one. Many will send their children to international schools—launch pads, it is hoped, for them to join the global elite. For these young ones, "Singaporean" is just one of a patchwork of identities they hope to stitch together as they journey through life.

Of course, the rise of transnational migrants is a global phenomenon—but their impact on Singapore has been significant because of the country's relative youth and small size. Moreover, as the incomes of the upper- and middle-classes have risen, it is likely that many native Singaporeans have also conceptually—if not yet practically—joined the ranks of transnational migrants, as comfortable roaming the streets of Bangkok and Hong Kong as they are Singapore. While first and foremost Singaporean, they are also embracing the ideas, habits, and vernaculars of other cultures.

And that, strangely, represents the optimism in this identity story. There are few countries in the world where race, religion, and language are depoliticised to this extent, where it is so easy to set up a business, where people from all over the world can visit so seamlessly.

Through policies that unintentionally undermine national identity, and ultimately nationalism, Singapore has unwittingly created a model for a future where nationhood, ethnicity, and religion should not matter. Each must be celebrated, but remain secondary to the higher human identity.

In other words, while there may never be a larger, *imagined* community within Singapore, people here will constantly be thinking about the larger, *global* imagined community (an affiliation that will vary by class, as described below). Some suggest that the Singaporean's greatest strength is as a global interlocutor. In this rapidly evolving multipolar world, Singaporeans can find common ground with more people than any other nationality. Simply put, they have more cultural touch-points with more people.

The Americans, so the argument goes, find it easier to deal with Singaporeans than with any other Asian. The Chinese, similarly, have less trouble communicating with Singaporeans than with people from other English-speaking countries. According to George Yeo, Singapore's former foreign minister, Singaporeans are experts at "code switching" when they move from communicating with, for example, a relatively introverted Asian to a gregarious Westerner.

## Embracing a Global Identity

At the heart of this transition from a solid albeit nascent national identity to the more fluid global city identity is a major paradigm shift. It is worth considering this shift using the framework of vulnerability and resilience.

When Singapore first gained independence, the vulnerability perspective demanded that a cohesive national identity be forged. Many of the policies implemented then—such as the reduction of diverse clans and dialects into supposedly homogenous racial groups—may have been illiberal but were certainly politically expedient, as they helped to unite disparate groups in a turbulent time towards a common goal.

Today, given Singapore's rapid economic growth, its embrace of globalisation, and its dramatically altered population make-up, hanging on to this vulnerability perspective will lead to suboptimal outcomes in terms of identity and multiculturalism. Many of the identity-related vulnerabilities of the 1960s—such as irredentism by Malaysia and inter-clan disputes in Singapore—have almost completely disappeared.

Instead, in this era of transnational migrants and multiple identities, a resilience perspective will allow the creation of a strong and confident yet fluid Singaporean identity. It has to be an open, progressive identity, one that can easily absorb both temporary visitors and permanent migrants, local and foreign, without any preconceived notions about what constitutes a Singaporean.

This shift has implications for mindsets, personal interactions, and national policy.

The overarching mindset shift requires that Singaporean identity no longer be conceptualised as an immutable, narrow, territorial-bound set of markers and values. Instead, identity is evolving in tandem with the global city's relentless change, a never-ending journey that maintains certain core precepts. For instance, even as the commitment to meritocracy is maintained, as earlier chapters have suggested, the expressions of meritocracy in society might change. In such a dynamic situation, the notion of all Singaporeans ever sharing a common culture is archaic.

Hussain Mutalib writes that "more often than not, the process of forging a common national identity not only takes time, but also, like the river, has its ebb and flow and is continuously changing its content and contours, depending on the kind of things the water comes into contact with as it moves along the river course. The same observation can be applied to Singapore's search for a common national identity."10

This shift will also have an impact on personal interactions. For instance, instead of viewing India Indians with suspicion for their alleged cronyism in recruitment policies, Singaporeans must start to realise that this might actually be how many cultures operate.

Not every society adheres devoutly to a strict paper meritocracy. Connections and networks matter, as do non-traditional interests and pursuits. "The India Indians are much better at looking after their own kind," admits one disgruntled Singaporean banker friend, "Singaporeans are more adversarial, afraid that others will get ahead, so we do not compliment or praise each other as much publicly."

With a rigid national identity lens, Singaporeans might complain more about India Indians upending our meritocracy. But from a global city identity standpoint, Singaporeans might be more eager to absorb lessons, and ultimately beat the India Indians at their own game—both in Singapore, and possibly in India. This is not to condone cronyism; rather, it is more a recognition that societal structures and incentives will always be different the world over.

Similarly, if Singapore embraces this global city identity, Singaporeans should not care if Ms Feng never learns any English. She does not have to sound like us to be one of us. Her time is probably better spent smashing balls than reading Shakespeare.

## Letting Go of Outdated Policies

The most obvious policy implication concerns integration. In a global city, it makes little sense, for example, to maintain ethnic quotas in HDB housing estates, when little ethnic enclaves have formed all over the country.

These quotas were useful when Singapore was emerging from the turbulent 1960s. Today, they are archaic, paternalistic and, perhaps worst of all, condescending. The policy's effective—though certainly unintended—messaging today is: "Foreigners and rich people do not have to integrate because they can take care of themselves. But Singaporean HDB dwellers must, lest you gang up and fight."

Meanwhile, the CMIO's reductionist tendencies render it irrelevant today. Attempts to homogenise, say, Singapore Chinese or Singapore Indians, mean that locals are streamlined into socially constructed racial buckets while newer Chinese and Indians migrants continue to express their unique identities. Perhaps there was a hope that these new migrants would eventually be absorbed into the CMIO fold. But given all the demographic and socioeconomic changes described above, this seems unlikely.

The CMIO model then has become a drag on Singapore's efforts to create a global city. It immediately limits the identities of locals while occasionally enforcing parochial notions of what a Singaporean should be. Perhaps it is better then to dispense with the CMIO model for one that acknowledges the demographics of a global city, with all its cultural and linguistic diversity.

On a related note, the government should no longer worry too much about maintaining a specific proportion of Chinese in the population. According to Chua, "[g]iven geopolitical conditions, the government has made a fetish out of changing demographics and has decided that the Chinese population should constitute approximately three-quarters of the total population at all times."[11] While there may have been some realpolitik justification for this approach in Singapore's early development, it is today completely out of kilter with the desire to build a global city.

The second implication concerns the state's role in identity creation. In order for Singapore to build a resilient global city identity, it has to allow ideas and opinions on identity to bubble up naturally. Society's appetite for top-down identity theorising is diminishing. This necessarily implies that non-governmental actors must feel that they can express themselves freely, particularly with regards to hitherto out-of-bounds topics (e.g., race). In describing the experience of Singaporeans living in Beijing, Lily Kong notes, "It is perhaps in the absence of state efforts to (re)invent traditions and rituals that construct the nation that the efforts of agency surface ... Agency thus finds itself space where structure does not dominate."[12]

Again, a vulnerability perspective suggests that the risk of uttering any ethnically inflammatory statement is sufficient grounds to bar all discussion. But a resilience perspective believes that the only way to strengthen the system is to air all opinions—positive and negative—in the belief that an open discussion will ultimately foster greater tolerance, trumping the risk of bigotry festering in silos.

The Little India riots on 8 December 2013, and the public discussion in its aftermath, actually demonstrated that Singapore's polity is mature enough to move beyond the old politics of race. First, the very fact that Singaporeans have grown to accept the presence of temporary "ghettos"—including South Asians in Serangoon Road or Filipinos in Orchard Road—is some proof that it is pointless to try and socially engineer neighbourhoods, whether in terms of its inhabitants or daily visitors. (Granted, this "acceptance" of their presence does not necessarily imply acceptance into the broader Singapore community—an issue complicated by notions of identity and class discussed here. Debates over the construction and location of foreign worker dormitories are testament to this.)

Second, while there were clear cases of racism and xenophobia against the alleged rioters online, these were subsequently overwhelmed by calls for tolerance and understanding. While bigots will always exist in every society, in this case they were almost instantly ostracised and had absolutely no ability to organise themselves beyond sporadic social media pow-wows.

## Prioritising Social Equity

But there remains one major problem with this transition from a national identity to a global city identity. Many have been left behind. Social inequality has risen rapidly over the past two decades.

The only way for all Singaporeans to accept the pros and cons of living in a global city is if they can actually participate in it. Indeed, if Singaporeans from all backgrounds had shared in the successes of the city's growth over the past decade, any supposed xenophobia would have been muted.

Addressing inequality in education, employment, and income remains this global city's greatest priority. Though the government clearly recognises this and has begun to take steps to address this, it will not be easy reducing social inequality. Singapore faces global trends—such as economic and technological change—that have created a "winner-takes-all", global market economy, where wealth is increasingly concentrated at the top.

Domestically, meanwhile, mindset changes are needed. But it will not be easy to convince Singaporeans to embrace a more redistributive socioeconomic model after decades of severe allergy to welfare.

And yet the alternative is dire. If Singapore is unable to reduce social inequality, lower income citizens will become increasingly disenchanted both with their economic prospects and their sense of belonging in this global city. That could lead to serious social friction of the sort that Singapore has never before witnessed.

Some believe that the creation and existence of two separate identity classes in Singapore is inevitable—one more nativist in outlook, the other with a global orientation. The latter group, no doubt, will consist of higher income foreigners and Singaporeans since they have the resources to move in and out of Singapore with ease. An underlying assumption of this school of thought is that Singapore's significant income and wealth inequalities are an inescapable facet of life here.

This essay rejects the possibility that this can ever be a harmonious, sustainable, long-term situation. Instead, the argument here is that, particularly for a country as small and dense as Singapore, it is imperative that the vast majority of people have a broadly similar conception of their place in the world. This can only happen if social inequities are reduced.

## All Roads Lead to a Global City

Given globalisation and the ongoing shift of economic power from the West to the East, it seems likely that all the global cities in the world—including Dubai, London, New York, and Singapore—will experience some form of identity convergence.

Global cities will start to look and feel more and more like each other, from the kinds of shops that are set up to the nature of business activities in them. They will attract people from the same talent pools. These global cities will be similar, but each with a local flavour. So are we witnessing the end of (national) identity, but the start of something new? It is doubtful, though, if a global city identity can ever inspire fervour like a national identity can.

## Less Emotional Attachment?

Therefore, perhaps by definition, it will be harder for Singapore to foster a sense of belonging to the country amongst "global citizens" than "national citizens". This has implications for many things, including emotional attachment, commitment to national military service, and emigration rates.

These are all tensions that will have to be managed by balancing the responsibilities of and benefits accorded to citizens vis-à-vis non-citizens. As both a global city and country, Singapore's challenge is unique. But in addressing it, Singapore can become a model for a tolerant, multicultural global city that values justice and equality.

## Is "Global City" the Only Path?

As a concluding comment, there is an underlying assumption in this essay that Singapore is on an inexorable path towards becoming a global city—if it is not already there. It is notable that there are Singaporeans who are deeply sceptical about this journey.

Some suggest an alternative course: rather than a "global city", Singapore as a "regional city". Among other things, this might imply a diminution in Singapore's global financial services sector as well as an increased focus on developing Southeast Asian economic and social linkages. The implication for Singaporean identity, then, will be one more closely aligned with the immediate region, as opposed to an East-West hybrid, or pan-Asian identity.

Others believe that Singapore should significantly alter its immigration and integration approach. Among other things, this could mean much tighter immigration laws coupled with a much more concerted integration effort, including language and national service requirements for first-generation migrants.

However, given Singapore's current developmental trajectory, and the PAP's continued dominance, it seems unlikely that there will soon be any major policy shift away from the "global city" aspiration. Nevertheless, these alternative developmental narratives could one day become more popular and have a more significant impact on policy.

## *Notes*

1. This piece was originally published on the Institute for Policy Studies' online platform, *IPS Commons*, on 23 Aug. 2012. It has been updated for this compilation of essays. The original version is available here: http://ipscommons.sg/index.php/categories/society/78-the-end-of-identity.

2. Ien Ang and Jon Stratton, "The Singapore Way of Multiculturalism: Western Concepts/ Asian Cultures," *Sojourn: Journal of Social Issues in Southeast Asia* 10, no. 1, "Post-Modernism and Southeast Asian Scholarship" (April 1995): 78.

3. Chua Beng Huat, "Multiculturalism in Singapore: An Instrument of Social Control," *Race & Class* 44, no. 3 (2003): 74.

4. Aaron Koh, "Imagining the Singapore "Nation" and "Identity": The role of the media and National Education," *Asia Pacific Journal of Education 25*, no. 1 (2005): 75–91.

5. Percentage of citizens in total population, 2011: 62.2 per cent (from government sources). Percentage of citizens that are born in Singapore, 2011: 73.6 per cent (my own calculation). Therefore, percentage of total population that was born in Singapore, 2011: 45.8 per cent. For more detail on the assumptions in my calculation, *see* "What percentage of Singapore's total population was born in Singapore?," www.sudhirtv.com.

6. Samantha Lo aka "The Sticker Lady" is a Singaporean artist who ran afoul of the law because she displayed her art on public fixtures. She painted "MY GRANDFATHER ROAD" on several roads, and created circular, black-and-white stickers with captions such as "Press to time travel" and "Press once can already", which she stuck on pedestrian crossing buttons.

7. Stephan Ortmann, "Singapore: The Politics of Inventing National Identity," *Journal of Current Southeast Asian Affairs* 28, no. 4 (2009): 39.

8. "Ban on 'Sex.Violence.FamilyValues' lifted, movie given R21 rating," *Yahoo! News*, 11 Jan. 2013.

9. Mike Featherstone (1993), "Global and Local Cultures," in *Mapping the Futures: Local Cultures, Global Change*, ed. Bird, J. et al. (London and New York: Routledge, 1993), 182.

10. Hussin Mutalib, "National identity in Singapore: Old Impediments and New Imperatives," *Asian Journal of Political Science* 3, no. 2 (1995): 29.

11. Chua Beng Huat, "Multiculturalism in Singapore: An Instrument of Social Control," *Race & Class* 44, no. 3 (2003): 69.

12. Lily Kong, "Globalisation and Singaporean Transmigration: Re-Imagining and Negotiating National Identity," *Political Geography* 18, no. 5 (June 1999): 585–6.

PART 2

# POLICY ALTERNATIVES
# FOR POST-CONSENSUS
# SINGAPORE

# 6

# WHAT'S WRONG WITH SINGAPOREANS?

*Linda Lim*

The recent population policy debate has thrown up a number of references to the inadequacy of Singaporeans—by quantity or quality—for many jobs in the country, resulting in the heavy dependence on foreign workers (both labour and talent) that has caused such controversy. In this essay I focus narrowly on examining the common assertion that Singaporeans' deficient labour market behaviour is partly to blame for our population conundrum: while not assuming that this is accurate, I consider what the causes might be if it were, and suggest some potential policy solutions.

## "Low-Skill" Jobs

The standard economic rebuttal to the complaint that Singaporeans do not want to work in low-skilled jobs in sectors such as construction, retail, F&B, cleaning and domestic service, is that the jobs pay too little to compensate for their perceived low status and difficult working conditions, including being physically arduous and often requiring long working hours. In other rich countries, wages for these labour-intensive jobs are much higher than they are in Singapore—in both absolute terms and relative to local median wages—their status is not so low, and technologies, business processes, and customer as well as worker behaviour have evolved such that locals are found in these jobs. They also attract foreign-born workers, but these are almost always permanent immigrants with an incentive to assimilate, not transients holding temporary work permits with no possibility of permanent settlement.

There are two major economic reasons for why wages, working conditions, and worker and consumer behaviour in Singapore have not evolved as they have in other countries at a similar income level. First, wages at the low end of the labour market have been depressed by massive inflows of foreign workers from much poorer neighbouring countries in South Asia, Southeast Asia, and China. Second, housing and living costs in Singapore have risen much more rapidly than median and below-median wages, in part due to a similar influx of medium- and high-skilled foreign workers as well as foreign investment in the property market. Singaporeans at the lower end of the income distribution have to bear much higher living costs than temporary foreign workers whose housing and other costs are "subsidised" (i.e., provided free) at on-site workplaces (for construction and domestic service workers) or dormitories (for factory workers); in the case of Malaysians, they can commute daily from lower-cost Johor. For Singaporeans, housing prices as a multiple of annual income is one of the world's highest, even for "public" housing in government-built Housing and Development Board (HDB) flats.

There are also social reasons for Singaporeans' reluctance to take such jobs. For one thing, they are associated with lowly skilled transient foreigners, and for another, the whole social development of the nation has led youth and their families to despise manual and menial jobs. Given the vast income disparity between Singapore and its neighbours, and the well-known migrant self-selection bias, it is also likely that many of the foreign workers—especially in retail, food-

and-beverages, and domestic service—have higher educational and social backgrounds in their home countries than Singaporeans who must compete with them at the low end of the skill ladder. Thus, a Singaporean at the 10th percentile distribution of "talent", education, and skills may be competing with a Chinese or Filipino at the 70th percentile distribution of a much larger home population; he or she is also much cheaper.

The persistent labour-intensity of these "low-skill" jobs also depresses productivity, preventing wages from rising. For instance construction, which is a "medium-skill" and medium or high wage job in other rich countries, is an extremely low wage and low skill job in Singapore. Construction sites are populated entirely by temporary foreign workers from the poorest countries, mainly Bangladesh; like Singaporeans, Filipinos, Malaysians and even Indonesians disdain such jobs. Given low wages and high rents, it is the private and government-linked property developers who benefit from the cheap foreign worker policy are. This aggravates already widening income and wealth disparities in Singapore (by International Monetary Fund estimates, the richest country in the world with a per capita GDP of US$61,567 in 2013).

In all high income societies, and particularly their large cities, services account for the vast majority of GDP, income, and jobs. As incomes rise, so does demand for consumption of personal as well as commercial services. University of California, Berkeley economics professor Enrico Moretti argues in his book *The New Geography of Jobs* (2012) that every high-tech job in a metropolitan area in the US translates into five local service jobs (lawyers, cab-drivers, hairdressers, yoga instructors, massage therapists etc.) whereas one job in traditional manufacturing generates only 1.6 additional local service jobs. But these service jobs need not be low-pay, or even low-skill.

For example, consider that Singapore's per capita GDP is now higher than the US's (US$51,248; still the third-highest in the world, and also unequally distributed). But in the small Midwestern town where I live, Ann Arbor in Michigan, where prices are generally lower than in the large coastal cities and the minimum wage is US$7.40 an hour; self-employed limo drivers are paid $60 for a 25 minute trip to the airport, exercise instructors and massage therapists $70 to $80 for a one-hour private session, hairdressers more than that depending on the particular service, carpenters $40 to $110 per hour depending on their certified skill level, and house-cleaners a minimum of $25 an hour. Wait-staff compete to wait tables in high-end restaurants where a 20–25 per cent tip (depending on quality of service) is the norm. These jobs are not considered low-skill—in fact many of these workers have some college education or even postgraduate degrees, and pride themselves on the professional standards of the service they provide. They are not only regarded as the social equals of the professionals who employ them, but are even somewhat admired as entrepreneurial, self-employed, small-business-owners who easily earn more than white-collar clerical and administrative employees in the large institutions in town (e.g., in the University of Michigan where I work, undergrads earn $11 an hour for temporary assistance, master's students $14 an hour, and PhD students $18 an hour). Needless to say, the cost-of-living—particularly for housing, cars, and even food—is much lower than it is in Singapore, so living standards are also much higher.

This situation is not peculiar to the US. In other high income countries like Japan and Western Europe, jobs like cleaning and waiting tables are—depending on the country—mostly occupied by locals or permanent immigrants, rather than transient workers though those also exist. Wages in these jobs are much higher than in higher-income Singapore because of state regulation, union bargaining, market-determined scarcity, or a combination of all three.

## "Medium-Skill" Jobs

Competition between Singaporeans and foreigners, whether short-term transients or ostensibly longer-term Permanent Residents (PRs) who are expected to eventually become citizens, is greater in a range of "medium-skill" jobs such as retail services, white-collar office jobs and technician-level occupations where, once again, Singaporeans are found wanting in numbers or quality. As with "low-skill" jobs, Singaporean workers here must compete with foreigners who are "higher" in the distribution of skills and talent in their home countries, but willing to work for lower salaries than locals.

One area in which Singaporeans at this level of the labour force reportedly "fall behind" their foreign co-workers is in language capability and communication skills (which also include positive attitude and social skills). Singaporeans' English language skills are weaker than those of Filipinos, Indians, and Westerners, while their Chinese language skills are inferior to those of mainland (PRC) Chinese. This is arguably a legacy of decades of ineffective bilingual education, as well as the existence and widespread usage of Singlish.

However, Chinese Malaysians do not appear to suffer from this inadequacy, despite the existence and use of a similar Manglish. Indeed, many Malaysians, certainly those working in Singapore and China, are often multilingual not just in standard English and Mandarin (some 90 per cent of Chinese Malaysians under the age of 40 have studied in Chinese-language schools—which for the most part no longer exist in Singapore), but also in Malay and various southern Chinese dialects.

Beyond language competency, some employers complain about attitudinal, social, and cultural issues, especially among younger Singaporeans, who are said to lack polish and finesse in customer-relations roles, behave in a "spoiled" manner and have an "entitlement mentality". These prevent them from being as effective as eager individuals with similar education and skill levels from other countries. Migrant workers in Singapore have invested a lot in the entrepreneurial activity of working abroad, and given the enforced limited duration of their stay, have every incentive to work hard and long hours to maximise the accumulation of savings that can finance a better life at home when they return. Visa restrictions also make it hard for them to "job hop" so they appear to be more loyal workers whose productivity naturally increases with time on-the-job. By contrast, Singaporeans lack "staying power", tenacity, and loyalty; they are "spoiled for choice" and frequently "job hop," which itself limits skills acquisition and enhanced productivity.

Countering this, in both medium- and high-skill jobs, Singaporeans also complain about discrimination by employers or managers who disproportionately favour nationals from their home countries, as reflected in "hiring clusters" by nationality that even if inadvertent might discourage non-nationals, including Singaporeans, from working in such environments. From the employers' perspective however, Singaporeans may simply lack the cultural understanding and experience to work in and manage diverse multicultural teams. A recent report by the Tripartite Alliance for Fair Employment Practices recommends that Multinational Corporations (MNCs) nurture Singaporean talent by giving junior employees overseas postings, providing "cross-cultural mentoring", and "global opportunities in Asia" for Singaporean staff; that these constitute half of the recommendations made suggests that they are areas in which Singaporean workers need improvement.

The 2012 Gallup poll, which ranked Singapore as the "most emotionless" society out of over 140 countries in the world, may also explain why some employers complain about Singaporean employees' "low EQ" (Emotional Quotient) and poor teamwork. As one human resources (HR) trainer put it, "You can easily tell the Malaysian Chinese from the Singaporean Chinese in any organisation; the Malaysians are more caring and sensitive to the views and emotions of their co-workers and generally have the respect and support of their team members and stakeholders. Singaporeans tend to focus on process and results, neglecting the emotions of those they work with, and often feel and act superior to people from other countries."

If it is possible to generalize from this comment, reflect Malaysians' (or at least those who work overseas) awareness of the need to understand people who are different from themselves, and to negotiate a complex multiethnic, multicultural and multireligious society; MNCs have told me this makes them highly flexible and desirable employees who "can be located anywhere"). At the same time, Singaporeans' belief that they are indeed "the best" in almost everything, as judged by the many international rankings constantly highlighted by the government and media, may lead to both an assumption that their own behaviour represents "best practice" that others ought to emulate, and a sense of superiority, especially to people from their less-developed Asian neighbours.

Finally, employers complain that Singaporean workers are "only interested in money"—an extrinsic motivator—rather than the intrinsic drives such as challenge, learning, and personal satisfaction; this also makes them more likely to "job hop" when offered higher pay elsewhere. In contrast, foreign employees, especially from less-developed Asian countries, are "hungrier" and more eager to learn, advance themselves in their current organisation, and acquire transferable skills that will enable them to stay in Singapore or do better when they return home.

## "High-Skill" Jobs

Professional, management, executive and technician (PMET) jobs include both medium- and high-skill occupations, as reflected in their accounting for 40 per cent of the Singaporean labour force, though university graduates account for just 25 per cent of current age cohorts (and a lower proportion of older cohorts). The high end of the income distribution (say the 15 per cent of the population who reside in private residential property) includes many self-employed individuals or entrepreneurs with lower educational levels, reflecting the upward social and economic mobility of previous generations.

Excluding these, Singapore has always had a shortage of highly skilled PMETs, reflecting in large part the global and regional role of many businesses in the country—the demand for skills (reflecting a larger global or regional market) exceeds supply (limited by the small local population)—with the gap being filled by expatriates with high or specific skills not found in the Singaporean population. Over time this dependence on highly skilled foreigners has probably increased as both foreign and domestic investment and employment creation reflect Singapore's shifting comparative and competitive advantage toward more skill-intensive activities (raising demand for skills), and increased overseas job or emigration opportunities for skilled Singaporeans (limiting the increase in supply).

For example, many sectors promoted for foreign investment by Singapore government agencies—such as the life sciences, pharmaceuticals, high-tech electronics, petrochemicals, financial services, information technology and digital media—to serve regional or global markets have such a high demand for specific skills that there is no way it can ever be met by the local population, especially as so many different sectors are being simultaneously promoted, resulting in extreme excess demand.

Many MNCs would rather relocate home- or third-country nationals—already in their organisation with the requisite technical skills, domain knowledge, professional experience and company-specific connections—to Singapore than hire and train native Singaporeans who might not be as globally mobile—especially as their salaries and tendency to switch jobs (given strong excess demand) may be higher.

There are also complaints from some employers that many local Singapore university graduates lack sophisticated language competencies, social skills, diversity of thought, and a multicultural outlook. As one such MNC recruiter told me, "Singaporeans all think alike, that's why we need to hire expats."

Finally, the overall skills shortage in Singapore is exacerbated by talent diversion into the large state sector, encompassing a relatively well-remunerated civil service, statutory boards, and government-linked companies (GLCs). This sector, especially the civil service and statutory boards, is still very much the preserve of Singaporeans and offers high status and job security relative to the global-market driven vagaries of MNCs for whom Singapore is mostly a minor and replaceable node of activity. (In recent years, GLCs themselves have also increasingly resorted to hiring foreigners in both high-skill and leadership positions as well as low-skill ones.)

In contrast, the national private sector of entrepreneurial and corporate employers is much smaller, less-developed, and lower-paying than in other high income developed economies including those of Japan, Korea, Taiwan and Hong Kong, and even middle income ones such as Malaysia and Thailand, arguably due to crowding out by the relatively large state and quasi-state sector, as well as by MNCs. Among the highly-educated in the private sector, many if not most are employed, not as entrepreneurial or operational managers in value-creating, profit-making private businesses (outside of the property sector whose returns are based on scarcity values yielding monopolistic rents), but in the professional services (law, banking and finance, consulting, auditing and other business services), which rely on the same academically-based analytical skills privileged in the state sector, and disproportionately serve bureaucratic state agencies, GLCs, and MNCs.

## What Can Be Done?

Most of the policy discussion so far has focused on how to increase labour productivity in Singapore such that it enables and justifies higher wages that will attract Singaporeans into low- and medium-skill jobs. It is not that difficult to come up with concrete suggestions since Singapore's labour-intensive services sector is manifestly less efficient than in other countries, as is apparent to even the casual observer of restaurants, retail outlets, and construction sites. But productivity increases by private sector employers alone are not enough to change a labour market situation many decades (and two generations) in the making. Here I will concentrate on government policy initiatives that can have a broader impact.

## Reduce State-Promoted Growth Distortions

The main cause of the excess demand for labour at all skill levels in Singapore is GDP growth that is too aggressive for the extremely limited, already fully-utilised land and people resources of a high income city-state. This growth has been driven largely by a state investment promotion policy that in the past decade alone has brought to Singapore two large casinos ("integrated resorts"); large-scale pharmaceutical manufacturing; life sciences projects; and IT, digital media, and "creative industries"; on top of expansions in financial and educational services; and continued evolution of the electronics manufacturing sector. Most recently, "Big Data" and even a "space industry" are being promoted to foreign investors.

Regardless of the Total Fertility Rate (TFR) of its native population, no city in the world with only 3.5 million people (Singapore's population in the beginning of the twenty-first century) and 716 square kilometres of land can absorb such massive and diverse investments, and the employment they require, in just ten years. As I have argued elsewhere, it is not possible to be a "jack-of-all-hubs" since excess demand will eventually push up costs and reduce competitiveness for all. Also, since Singapore does not possess a market-based comparative advantage (a relative abundance of the specific resources require) or a competitive advantage (a large local market or comprehensive supply-chain) in these sectors, these investments have had to be subsidised by tax and other investment incentives, including the liberal importation of labour and talent. There is no way that native Singaporeans, even if they did not suffer the deficiencies mentioned above, could have filled the employment requirements of the multiple state-promoted sectors.

At the same time, the growth of these sectors, and the massive influx of foreign labour and talent needed to man them, predictably raised the living costs of Singaporeans and reduced their quality of life, through decreased housing affordability, increased physical congestion, transportation bottlenecks, environmental degradation, and loss of historical and cultural assets, which were bulldozed away to accommodate the new foreign industries and their mostly foreign employees. The fact that some Singaporeans may have gained—from the resultant asset inflation (once touted as a benefit to the general population) and sophisticated lifestyle options resulting from or enabled by the foreign influx—is offset by the declining real incomes and well-being of others, particularly those in the bottom half of the income distribution. Even property owners' gain is at best a one-generation phenomenon, since most families own only a single property and are faced with sharply rising replacement housing costs.

Thus the most important solution to the excess demand for labour problem is to reduce state agencies' microeconomic management of investment allocation through targeted sectoral subsidies. This will also make macroeconomic management—of inflation, interest rates and the currency—less difficult and more effective. Dependence on foreign labour and talent will be reduced (not eliminated), due to overall reduction in excess demand. Also reduced will be the economy's risky reliance on the questionable ability of bureaucratic actors to correctly pick and predict the sectors likely to be successful in the global marketplace, especially at the highly uncertain technology frontier at which Singapore is now perched.

Over time, the misallocation of resources directed by state policy distortions should be mitigated. Economists' "first-best" option to avoid allocative inefficiency is to maintain a single corporate tax rate for all industries (Singapore can lower its already low rate if necessary to attract more investment). Market forces will then decide which businesses take root in the country (i.e., those that makes financial sense sans subsidies). A more market-oriented economy will also encourage private sector innovation and entrepreneurship, which are the primary drivers of growth in high income, post-industrial societies.

## Reshape the Education System

Nearly all employers who mention Singaporeans' uniformity/conformity of thought attribute it to the educational system, which is (a) exam-oriented, focusing heavily on narrow "teaching-to-the-test" skills from a very young age; (b) highly-tiered, with screening of students for academic ability beginning with the Primary School Leaving Examination (PSLE) at age 12 and continuing through the teenage years; (c) heavily-dependent on private tuition, which over 90 per cent of all schoolchildren undertake, (d) increasingly ineffective as a channel of upward social and economic mobility, given "streaming" by performance, unequal distribution of state and private resources, and the varied cost and quality of tuition.

All this effort has resulted in Singapore students regularly topping global charts for performance in science and mathematics. Yet, according to some employers, Singaporeans still fall short of global standards, necessitating the hiring of foreigners instead of Singapore university graduates even when the latter are available and applying for the same jobs. Employers also note that it is difficult to differentiate among Singaporean job applicants, especially university graduates, since they typically have uniformly high grade point averages (GPAs) and make very similar curricular choices. Ironically, this may result in grades and high test scores being dismissed, ignored, or under-weighted by recruiters—a poor payoff for the years of expensive private tuition and stress suffered by students and their families.

At the high end of the labour market (e.g., MBAs and PhDs), employers in the US (including those that recruit for positions in Singapore) have told me that "perfect grades" are sometimes viewed negatively as they indicate that the candidate "thinks grades are important" and "did not take any risks" as in attempting courses out of their normal range of competency. At a minimum, once every applicant has the same grades, for the same courses, this achievement ceases to be an asset for the individual. Employers in Singapore also note that local university graduates in particular fields of specialisation (e.g., finance) tend to have "identical resumes", down to extracurricular activities, internships, and philanthropic and entrepreneurial ventures; they suspect these are artificially "managed" by career counsellors at their schools or universities.

Employers also note that competitiveness for jobs in a "knowledge society" relies not only on academic and technical competencies, but also on broad general knowledge, social and conversational skills, cultural flexibility, openness to new ideas, and contextual intangibles such as a "sense of humour". Singaporean university graduates apparently lack many of these traits, being "cookie-cutter", "risk-averse", "not at all entrepreneurial", "provincial", "materialistic", and simply "boring". Employers in the US have also told me that they expect MBA job candidates to be "interested and engaged in the world", able to converse about "the news of the day", to "have opinions/a point of view", and to present unique, value-added contributions to the employer.

Put simply, in the local or global job market, Singaporeans with better grades and learned competencies may lose out to savvier, street-smart foreigners from more diverse backgrounds who have inferior paper qualifications (e.g., lower grades, degrees from less reputable foreign universities in the West, China or India). This suggests that the educational system should be liberalised and diversified—not just for a few elite school or gifted stream students—but for the student population as a whole. The goal would be to minimise emphasis on test scores in a few subjects, reduce reliance on private tuition, and encourage/allow students to explore a wider range of academic and non-academic interests and activities in a non-competitive context. Over time, this should result in a more diverse and competitive highly skilled workforce.

Take, for example, the current hand-wringing over the precipitous decline in students electing to take Literature at 'O' or 'A' levels in Singapore. Two of the reasons offered are relevant to this discussion: (a) the perception that literature is "useless" for job-hunting purposes, and (b) it is hard to get an 'A' in the subject, which looks bad on paper.

But in addition to its intrinsic value in enhancing one's enjoyment of life, consider the benefits of studying literature in the search for PMET jobs: (a) it improves vocabulary and language ability (improving Singaporeans' alleged poor communication); (b) it facilitates participation in conversation and encourages engagement with the world (an important factor in selecting colleagues, as in the "Would you want to sit next to this person on a 20-hour flight?" question); (c) it "widens horizons", giving exposure to different times, places and subjects that develop imagination, tolerance and flexibility (all important workplace characteristics); (d) it promotes understanding of "the human condition" (important in analysing interpersonal situations and relationships in job or social situations, and in understanding customers), (e) it trains one to think critically (the single quality corporate recruiters look for and appreciate in MBA job candidates).

Perhaps it is not surprising, then, that at least in the US, English Literature majors have gone on to successful careers in diverse fields beyond the obvious ones of arts (Steven Spielberg) and journalism (Bob Woodward). In politics, the former US Treasury Secretary and Goldman Sachs chair (Hank Paulson) and the former US presidential candidate and CEO of Bain & Co. (Mitt Romney); in business, the former CEOs of Disney (Michael Eisner), Avon (Andrea Jung), and Xerox (Anne Mulcahy). At the *Wall Street Journal's* February 2012 "Unleashing Innovation" summit in Singapore, conference participants ranked the fields of study that were "the best preparation for a life of innovation": Literature ranked third (16 per cent) after Engineering (44 per cent) and History (34 per cent). None suggested the undergraduate business or finance major, the most popular fields of study in both Singapore and the US.

To improve Singaporeans' multicultural facility, Singaporeans could be facilitated and encouraged to learn more about their neighbouring countries through geography, history and language classes in school and through study-abroad programs. Second and even third language learning should not be limited simply to one's "mother tongue" and the languages of developed countries (like French, German, and Japanese), but broadened to include the languages of neighbouring countries. Besides Southeast Asia being the most likely locations for Singaporean entrepreneurs venturing outside the small and saturated domestic market, having language and cultural knowledge of the region would be a unique differentiating advantage for Singapore and Singaporeans when competing with other developed countries, and also companies and entrepreneurs from China, India, and Korea who are already venturing to the region.

In addition to its schools, Singapore's universities have also climbed the international rankings, most of which are overwhelmingly based on the number of faculty research papers published in Western academic journals. While this might have value in some contexts, it is not clear how high research university rankings translate into the employability of graduates in an essentially global labour market (given the competition with easily-hired foreign talent in Singapore).

In the rest of the labour market (i.e., the 75 per cent of Singaporeans who are not university graduates, though most would have attended polytechnics and other non-degree tertiary training institutions), the problems as I see them are (a) Time and money wasted in being force-fed a diet of rigid test-focused academics best suited to sorting out the top 1 per cent, 10 per cent or 20 per cent of students by those metrics, instead of being given the opportunity to explore diverse modes of learning and develop complementary/compensating as well as basic standard skills; (b) Low self-esteem, and a sense of inferiority and even failure at "not making it", bred at a very young age (e.g., from being branded as a "normal" versus "express", "special" or "gifted" stream student), which then discourages further interest in learning.

While recent changes proposed by the Ministry of Education (e.g., promoting arts education and a "love of learning", developing "self-confidence" and "well-rounded" students, increasing recognition of "multiple intelligences") are in the right direction, they are still too often couched in terms of (a) "helping" "weaker" students (judged by existing metrics) and (b) social mobility, rather than, for example, in terms of (a) enabling the fullest attainment of human potential for its own sake and (b) maximum advantage in a diverse and dynamic labour market. The sense of inferiority imbibed by "weaker" students encourages later over-investment in acquiring a "university degree. Although the degree still has value in terms of expanding mental horizons, facilitating "re-skilling", and as a "consumption good"', it is often not suitable or necessary from an economic perspective.

## Reframe Meritocracy and its Rewards

The issues in the education sphere are related to the philosophy of meritocracy that Singapore's founding fathers entrenched in the nation's founding principles nearly half a century ago. It has been much discussed amid growing concerns over widening and high-by-global-standards income and wealth disparities; I will not revisit the subject here, except with respect to its labour market implications.

Meritocracy as it has been defined and practiced in Singapore has been narrowly weighted toward academic achievement (i.e., measured by grades). This "race to the top" culminates for a very select few in government scholarships to study at prestigious universities abroad (predominantly in the West especially the US and UK), following which they serve out bonds in the civil service, through a career path through which the most elite "Administrative Officers" (AOs) are "fast-tracked".

"Scholars" and "AOs" make up a small proportion of the large civil service, but they are disproportionately influential in policymaking, commanding status, power and high salaries (pegged to the top of the private sector incomes of their university cohort). This, together with non-scholar appointments, results in the civil service "capturing" a disproportionate number of high academic achievers, thus "crowding out" private sector employers as previously noted. Later in their careers, many top civil servants without private business experience also end up in the well-compensated senior management ranks and on the boards of statutory boards and government-linked companies (GLCs), which are among the most prestigious employers in the country.

The status, power, and income commanded by senior civil servants and GLC functionaries in such a small but heavily state-centric society naturally has a strong demonstration effect on the aspirations of many Singaporean students and their parents. Significantly, because the "merit" on which such career rewards is based is academic achieve- ment at an early age, its influence cascades through the educational system and society as a whole. Beyond those at the very top of the academic ladder, university education is highly-prized and almost a stronger marker of success than income and wealth.

The Singaporean version of meritocracy has been criticised for its narrow definition (traditional academic achievement) and for being based on input measures (exam performance, prestigious degrees) rather than performance outcomes (e.g., in the civil service, the oper- ational success of particular policies). In the real world of business, on the other hand, performance outcomes are and should be every- thing: prior academic results and excellent classroom performance are of limited relevance. There is also the risk that long years of academic education (e.g., for polytechnic graduates who later go on to obtain a university degree) reduce their entrepreneurship since it reduces savings-based start-up capital and raises the opportunity cost of striking out on one's own.

More generally, a meritocratic scheme based on rankings runs the risk of being demotivating: by definition, the majority of the population will be "average" or "below average" and thus self-deserving "failures". Even if the criteria in establishing "merit" were broadened beyond the academic to include, for example, artistic and sports achievements, the fundamental problem of competitive ranking to establish one's merit relative to others remains. It perpetuates not just elitism among the "winners", but also defeatism, envy, and demotivation among the "losers", who may in fact simply be ordinary. It also discourages the kind of diverse individuality that many employers say they seek, especially in so-called "higher" skilled jobs (such as management, design, and innovation) that require flexibility, creativity, imagination, and an ability to deal with ambiguity and different types of people.

Reframing, if not altogether discarding, meritocracy in Singapore from a labour market perspective suggests that market competition, rather than state-dictated metrics, should decide what constitutes successful performance. Together with the removal of policy distortions (e.g., state industrial policy incentives to produce and employ certain types of skilled persons, and other labour market interventions), over time scarce labour resources should be allocated more efficiently, with students/workers specialising in diverse fields where they have individual interest and ability, and which the market will reward.

## Resize the State Sector

As previously noted, education and meritocracy in Singapore are linked to the size, status, power, remuneration and job security of the state sector—civil service, statutory boards and GLCs—that influences if not sets the aspirational standard for many Singaporeans, and diverts talent and skills from the private sector. Some thought should be given to how this state and quasi-state apparatus may be resized to reduce its impact on the private job market. For example, GLCs and other state-related enterprises (such as those run by the National

Trades Union Congress or NTUC) should not crowd out private enterprises in product or factor markets, or be given any advantage over them, while civil servants should not be given carte blanche entry into senior corporate leadership positions without having demonstrated success in private business operations.

In the Singapore context, lack of political "turnover" in a one-party state may also have contributed to both the conformity of thought and the aversion to risk that has been noted among Singaporeans. The culture of fear from life under a patriarchal-authoritarian regime—where freedom of expression was curtailed and a few were punished for dissident political views—may have diminished in recent years. But the cultural and political habit of conformity persists both inside the government—for example in the groupthink that understandably prevails in a monolithic state bureaucracy and a polity that has faced no competitive challenge for nearly a half-century—and in society, for example in Singaporeans' oft-remarked-upon interest only in "food and shopping", which in other societies tend to recede with affluence and education. The diversity of thought that employers value—especially in "knowledge" and "creative" industries, and which have tended to become a larger part of the GDP and value-chain in affluent and well-educated societies—can be encouraged with further liberalisation of the media as well as the education system, and by greater tolerance of diverse views, opinions and humour in public fora.

## Caveats and Conclusions

This essay has a very narrow focus: to unpack the complaint of many employers and human resources professionals that "there are not enough good Singaporeans to hire," forcing them to rely heavily on foreign labour and talent. I argue, firstly, that labour market distortions resulting from government policy—specifically the excess demand for labour and talent resulting from an investment-heavy growth model enabled by liberal import of foreign labour and talent—are the main reason for the shortage of local talent that many employers experience. Secondly, compared to other countries, a significant proportion of scarce local talent is siphoned away by the large state and quasi-state sector, and by MNCs, often to work overseas. Thirdly, education in local institutions, and sociocultural forces accompanying the economic development of the past three decades, may not have adequately prepared Singaporeans for the kinds of skills, qualities, attitudes, and work habits that employers increasingly require, especially in regional or globally-oriented businesses that must rely on innovation rather than cost to compete.

In seeking to explain "what's wrong", I argue that the presumed labour market deficiencies of Singaporeans are embedded in the entire unique state-driven and state-centred economic, social, educational, and political system in which they have lived for over two generations. This is the only possible explanation for why Singaporeans are supposedly so different—from people in other rich countries, and in other Asian countries (particularly Malaysia, which is culturally as well as genetically similar)—that local as well as multinational employers prefer hiring foreigners of various nationalities instead, making the liberal foreign-labour-and-talent policy "inevitable".

This is not to say that the "Singapore system" has had no advantages—it clearly does, especially in the era of mass manufacturing and cost-based competition—but that is not the subject of this essay. Neither is it my contention that all or even most Singaporeans exhibit the deficiencies discussed here. One can even argue that there is in fact nothing wrong with Singaporeans in terms of their labour market behaviour and performance (beyond the economically rational response of shunning low wage, low-status jobs that cannot cover their costs of living). I will leave that argument to others.

# 7

# ADAPTING TO OUR POPULATION CHALLENGES

*Donald Low*

In Robert Zemeckis's 1989 blockbuster, *Back to the Future II*, Marty McFly and Doc Brown travel to the year 2015. The future that was depicted in the movie bears some similarities to our world today: ubiquitous security cameras, wall-mounted flat-screen TVs, the ability to watch six channels at the same time, video games that do not require the use of hands, and the popularity of plastic surgery. But many other features of the future imagined by Zemeckis and his team are almost comically divorced from the reality we know today: flying cars, hover boards, clothes that automatically dry and adjust to the wearer's size, shoes with automatic laces, ovens that hydrate mini-pizzas, oddly shaped and coloured buildings, and so on. Above all, Zemeckis and his team missed what were perhaps the most important innovations of the last 25 years—the internet and the near-universal access we have to it thanks to cheap telecommunication technologies, and the speed at which information is spread and amplified through social media.[1]

When thinking about the future, a great dose of humility and an appreciation of the limits of human cognition and imagination are in order. The Danish physicist Niels Bohr famously said, "Prediction is very difficult, especially about the future."

The reason we frequently get our predictions wrong is that the human mind reasons by analogy and extrapolation. We are drawn to internally consistent "stories" about the world as we know it, and we tend to project these stories into the future, often in a linear and mechanistic fashion. But just because a story is consistent or coherent does not make it correct as a prediction of the future.

Daniel Kahneman, the Nobel Prize laureate for Economics in 2002, puts it this way, "[T]he exaggerated expectation of consistency is a common error. We are prone to think that the world is more regular and predictable than it really is, because our memory automatically and continuously maintains a story about what is going on, and because the rules of memory tend to make that story as coherent as possible and to suppress alternatives. Fast thinking is not prone to doubt." Kahneman goes on to argue that our deeply-ingrained, psychological desire for coherence (or consistency and predictability) breeds overconfidence: "Confidence is a feeling, one determined mostly by the coherence of the story and by the ease with which it comes to mind, even when the evidence of the story is sparse and unreliable. The bias toward coherence favours overconfidence. An individual who expresses high confidence probably has a good story, which may or may not be true."[2]

These findings from the behavioural sciences were very much on my mind during the population debate in February 2013—both inside and outside of Parliament. Much of the debate centred on the government's dire predictions of Singapore's future as an ageing society. One of the main assumptions of the Population White Paper was that as Singapore ages, our economy would lose vibrancy, exciting jobs would dry up, and young, talented Singaporeans would leave the country in search of better opportunities elsewhere. To prevent this apocalyptic scenario, the argument goes, Singapore needs to maintain relatively high levels of immigration and keep its doors open to foreign workers. Worsening old age dependency ratios were frequently cited to remind Singaporeans of an economically dire future if we did not accept a larger population comprising a larger share of foreigners.

During the debate, I was struck by how policymakers, businesses, experts and citizens made confident predictions of the future. Rather than think about the future in probabilistic terms, we tend to zoom in on a single scenario, usually one extrapolated from the present we are familiar with. Even when we remind ourselves that the future is uncertain and we adjust our scenarios to take this into account, the present exerts a strong anchoring influence. Consequently, the adjustments we make are insufficient, and we *systematically* underestimate the extent, rate, and possibility of change. For instance, the government's projections in the White Paper were strongly influenced by Singapore's current growth model, while its projections of future labour demand reflected firms' current demand for foreign labour. Meanwhile, citizens' perceptions of quality of life in the future were similarly influenced by their current lived experiences of congestion and crowdedness.

## Population Ageing and the Economy

Our deep neurological tendencies to extrapolate from our current experiences can lead to fundamental misdiagnoses. Take the ageing population for instance. Is it really the case that an older population and a shrinking workforce portend economic doom for Singapore? In this essay, I argue why this may not be so and suggest four rules of thumb for thinking about our ageing population.

### *No Need for Alarmism and Pessimism*

First, there is no need for much of the alarmism and pessimism that surrounds much of the current discourse on the ageing population. Demography is not destiny; the international evidence does not support demographic determinism. Just as there is no necessary link between a baby boom and an economic boom, there is also no necessary reason why an ageing population will lead to economic stagnation. If demographic determinism were correct, one would expect

African countries to be the fastest growing economies today because they had and still have the highest birth rates since 20–30 years ago. We would also expect the world's oldest nation today—Germany—to be in terminal economic decline. Far more important than demography in explaining a country's economic prospects are the quality and flexibility of its policies, institutions, and markets.

## An Ageing Future is Unavoidable

Second, an ageing population for Singapore is already *locked in*. There is very little we can do in the short to medium term to reverse or mitigate the onset of an ageing population. While the government should try to boost our birth rates, the fact that it has not succeeded in the last 30 years suggest that this is not something that policymakers can easily or predictably engineer. Besides, babies born today will not reach working age until 20 years later; an immediate increase in our total fertility rate does not improve the old age dependency ratio. But most importantly, our birth rate is probably influenced more by our economic model, the social compact, and wider norms (e.g., of gender equity and employer attitudes) than by any pro-natal incentives government can introduce.

What about increasing immigration as a way of mitigating the decline in the working-age population? Yes, that works— but only up to a point. Judging by Singaporeans' reactions to the White Paper, I suspect that we are nearing the point beyond which Singaporeans will not accept the congestion and competition for public goods, the depressed wages and inequality, and the dilution of national identity that liberal immigration and foreign worker policies entail. So even if our physical carrying capacity is not yet near its maximum limit, society's absorptive capacity is probably nearing a critical threshold.

## Think Adaption, Not Mitigation

Given the inevitability of a rapidly ageing population, I believe it is far more useful to discuss how we should *adapt* to it rather than how we can avoid it. The key question we should ask ourselves is not how we can delay or mitigate population ageing, but how we make our economy and society more resilient by adapting our policies, institutions and markets (especially our labour markets).

The debates in most Organization for Economic Co-operation and Development (OECD) countries with respect to population ageing have seldom centred on increasing immigration to mitigate or avoid ageing. Instead, the most successful of these countries in Europe have focused on reforming their pension systems, increasing the labour force participation among older persons, and buttressing the ability to finance their welfare states.

It is quite common for Singapore's policymakers to paint the European economies as sclerotic, their governments as paralysed, their welfare regimes as incentive-destroying, and their societies as rigid and inflexible. But a deeper study of the better governed and highly competitive smaller European countries would lead one to the conclusion that these societies have been quite deliberate and disciplined, adaptive and agile in addressing the challenges of ageing. Sweden for instance has reformed its pension system, turning it from a defined benefit system to a defined contribution one. The system now responds automatically to rising longevity, and provides strong incentives for older people to work for longer. These reforms, long regarded by experts as economically sensible but politically unpopular, were consistently pursued by successive Swedish governments across party lines for over two decades—reflecting a high degree of social and political consensus.

## Sufficient Fiscal and Institutional Resources

Fourth, if we focus on adaptation rather than mitigation, we shift the discussion away from the current emphasis on fertility and immigration to a broader, more fruitful discussion on more critical issues: how we should reform our growth model, assure Singaporeans of retirement security, increase labour force participation among older and female Singaporeans, enhance our health and long-term care financing system, and make intelligent use of our fiscal reserves.

## The Adaptive Challenges of Slower Growth

On reforming our growth model in particular, the choice for Singaporeans is between persisting with the current growth model with a high reliance on foreign labour versus one with slower growth based on a growth model that relies largely if not entirely on productivity growth. This slower growth model entails more adjustment pains for businesses that are now heavily reliant on foreign labour and possibly higher costs for households (in the short term at least). But it should also result—after a period of adjustment—in a fairer distribution of incomes, higher wages, less reliance on low-skilled foreign labour, and faster productivity growth than in the past decade.

The slower growth model that I propose presents a major adaptive challenge for Singapore—not just for businesses, but also for middle class Singaporeans who have enjoyed many affordable services that are not available to residents of other rich cities. These include cheap hawker food, live-in maids, cleaners, security guards, a relative abundance of service staff in restaurants and retail shops, and many other non-tradable services that middle class Singaporeans take for granted. But as profound and complex as this challenge may first appear to be, we should not underestimate the capacity of the economy and society to adapt, and to do so more quickly than linear projections from our recent past would suggest.

More importantly, given our limitations of size, we will eventually reach our physical carrying capacity limits. If so, it would be prudent for us for start adapting to a future of zero population growth *today*, rather than postpone the adjustment challenge to future generations, at which point the extent of change and the adjustment pains would only be greater. The sooner we begin this process of adaptation, the better prepared we are for a future where economic growth is driven mostly, if not entirely, by labour productivity gains.

In transiting to such a future, we can draw confidence from the fact that we have considerable fiscal resources. A significant part of our reserves are the result of fiscal surpluses generated in the 1980s and 1990s—the period when the baby boom generation was the most productive economically. Indeed, we should view our reserves as a transfer of savings from the baby boom generation to the state and to future generations of Singaporeans. Now that the baby boom generation is entering retirement, it is only reasonable that the state reverses part of that transfer. Continuing with a strategy of growing our reserves implies a negative discount rate (i.e., that we favour the interests of a future generation, one which is better educated and richer, over the interests of the current generation that has immediate needs). This is neither sensible from an economic perspective nor equitable from an intergenerational one.

## Re-Imagining our Ageing Future

The baby boom was a one-off demographic phenomenon. The baby boom generation gave us a one-off demographic dividend in the 1980s and 1990s in the form of rapid economic growth and the accumulation of large fiscal surpluses. Now that this generation is entering retirement, it presents Singapore with a demographic "burden". But this burden is entirely manageable, and there is no need to view the ageing future with pessimism, alarmism or fear. That one often does is a reflection of the very human tendency to predict the future based on current experiences, assumptions, constraints, and beliefs. And when the imagined future seems bleak, the tendency is to try to pre-empt, mitigate or avoid it. These instincts are common and affect everyone, but policymakers should try to resist the pull they exert on our minds.

Rather than rely on avoidance or mitigation efforts in procreation and immigration, we should respond to our ageing demographics by reforming our growth model, the Central Provident Fund (CPF) system, the health and long-term care financing system, and the reserves protection framework. Adaptation, not mitigation, holds the key to Singapore's population challenges.

## *Notes*

1. I wrote this essay in March 2013 partly in response to the debate on the Population White Paper. It was based on a paper I had prepared for the Institute of Policy Studies on the economic impacts of an ageing population.

2. Daniel Kahneman, "Don't Blink! The Hazards of Confidence", *New York Times Magazine*, 19 Oct. 2011.

# 8

# RETHINKING SINGAPORE'S HOUSING POLICIES

*Donald Low*

Public housing policies in Singapore have been highly successful in enabling home ownership for the majority of Singaporeans and in giving citizens a stake in the country. The proportion of the resident population living in public housing is about 85 per cent, of which the large majority (around 95 per cent) own the flats they occupy. Equally notable is the fact that the opportunity to own homes has not been limited to those in the higher or middle income groups; lower income Singaporeans have also benefited from home ownership policies.[1]

Singapore's unusual success in providing affordable housing for the vast majority of a highly urbanised population is the result of innovative, activist government policies rather than a reliance solely on market forces. Along with education and healthcare, public housing was seen as a merit good deserving of state provision and subsidisation. Various other factors also contributed to the successful provision of affordable public housing.

## Housing for All

First, strong economic growth enabled rising incomes across-the-board and generated social improvements for all segments of the population. The People's Action Party (PAP) came into power in 1959 with a manifesto of providing employment and housing for all. Unlike most other developing country governments that saw housing as a social problem to be addressed only *after* economic growth has been achieved, the PAP government considered both objectives (of growth and housing) of "equal and symbiotic importance."[2] The provision of affordable public housing is perhaps the clearest manifestation of Singapore's "growth with equity" story.

The government also pursued housing policies that were comprehensive and effectively integrated with broader socio-economic objectives. The Housing and Development Board (HDB) did not see itself just as a developer of rental housing for those who could not afford privately developed housing. Instead, it sought to "encourage a property-owning democracy in Singapore and to enable Singapore citizens in the lower and middle income group to own their own homes" (HDB Annual Report, 1964).

The government's comprehensive approach to public housing is also reflected in the policy to allow Central Provident Fund (CPF) savings to be used for financing house purchases. This allows many first-time home buyers to pay their monthly housing loan mainly, if not entirely, from their CPF savings. The integration of the CPF system and the housing system has not only promoted high levels of home ownership in Singapore, but has also been an important source of financial security for Singaporeans. Indeed for lower and middle income Singaporeans, the homes bought with their CPF monies are the most visible expression of social security, Singapore-style.

Inclusiveness was also achieved by ensuring that HDB flats were affordable for their intended target groups. The government committed to set the price of new four-room flats at a level that was affordable for 70 per cent of Singaporean households while the price of three-room flats would remain affordable to 90 per cent of households. Singapore's housing programme catered to almost all segments of society. All Singapore citizens who do not already own homes and whose monthly household income falls below specified income ceilings are eligible to rent HDB flats and are also eligible for special subsidies in the form of grants to make it possible for them to close their financing gap for a new home.

## New Socioeconomic Realities

The social contract that has enabled home ownership for the vast majority of Singaporeans is now coming under stress. In recent years, home prices have risen at a much faster rate than median or average incomes. The reasons for this phenomenon are complex, but most agree that the explanation lies in part with wider economic and policy factors—rapid economic growth, more liberal immigration policies, and low interest rates resulting from loose monetary policies in developed economies in the aftermath of the global financial crisis. One government response would be a combination of well-timed policy interventions. On the demand side, this involves prudential or anti-speculative measures aimed at cooling the property market. On the supply side, the government would release more residential land and ramp up the development of public housing flats.

While these policy interventions are certainly useful, a more fundamental rethink of public housing policies in Singapore is also in order. This is because alongside the cyclical factors, there are significant changes to many of the socioeconomic and demographic assumptions that guided the formulation of public housing policies in the first 40 years of nationhood. For instance, while Singapore's population was young and growing rapidly up to the 1990s, the growth of the population henceforth is likely to be more moderate (if we exclude the impact of immigration).

Singapore is also ageing rapidly. This will have far-reaching implications not only on the rate of household formation, but also on the types of public housing we provide, the community-based services that have to be developed to help older Singaporeans age in place, and the ways in which older households are able to monetise their housing assets. These longer-term, structural changes suggest that housing policies should not be overly driven by cyclical or short-term considerations, but should be informed by longer-term trends. For example, as the population ages, the current policies to encourage home ownership have to be adjusted to enable Singaporeans to monetise their housing assets. At a minimum, the government has to develop more monetisation options for the majority of older Singaporeans who own public housing, as well as develop a more affordable rental market.

Beyond demographic changes, policymakers must also consider whether home ownership is still the best way of providing social security and of building a stake-owning society. In the context of greater inequality, slower income growth for the lower and middle strata of society, and increased economic and employment volatility, it is by no means clear that home ownership is still the most appropriate way for the state to redistribute incomes or to provide a measure of retirement security to Singaporeans.

The primary way in which home ownership might contribute to retirement security is if house prices appreciate over time. Public policy so far has encouraged this; the government argues that rising house prices represent an increasing store of wealth that can be unlocked by home owners to finance their retirement needs. But this assumption can be seriously questioned on at least two levels.

First, it is by no means assured that the older Singaporeans who need to monetise their housing assets can do so at the right time in the housing cycle. In view of how volatile house prices can be, it seems rather risky to expect Singaporeans to lock up so much of their wealth in housing on the assumption that they can easily monetise an illiquid asset at a time of their choosing. As the population ages rapidly in the next two decades, a surge of elderly Singaporeans (the population above 65 is expected to more than triple in the next 20 years) seeking to monetise their housing assets might easily cause prices to fall sharply.

A second and more fundamental objection to the use of housing as a form of retirement security is that it is highly regressive and inequitable. The people who benefit the most from housing as a form of social security are those who have the means to own more than a one piece of property. It seems quite unfair that a citizen's retirement security should be so dependent on whether the individual had the resources and risk appetite to invest in housing at an earlier age. Since one can never be sure that house prices would rise in perpetuity, house price appreciation is, at best, an indirect and inefficient way of providing retirement security. At worst, it accentuates inequality as the current system favours those with more housing assets.

The government has a general aversion to intergenerational transfers through the fiscal system (of taxing the young to pay for the benefits of the old); this is why Singapore does not have the tax-financed pensions found in most developed countries. But the current approach of relying on house price appreciation to finance the retirement of the elderly is de facto a form of intergenerational transfers too since it is the next generation that has to bear the burden of rising house prices. The question then is not whether we should have the young pay for the retirement of the old; this already occurs under the current system of relying on housing as a form of retirement security. Rather, the real question policymakers should ask is whether the country is better off with an explicit system of taxes on the working population to pay for the retirement benefits (e.g., basic pensions) of the old or with the current implicit system of relying on house price appreciation to finance the retirement needs of the old. Framed this way, it is by no means obvious that the current strategy of providing retirement security via housing is more sustainable or superior.

## Unintended Consequences of Home Ownership

The collapse of the housing bubble in the US in 2007–09 also provides a cautionary tale of how an unhealthy fetish for home ownership, combined with relatively weak social safety nets and low interest rates, can be a source of economic and financial instability. The former chief economist of the International Monetary Fund, Raghuram Rajan, has argued that the main governmental response to rising inequality in the US was to expand lending to households, especially low income households, to support the objective of increasing home ownership. He suggests that promoting home ownership became a convenient substitute for the policies that really address the problem of inequality—improving access to quality education and strengthening social safety nets. Although politically expedient, the government's home ownership objective fuelled increasing leverage and drove financial deregulation, setting the stage for the collapse of the housing bubble and the financial crisis.[3]

Policies to promote home ownership in Singapore are mostly still prudent and financially sustainable; Singaporean households are also not heavily leveraged in making their home purchases. Neither do we have policies, such as the tax deductions for mortgage payments in the US, which artificially boost demand for housing. Nonetheless, the US's experience suggests that home ownership is *not* an unambiguously good thing that the government should aim to maximise. While home ownership is generally desirable given its benefits in terms of sociopolitical stability and giving citizens a stake in the country, we should also be cognisant of its limits.

In particular, home ownership is probably not appropriate as a substitute for social insurance against the risks of unemployment, ill health, or retirement. We should also be careful about encouraging home ownership for *all* segments of the population. Among lower income households in particular, home ownership may neither be financially prudent nor the best way of providing them a measure of social protection.

Yet another structural issue that policymakers need to consider is the relationship between home ownership and asset appreciation. As the majority of Singaporeans became home owners, policymakers may have conflated the goal of home ownership with that of asset appreciation. This is mostly misguided. While house price inflation provides a boost to consumption because of the wealth effect, this benefit has to be weighed against its costs. Not only do rising house prices cause anxiety for new households looking for a home, but they also have socially corrosive effects. For example, if house prices increase more rapidly than wages over a sustained period, people may begin to view financial speculation or investing in property as a more reliable way of securing income gains than through their own labour. The increase in speculative activity and the shift in social attitudes with respect to how money can be made (rental income and capital gains instead of wages) erode society's work ethic, increase status competition and envy, and divert society's resources from productive activities to less productive and potentially destabilising ones.

The basic dilemma for our housing policymakers is that as a global city with liberal immigration policies for skilled individuals and open capital markets, high-end private property prices in Singapore will rise towards those in other global cities. These forces in turn exert upward pressure on mass market private home prices, and to some extent, HDB resale prices. Given Singapore's newfound status as a global city, the government has to be a lot more deliberate and activist in managing both HDB and overall house price appreciation. Sky-high private property prices exacerbate the sense of inequality, reduce social mobility, and increase the risks of destabilising housing booms and busts.

## A New Approach to Housing

These structural changes suggest that a new approach in public housing is needed. The new approach should include the following features. First and foremost, the HDB should once again embrace affordable housing for the majority of Singaporeans as its primary mission. While improvements in the design of HDB flats are desirable, they should not come at the expense of affordability.

To ensure affordability, the government should strive to keep the house affordability index (which is the ratio of house price to the buyer's annual income) well below four, preferably around three. New entry-level three-room flats in non-mature estates should be affordable for the 21–30 percentile of households with annual incomes of around $40,000. This suggests a new flat price of around $120,000, which was the price of such flats about a decade ago. Given the real possibility of slow median wage growth relative to house prices, the first order of business for HDB should be to restore and maintain the affordability of housing for the majority of citizens. Indeed, the prices of new build-to-order (BTO) flats and recent announcements by the Minister for National Development suggest that this is the direction the government is already taking.

Second, the government should discard its implicit but long-standing goal of asset appreciation and end its reliance on housing as a de facto form of retirement funding. Compared with other markets, the housing market is particularly prone to speculative booms and busts. Relying on such a volatile market to deliver retirement security—where surely one of the key goals of public policy must be to shelter citizens from the vagaries and uncertainties of the market—not only creates too much risk to citizens, but is also highly regressive and inequitable. Instead of pursuing asset price appreciation, the proper goal of housing policy should be to maintain price stability. The lesson from Japan's lost decade in the 1990s and the 2000s is *not* that a country is destined to stagnate because of its ageing demographics. Rather, the real lesson is that a real estate boom and crash often has long-lasting, deleterious effects on the economy.

Third, public housing policy needs to be rethought in the context of significant demographic and economic changes. When the population was young and incomes were rising across the board, public housing was an efficient and incentive-compatible way of spreading the fruits of economic growth. It was also a good way of helping Singaporeans achieve social mobility and build up their assets for retirement. But the rapid ageing of the population suggests that focus of government policy has to shift from enabling asset accumulation to helping Singaporeans unlock and monetise their housing assets. Just as importantly, slower income growth and relative wage stagnation for a sizeable segment of the workforce highlight the need for more social transfers and direct redistribution via the conventional route of taxes and social transfers.

Fourth, the government also needs to ensure an affordable rental market for a wider range of households (and not just lower income groups). The undersupply of housing in recent years, combined with liberal immigration policies, has made rental housing in Singapore increasingly unaffordable. This risks making Singapore unattractive to the middle-skilled immigrants that it wants to attract. The relative dearth of affordable rental options also makes it harder for young Singaporean couples to settle down and raise families. Given the country's global city ambitions and its desire to encourage Singaporeans to marry and have children, the single-minded obsession with home ownership is becoming quite anachronistic. More than before, housing policies in Singapore need to offer a greater *variety* of options to meet the increasingly diverse needs of its population.

All the changes proposed here require the government (and Singaporeans too) to discard its old paradigms about housing, and to recognise that the context Singapore faces today is quite different from the context it faced in the 1960s when the country's policies and institutions in housing were first established. While these policies and institutions worked remarkably well in the first 40 years of independent Singapore, they are becoming increasingly ill-suited for the country in light of rapidly changing social, economic and demographic realities. Relative to how much the context has changed and is changing, housing policies and institutions—and the objectives that they are designed to achieve—have not kept up.

This gap between what the context requires and what policy delivers is at the heart of explaining why, after 50 years of undoubted achievement in the provision of public housing, housing is once again a source of uncertainty and insecurity among citizens. This gap cannot be closed simply by the property cooling measures the government has introduced in the last two years; the laudable efforts by the government to increase supply and maintain the prices of new BTO HDB flats are also unlikely to be sufficient. Instead, as this essay has tried to argue, what is required is quite a fundamental and thorough relook at the objectives of housing policy in Singapore.

## Notes

1. This essay was originally published on *IPS Commons*; a shortened version of it was reproduced in *Today* newspaper on 3 June 2013 (http://www.todayonline.com/commentary/rethinking-singapores-housing-policies).

2. Belinda Yuen, "Squatters No More: Singapore Social Housing," *Global Urban Development Magazine* 3, no. 1 (2007).

3. Raghuram Rajan, *Fault Lines: How Hidden Fractures Still Threaten the World Economy* (Princeton: Princeton University Press, 2010).

# 9

# BEWARE THE INEQUALITY TRAP

*Donald Low and Yeoh Lam Keong*

Whether measured by the Gini coefficient or by the ratio of incomes between the top and bottom 20 per cent, the evidence points to increasing income inequality in Singapore in the last decade. Government redistribution in the form of taxes and transfers has not slowed the increase in inequality sufficiently. Even after taking into account government redistribution, Singapore society was more unequal in 2012 than it was ten years ago before government redistribution, as measured by the Gini coefficient.[12]

Not only is income inequality rising, there are also certain aspects of our inequality patterns that are especially worrying. To begin with, the increase in income inequality is accompanied by wage stagnation for some segments of the workforce. Between 2001 and 2011, the median incomes for full-time employed citizens increased by just 11.2

per cent in real terms (or 1.1 per cent in annualised terms), while the 20th percentile had hardly any increase at all.[3] Including part-time workers would likely show wage stagnation extending to a larger proportion of the workforce.

Second, there are concerns that social mobility in Singapore has declined. Inequality is more tolerable if social mobility is high. Singapore's policymakers have also tended to place greater emphasis on social mobility when discussing rising inequality, arguing that the former ameliorates the effects of the latter. But evidence from other countries suggests that more equal societies are also more mobile. Intuitively, this makes sense too: it is easier to climb the income ladder when the rungs are spaced more closely together. Even if policy-makers care only about social mobility and equality of opportunity, they cannot ignore distributional concerns altogether.

Third, as a growing wealth of research indicates, people's well-being are affected as much by inequality—or relative incomes—as by absolute incomes. Even if absolute incomes are rising across-the-board, rising inequality alone reduces subjective well-being.

Fourth, a more unequal distribution also makes it more difficult to have coherent policies that all segments of society can rally behind. Income stratification, especially if combined with low social mobility, may polarise societies as different income groups begin to see their interests as conflicting. Lee Kuan Yew alluded to this in September 2011 when he said at a students' forum that in a more stratified society, "What's good for the middle income will be seen by the lower income as unfavourable ... What is good for the higher income will be resisted by the middle income."[4]

Singapore's social policies—founded on the ideas of individual responsibility, economic growth and jobs for all, and a social security system that emphasises savings and home ownership—have served Singaporeans well. They have enabled Singapore to achieve "growth with equity" and delivered high standards in education, housing, healthcare and our social infrastructure without imposing a huge burden on public spending. But in the face of significant changes in our operating context—globalisation, rapid technological change, a maturing economy, an ageing population, greater economic volatility, and a more uneven distribution of the fruits of growth—our social compact needs to be re-examined and re-formulated.

## Targeted versus Universal Approaches

In much of the policy discourse on inequality, the emphasis in Singapore has been on what (more) the government should do for the poor. The implicit assumption here is that the state's role should be confined to poverty reduction, and that inequality by itself does not merit policy action. This is consistent with the Anglo-Saxon or "residual" model of social welfare. In this approach, social transfers are means-tested rather than universal; they are also financed by general taxation rather than social insurance. This model envisages a smaller, less redistributive state since the aim of policy is not to achieve more equal outcomes but to ensure no one falls below a certain level. This approach is also more ambivalent about the need for more government redistribution in the face of rising inequality, especially if real incomes of the poor are not falling.

Policymakers in Singapore generally subscribe to this more targeted approach of social welfare. They believe that government assistance should be limited, that it should only help those least able to afford basic services. There is also little questioning of the assumption that more extensive benefits will erode the work ethic, undermine self-reliance, and impose an increasing strain on Singapore's (scarce) fiscal resources. The case for this residual model of social welfare is augmented further by the emphasis on the family as the first line of defence after the individual has exhausted his means, and by concerns over the fiscal sustainability of inter-generational transfers.

A second approach, favoured by the northern European countries, espouses the principle of inclusion and relies more on universal programmes—sometimes financed by social insurance—that benefit the large majority of their populations. Even if benefits (say, pension benefits) are differentiated by the amount of contributions the individual has made, this model is based on the idea of universal rights to such benefits. Such systems also emphasise the government's role in redistributing incomes, and in fostering solidarity and social trust.

The importance of social trust has become widely accepted in the social sciences in recent years. One reason for this is that generalised trust in society is correlated with a number of normatively desirable things. For instance, people who believe that in general most other people in their society can be trusted are also more inclined to have a positive view of their public institutions, to participate more in their civic and political organisations, to give more to charity, and to be more tolerant of minorities and people of a different ilk.

In a 2005 paper, Bo Rothstein and Eric Uslaner suggest that countries with more inclusive social programmes enjoy higher levels of social trust for at least three reasons.[5] First, because universal programmes are more redistributive than means-tested ones aimed at the poor, they result in much lower levels of economic inequality once government taxes and transfers are taken into account. Second, since universal programmes are based on the principle of equal treatment and minimise bureaucratic discretion, they increase the sense of "equal opportunities" more so than means-tested programmes. The greater use of social insurance—often with the state under-writing the premiums of lower income and other disadvantaged citizens—also enhances the sense of citizenship and access to opportunities. Third, means-tested programmes often accentuate class and racial divisions within a society, and lead to less generalised trust. By contrast, universal programmes enhance solidarity and the perception of a shared fate among citizens.

Rothstein and Uslaner also contend that societies with a high initial level of high inequality are less likely to establish universal social programmes that enhance social trust. The logic of why inclusive programmes are more redistributive than programmes narrowly targeted at the poor is complex and somewhat counter-intuitive. This makes it difficult for the advocates of these programmes to attract support from disadvantaged groups. Second, inclusive programmes also extend benefits to better-off groups. In a society with an already high level of inequality, it is difficult to explain why scarce public resources should go to the middle class. Rothstein and Uslaner predict that societies with high initial levels of inequality are likely to find themselves stuck in an inequality trap characterised by low levels of social trust, a reluctance to embrace more inclusive social programmes, and a continued reliance on targeted programmes that make a sharp distinction between those entitled to benefits and those who are not.

To be sure, universal social programmes have their disadvantages too. Broad-based benefits in childcare, healthcare, pensions, and unemployment protection cost more than means-tested ones. In northern European countries, generous benefits have to be financed by a wide range of higher taxes and social insurance contributions. But policymakers should weigh the costs of inclusive universal programmes against their benefits in terms of fostering norms of fairness, and in promoting social trust, citizenship and solidarity. Whether the costs of such programmes exceed the benefits is an empirical question rather than a theoretical one, which can be resolved by first principles.

## Relevance for Singapore

It would be all too easy for Singaporean policymakers to dismiss the universal model of social spending as too costly, too corrosive of its work ethic, too destructive of its competitiveness, and too unique to the cultural contexts of northern European societies. In Singapore's multi-ethnic context, given the heavy reliance on foreign investments, policymakers here may argue that the country cannot afford the aggressively redistributive model of high taxes-and-transfers practised by the large welfare states of Europe. Furthermore, some of these countries have begun to adopt policies rather similar to Singapore's, suggesting that not all is well with their universal models of social spending. For instance, pension reform in these countries often involves the introduction of individual savings accounts (much like the Central Provident Fund, or CPF, accounts) to counteract the heavy reliance on social insurance and general taxation, and to reduce long-term pension costs.

Notwithstanding the differences in our respective contexts, there are lessons from the northern European experience that are instructive for us. The first is that, in considering the design of social programmes, the technocratic objectives of efficiency and getting incentives right should be complemented by a deeper, more nuanced understanding of the wider societal benefits that inclusive social programmes may generate. In theory, means-tested programmes promise to limit moral hazard and "deadweight funding". In practice however, they often result in high administrative costs, stigmatisation, and rent-seeking behaviours. For instance, the British government's efforts in the early 2000s to put state pensions on a means-tested basis resulted inadvertently in people saving less so as to qualify for higher pension entitlements.

Pursuing a more inclusive approach to social spending can strengthen norms of fairness, promote social trust, and foster an egalitarian ethos. Within such an approach, there is still room to structure benefits progressively. Take eldercare for instance. Instead of relying only on means-tested subsidies (as per the current regime), we should consider a basic tier of benefits for all older citizens who require long-term care, combined with means-tested subsidies for those with lesser means. Progressive universalism, or the idea that means-tested benefits should be supplemented with basic benefits that are provided to all, could be the philosophy that underpins our new social compact.

Secondly, our policymakers should worry less about cost containment and more about cost-effectiveness. A cost containment approach focuses on keeping social spending as low as possible in the belief that transfers, once provided, fuel over-consumption and an insatiable demand for more subsidies. While it is certainly true that badly designed transfers create the wrong incentives, one should not conclude that tightly means-tested benefits are necessarily superior. The critical question to ask is not how we can keep social spending on a tight leash, but what kinds of social spending would deliver the greatest social benefits, and how these should be designed. Applying this broader cost-effectiveness approach—to areas like childcare, healthcare, eldercare, pensions, and unemployment support—may well result in social policy choices quite different from the ones we have made.

The concern for Singapore is that in the government's unwillingness to question certain long-held assumptions about our social policies—the fear of moral hazard and over-consumption, the aversion to intergenerational transfers, the reluctance to make more use of social insurance, and the mostly unquestioned faith in targeting—it consigns Singapore to the inequality trap predicted by Rothstein and Uslaner. While the current approach is fiscally sound, it does not take sufficient account of the societal benefits of inclusive social programmes in areas such as childcare, healthcare, eldercare, and pensions.

Singapore's own history also suggests that large-scale, (near-) universal social programmes have generated the largest benefits. Our public housing programme, a heavily subsidised basic education system, and the large investments in public health, water, and sanitation were all public programmes that were universal or near-universal, rather than targeted or means-tested. They fostered a sense of citizenship and helped to create the societal conditions that legitimised growth-enhancing policies.

We need the same boldness and enterprise in using public monies to achieve desirable social ends to be applied to the policy challenges of our time—securing the retirement needs of an ageing population, raising the incomes of our less skilled workers, and addressing the health and long-term care needs of older Singaporeans. A penny-pinching and targeted approach to these challenges may enable the government to maintain healthy surpluses, but it will also result in many missed opportunities to improve the welfare of our citizens, reduce inequality, and bolster social trust. To avoid the inequality trap, we need not just expanded social safety nets, but also more inclusive, even universal, ones.

## Notes

1. An abbreviated version of this essay appeared in the *Straits Times*'s Opinion pages on 14 December 2011.

2. Department of Statistics, Key Household Income Trends, 2012, 12, http://www.singstat.gov.sg/Publications/publications_and_papers/household_income_and_expenditure/pp-s19.pdf.

3. Ministry of Manpower, Report on Labour Force in Singapore, 2011, 23–24, http://www.mom.gov.sg/Documents/statistics-publications/manpower-supply/report-labour-2011/mrsd_2011LabourForce.pdf.

4. *Straits Times*, "Mr Lee: Beware rifts that hinder progress," 6 Sept. 2011, 1.

5. Bo Rothstein and Eric M. Uslaner, "All for All: Equality, Corruption and Social Trust," *World Politics* 58, no. 1 (Oct. 2005): 41–72.

# 10

# NEW OPTIONS IN SOCIAL SECURITY

*Donald Low*

Singapore's social security system is premised on the principles of individual and family responsibility, community help (sometimes referred to as the "Many Helping Hands Approach"), and government assistance as a safety net of last resort. Besides housing and healthcare, the main expressions of our social security system are the Central Provident Fund (CPF) system—to help Singaporeans achieve a certain degree of retirement adequacy—and more recently, Workfare—to encourage low wage workers stay in work. For the chronically poor and others requiring targeted assistance, various programmes under the umbrella of ComCare have been developed in recent years, and delivered at the community level.[1]

## Weaknesses of our Social Security System

The three main innovations in our social security system over the last few years have been the Workfare Income Supplement (WIS), CPF LIFE, and the various efforts to enhance and increase the coverage of MediShield. The first addresses the problem of wage stagnation among low income earners through the government topping up the wages of low wage workers; the second addresses longevity risks by introducing social insurance into a system that has otherwise relied mainly on individual savings; while the third addresses the risks of catastrophic illnesses by increasing insurance benefits for a wider range of medical conditions and treatments, and by extending coverage to previously excluded citizens.

These measures are important steps in strengthening our social security system. But the system still has significant gaps and is not sufficiently robust for three main reasons.

First, Singapore's social security system provides *hardly any protection against the risks of involuntary unemployment.* Workfare is aimed at employed, low-wage workers in the formal sector (roughly corresponding to the bottom fifth of the income distribution). CPF savings cannot be withdrawn before the individual reaches the age of 55. Even the subsidies that the government channels into various training programmes are mostly mediated through employers. While the unemployed are not excluded from these training subsidies, the principle of co-payment requires them to fork out their own monies to benefit from government subsidies in training and skills upgrading. We should think hard about how we can provide lower- and middle-income Singaporeans better protection against the risks of involuntary unemployment without creating significant risks of moral hazard.

Second, for the majority of Singaporeans, our social security system *relies mostly on the principle of individual savings.* With the exception of the subsidies in healthcare, Medishield and CPF LIFE, Singaporeans do not fully benefit from social insurance and the power of risk-pooling to deal with contingencies such as a loss of earnings, disability, or an extended period of illness. They are almost entirely reliant on their own accumulated resources to deal with such episodes of income instability. While self-reliance is a good principle in general, if taken to extremes, it may neither be efficient nor just. We should think hard about how our social security system can find a better balance between individual savings, social insurance, and direct subsidies.

Third, despite Singaporeans having one of the world's highest savings rates and highest social security contribution rates, *many Singaporeans struggle with attaining retirement adequacy*. For instance, among active CPF members who reached 55 years old in 2009, only 37.5 per cent had met the Minimum Sum stipulated by the government with *both* cash and a property pledge, and only 20 per cent could meet the Minimum Sum wholly in cash. This means that four out of every five active CPF members who turned 55 in 2009 did not have sufficient cash to meet their basic needs in old age if they did not have sources of financial support other than their CPF savings.

This lack of retirement adequacy has different causes for different segments of the population. Among lower-middle to middle-income Singaporeans, this is, in large part, due to the fact that so much of their CPF savings are locked up in housing. While housing represents a store of value that can be unlocked for retirement needs, this presumes that monetisation incurs relatively low costs. The fact is monetisation options are currently quite limited, not to mention households that need to unlock their housing assets may be doing so in the wrong part of the property cycle. While the lease buyback scheme introduced by government in 2008 is a step in the right direction, it is also incumbent on the government to develop more monetisation options for older Singaporeans.

Among the poorest Singaporeans, poverty both in terms of difficulties meeting basic needs (i.e., the bottom 10 per cent of working households) and the lack of retirement adequacy (i.e., the bottom 30 per cent of working households) arises from the fact that their wages are barely enough to cover basic needs. The solution for this smaller segment of the population will probably need to be some combination of increased Workfare (especially the cash component), direct subsidies to meet their basic needs, and government assistance to pay for medical and longevity insurance.

## Principles for Reforming our Social Security System

Singapore's social security system needs to be enhanced and reformed along two key principles. First, in the context of intensifying global competition, low-wage competition and rapid technological change, Singapore is likely to experience a more rapid pace of economic restructuring, increasing economic volatility and higher income inequality. If so, Singapore's social security system needs to be expanded to go beyond simply meeting the retirement, housing, and healthcare needs of Singaporeans to also providing a cushion and buffer against rapid economic change and adjustment. Such a social security system will facilitate the process of economic restructuring. It will also help our workers transit from one industry to another as the economy moves up the value chain, provide them greater protection against periodic bouts of unemployment and income instability, and enable them to save enough for retirement. Seen in this light, an expanded social security system is an essential counterpart of our basic economic strategy of globalisation and plugging into the global economy.

Economic restructuring and the creative destruction produced by it are not bad in themselves, a point emphasised earlier (*see* chapter 3, "Economic Myths in the Great Population Debate"). But such restructuring often creates winners and losers. The goal of public policy should not be to inhibit the processes of creative destruction, but to ensure that the state provides a compensatory mechanism for those who lose out from restructuring.

Second, well-designed social protection programmes can be achieved through the careful incorporation of social insurance into our social security system. The incentive effects of increased social protection have more to do with the *design* of social protection programmes than with aggregate levels of spending. Our own experience in healthcare financing provides a "model" for how the overall social security system should evolve. In healthcare, the government has accepted that it is neither efficient nor equitable for individuals to save for large medical bills arising from catastrophic illnesses, and it has—over time—expanded the use of medical insurance to deal with more of these risks and contingencies. In dealing with longevity risks, the government has also come to accept that such risks are best dealt with through risk-pooling and social insurance in the form of CPF LIFE.

The main alternative to the expanded use of social insurance—a greater reliance on direct subsidies financed by taxation—although necessary, is a less attractive one. The most useful subsidies are those that can be directed at incentivising work or training, like the current Workfare programme or the wage loss insurance scheme proposed below. While tax-financed subsidies are needed and will have to increase in some areas (e.g., in healthcare and in government support for the old), it should not be the principal source of funding for the enhanced social security system. To avoid moral hazard and over-consumption, tax-financed subsidies have to be rationed administra-tively— either through queues (i.e., "rationing by ordeal") or through some form of targeting (such as means-testing). These do not always foster social cohesion as they accentuate the distinction between those who are entitled to subsidies and those who are not. Social insurance, in contrast, can be designed to promote participation in the labour force. It also fosters a stronger sense of solidarity and citizenship since coverage is usually universal or near-universal.

Constructing a more robust social security system that provides Singaporeans greater protection against the uncertainties and vagaries of the global economy is an economic, not just a social, imperative. By providing Singaporeans greater social protection, the government builds public support for the tough policy choices necessary in global-isation and economic restructuring: attracting and integrating foreign talent, outsourcing or relocating lower value-added jobs, maintaining flexible labour markets, and increasing Singapore's integration into the global economy. A more robust social security system also gives Singaporeans a stronger stake in the nation, enabling government to use social insurance programmes to foster social cohesion.

## Addressing the Risks of Unemployment and Income Loss

A possible response to the weaknesses highlighted above is to argue that it is not a bad thing for our social security system to provide little by way of unemployment benefits. Among policymaking circles, it is often argued that unemployment benefits create moral hazard. Indeed, most research evidence suggests that increases in unemploy-ment benefits are associated with longer periods between jobs.

But even if our policymakers remain sceptical about the prospects of designing an incentive-compatible, labour market-friendly unemploy-ment insurance scheme, they cannot avoid this structural question:

how should our social security system help workers transit between sectors as the pace of restructuring intensifies? How can it provide greater protection against unemployment risks without creating moral hazard? Despite the fact that our labour market has one of the highest job turnover rates, our safety net for easing job transitions remains very weak. To address this lacuna in our social security system, we propose an unemployment savings programme and a wage loss insurance scheme.

An unemployment savings programme would be a relatively afford-able way of providing workers a degree of protection against short-term unemployment, while giving them a cushion as they search for new jobs. One of the main benefits of such a programme—besides the fact that it is consistent with the principle of individual responsi-bility—is that it gives the unemployed worker the liquidity to spend an optimal amount of time to seek a suitable job as opposed to taking up whatever comes first, regardless of its appropriateness and fit.

With middle- and higher-income workers, the contribution to the unemployment savings programme would probably amount to 2–3 per cent of their monthly incomes. For lower income workers (i.e., those in the bottom third of the workforce by income), the state would probably have to make most of the contributions on their behalf. In terms of benefits, the unemployment savings programme could be limited to, say, three months, and capped at half the worker's last-drawn salary, up to the CPF salary ceiling of $5,000 (i.e., the maximum benefit would be $2,500 for up to three months, subject to the indi-vidual having sufficient funds in his unemployment savings account).

In addition to unemployment savings, Singapore should also consider some form of risk-pooling to deal with unemployment risks. The conventional approach of unemployment insurance suffers from problems of moral hazard. An alternative to unemployment insurance is a wage loss insurance system. Wage loss insurance differs from conventional unemployment insurance in two main ways. First, bene-fits kick in upon re-employment, not unemployment, thus giving participants a greater incentive to find new jobs rather than stay unemployed. Second, benefits are set as a percentage of the difference between the participant's previous and current wage (and paid for a fixed period of time). The aim is again to encourage participants to re-enter the labour market soon, even at a lower wage, rather than hold out for a better-paying job. The main goal of wage loss insurance is to smooth over the incomes of workers who suffer job displacement and a decline in their earnings.

Wage loss insurance also acts as a subsidy for "firm specific" on-the-job training for the worker's new employer. Generalised retraining programmes may not only fail to guarantee a worker a job but also cost the worker the wages that he could have earned if he had accepted new employment sooner. In contrast, the retraining that a displaced worker receives on accepting a new job provides new skills that contribute directly to his performance. Yet another benefit of wage loss insurance is that it encourages workers to consider different types of jobs and sectors of employment. By encouraging the unemployed to broaden their job search, wage loss insurance can increase labour market mobility.

To facilitate the training that may be necessary for job transitions, it is also worth considering a wage loss insurance scheme that pays out a part of its benefits to the unemployed person's training programmes between jobs. Such benefits will help address the current problem of the unemployed having to fork out their own monies to participate in government-funded training programmes. It will also reduce reliance on direct subsidies for training and minimise the moral hazard problems that overly generous (and hard to monitor) training subsidies might create.

Introducing such a wage loss insurance scheme for low- and middle-income earners has four main benefits. First, it encourages the unemployed to seek re-employment quickly, thereby avoiding the moral hazard problems associated with conventional unemployment insurance. Second, it helps unemployed persons who wish to move to a new industry pay for their training, thereby increasing labour mobility. The training insurance functions as de facto individual learning accounts that workers can draw on for training purposes when they are laid off. Third, it provides greater protection against the risks of unemployment and income volatility without imposing a significant fiscal burden, since this programme can be financed mostly by employer and employee contributions, with government subsidies limited to helping low income workers pay their premiums. Fourth, it improves labour market flexibility by reducing workers' reliance on employer-provided retrenchment benefit schemes. Seen in this light, wage loss insurance is a way of making retrenchment benefits, which are currently dependent on employers, portable.

## Helping Singaporeans Attain Retirement Adequacy

Beyond the pressures created by globalisation, wage competition, and technological change, Singapore's social security system will also come under significant pressure from demographic changes. Many of today's older workers are unlikely to have built up sufficient retirement savings, and even if they have, may have invested too much in housing. As the population ages, our current policies to encourage home ownership will have to be adjusted to enable Singaporeans to monetise their assets. At a broader level, we should also question whether our current housing and CPF policies are contributing to an excessive allocation of the country's savings to housing. That our housing subsidies are not a particularly progressive or equitable way of providing citizens with retirement security is another reason to rethink the government's housing policies and the role of housing as the primary instrument of social security (*see* chapter 8, "Rethinking Singapore's Housing Policies").

For the poorest segments of our population, policy has to be finely balanced between providing more financial support and creating stronger incentives for those who can work for longer to do so. This suggests a two-pronged approach. First, for the "young old" aged 55–70, the government should significantly increase WIS so as to increase their annuities under CPF LIFE.

Second, for Singaporeans above 65 who do not meet the Minimum Sum, the government ought to introduce a basic retirement grant to enable them to participate fully in CPF LIFE. This grant can be pegged, for instance, at half the difference between the individual's CPF savings and the Minimum Sum. This retirement grant will not create large unfunded liabilities as it is likely that a higher proportion of future cohorts of retirees will attain the Minimum Sum. This helps to ensure that the fiscal burden of the proposed retirement grant does not rise unsustainably over time. The risks of moral hazard arising from such a retirement grant are also minimal since it is unlikely that working-age adults today will work less (and forego income and CPF savings) just to qualify for the grant at retirement.

Nonetheless, to reduce any work disincentive effects that may arise from introducing a basic pension for the very old, the government should consider increasing the WIS substantially for the bottom three deciles *for all age cohorts* to help those most exposed to wage stagnation and erosion save more for their retirement. A portion of these increased payments could also be used as premiums for the proposed wage insurance scheme, Eldershield, or any new insurance programmes introduced to address Singaporeans' long-term care needs. The rationale here is that risk-pooling is most effective if coverage is as wide as possible *and* members participate early in their working lives.

## Ensuring Intergenerational Equity

A third major area that needs to be carefully re-examined in the context of our baby boomers entering retirement is intergenerational equity and how our reserves can be optimally deployed to help us cope with an ageing society. Under the existing rules for the protection of reserves, the current government can use up to half the expected investment returns from the country's reserves. This rule is intended to preserve (and if possible, increase) the real value of our reserves.

On intergenerational equity, perhaps the most important fact is that it is the baby boom generation that contributed the most to the accumulation of national reserves. A significant part of our reserves is the result of fiscal surpluses generated in the 1980s and 1990s—the period when the baby boom generation was most economically productive. Indeed, we should view the reserves accumulated as a net transfer from the baby boom generation to the state. Now that the generation that contributed the most to our reserves is entering retirement, it is only fair from an intergenerational perspective that the state reverses part of that transfer. To impose the fiscal burden of looking after the needs of the baby boomers onto subsequent generations in the form of higher taxes while continuing to accumulate reserves is not only inequitable but also inefficient. It is inefficient because continuing with a strategy of growing our reserves regardless of context implies a negative discount rate (i.e., that we favour the interests of a future generation more than the interests of the current generation of baby boomers which has immediate needs).

Increasing the share of the investment returns that can be used by the current government (or more radically, setting aside part of our reserves for the baby boom generation) alleviates the fiscal burden on the working-age population for the next 20 years, allowing them to consider parenthood decisions with less worry about supporting their elderly parents.

A likely objection to the proposal to set aside part of our reserves to fund the needs of the elderly is that this represents a raid of our reserves, which the current Constitutional rules on the protection for reserves were designed to forbid. But this objection ignores the fact that the rules on the use of reserves were formulated at a time (the early 1990s) when Singapore was still generating large fiscal surpluses and the concern then was how we can set aside sufficient resources to deal with future contingencies. It is timely and necessary for government to review how the rules on the use of reserves should be adapted for a radically different context. In particular, the government should consider raising the share of investment returns that can be used by the current government *before* it contemplates tax increases to finance the expansion of social protection.

This discussion on intergenerational equity and how reserves should be invested suggests quite a different framing of the fiscal issues from the one the government has presented so far. It has highlighted the need to raise taxes at some point to finance the needs of a much larger elderly population and the greater demands for social spending. Such a framing is incomplete. It implicitly assumes that the current fiscal position is optimal and has little "slack" or redundancy. This ignores Singapore's considerable fiscal resources, which give the state plenty of room for fiscal manoeuvre. Rather than raise current tax rates, the government should first ask itself whether investing the nation's savings abroad yields superior returns than spending them on its own people.

The question of whether higher taxes are required also cannot be properly addressed until there is better information on national reserves and their expected future contributions to the national budget. While citizens probably do not need to know the exact amount of reserves the state holds, the government should at least inform the public of whether it is utilising the full 50 per cent of net investment returns (NIR) that it is entitled to, as well as what it expects future NIR and NIR contributions to be. Only with such information can citizens have an informed debate about whether increased spending must be financed by higher taxes.

Finally, even if taxes have to be increased, it is not apparent at all that the burden of tax increases should fall on citizens in the form of further GST increases. In the context of rising inequality and the fact that the very rich have been the main beneficiaries of income growth in the last decade, it would be equitable to increase progressive taxes rather than raise regressive consumption taxes. Raising progressive taxes could take the form of introducing a capital gains tax (also an efficient tax since it does not reduce work incentives), having a more progressive property tax system, or raising the top marginal tax rate on personal incomes.

## Rethinking the Trade-Off between Growth and Equality

A social compact that is appropriate to the realities of globalisation, skill-biased technical change, rising inequality, and low and median wage stagnation will be a more costly one requiring a larger state. Criticism of the ideas presented in here fall into one of two main categories: *cost* and *incentives*, or more specifically "who pays?", and "what incentive effects will these policy changes have on Singaporeans' work ethic and on Singapore's economic competitiveness?"

### Who Pays?

On the issue of who pays, the sceptic might argue that in the context of Singapore's ageing demographics, the proposed new social compact is fiscally imprudent or unsustainable. Against this line of argument, the first thing to highlight is that notwithstanding the failure of many developed countries to finance their generous social programmes on a sustainable basis, there are also notable success stories of developed countries organising their social protection programmes in a fiscally prudent way that does not produce serious work disincentives. Australia, Canada, Germany, Switzerland, the Netherlands, and the Scandinavian countries come to mind. Closer to home, Hong Kong, South Korea, and Taiwan all manage much larger social programmes without high direct tax rates or loss of economic competitiveness.

Second, Singapore starts from a much stronger fiscal position and has far more room for fiscal manoeuvre than almost any other country with a similar standard of living and GDP per capita (excluding the oil-rich states), even after taking into account its demographics. For instance, Singapore runs a very healthy structural surplus once land sales as revenue are included and one-time development expenditures are excluded—practices that are based on accounting conventions consistent with International Monetary Fund (IMF) guidelines.

More importantly, owing to its persistently high savings rate, Singaporeans have higher unencumbered official reserves (government reserves not backing any liabilities) on a per capita basis than almost any developed economy. Although the size of Singapore's financial reserves is not public information, they should still be growing quite rapidly due to a high national savings rate, stable long-term capital inflows, and the fact that it runs a managed exchange rate that tends to accumulate external reserves rapidly in the face of large current account surpluses.

Furthermore, the changes introduced to the government's spending rule in 2008 allow for the use of half of the expected long-term real returns of the reserves. The other half is ploughed back into reserves and invested to help grow its value for future generations. The growth in our unencumbered financial reserves would mean that by around 2030, when Singapore's elderly population share reaches a peak and our savings rate naturally slows, significant percentages of GDP should be available to the government as a current fiscal resource, while still allowing the protected reserves to grow at a pace commensurate with economic growth. The government should think deliberately about how these future revenues streams can be invested in our people rather than make piecemeal adjustments, or simply increase special transfers on a discretionary basis from year to year.

Third, from a national balance sheet perspective, many global economic policymakers have argued that it is not obvious at all that a strategy of reserve accumulation is still optimal for Singapore. In the short to medium term, bond yields are likely to remain depressed and equity returns will be volatile. Singapore also faces significant exchange rate risks when investing its reserves abroad. In this environment, the financial returns on the reserves, in Singapore dollar terms, may well be lower than what has been achieved in the past.

Compared to these financial rates of returns, the *social* rate of return on our investments in education, healthcare and social security may well be higher, especially in areas where public investments are starting from a low base (for example, in early childhood education and retirement security).

Even if we increased public spending from the current 16 per cent of GDP to around 25 per cent of GDP (say, over a 10–20 year time frame), Singapore would still be one of the smallest governments among developed economies. Public sector spending in advanced economies is usually well over 40 per cent; among advanced Asian economies, it is between 25 and 30 per cent. Furthermore, public spending of around 25 per cent of GDP is closer to Singapore's levels of public sector spending before the start of the 2000s: Singapore's government spending was about 25 per cent of GDP for most of the 1980s, and as recently as the late 1990s, it was still around 20 per cent. While public spending in Singapore does not need to increase to the levels of the large European welfare states, with careful fiscal management, Singapore can easily *return* to higher levels of government spending in the long-term without sacrificing fiscal rectitude.

## What Incentive Effects?[2]

A more fundamental critique than whether we can afford these social programmes is how they will impact our work ethic, economic competitiveness, and growth prospects. The central criticism against any expansion of social protection is that such increases are detrimental to the efficient operation of market economies and, over the long run, reduce people's drive, the economy's growth rates, and the country's living standards. For example, critics argue that the high income taxes that these programmes require represent a serious work disincentive among the most productive and educated segments of the population. A second line of argument holds that generous social transfers discourage work, especially among the less-skilled workers. Alongside these arguments about work (dis)incentives, critics also argue that there are deadweight costs associated with high overall taxes, which lower the rate of savings and investment in the economy, and discourage talents from moving to Singapore.

However, an extensive body of research has emerged to point out ways in which social protection programmes may actually *enhance* economic efficiency and growth. One strand of this approach argues that a great deal of social spending can be seen as a form of investment in human capital. This is most evident in education and training programmes but it also holds for healthcare and income support programmes that improve the economic conditions of the lower income and enhance their ability to take advantage of market opportunities. The fact that the largest welfare states, the Nordic countries, also invest the most in worker retraining programmes *and* have the world's most productive workforces (and competitive economies) is evidence that such social programmes can yield significant economic benefits.

Other scholars question the assumption that worker productivity is just a function of incentives. Psychologists have found that people care just as much about fairness and reciprocity. As more work is done in teams, measures that reduce pay disparities and competition between employees and encourage cooperation between them may be more effective in raising worker productivity. As economists George Akerlof and Janet Yellen found, wage compression (or smaller wage inequalities) at the firm level yield more harmonious labour relations and greater employee effort.[3] If this logic also operates at the societal level, social programmes that redistribute incomes or promote a sense of economic security among workers may contribute to labour productivity.

Yet another argument proceeds from the observation that the social benefits provided by employers (retrenchment benefits, for instance) represent an obstacle to labour mobility. In Scandinavia, the expansion of social insurance under public auspices has often been justified on the grounds that when such benefits are provided by governments rather than companies, workers are more willing to move between firms, providing for a more efficient allocation of labour.

Finally, the association between economic openness and the size of the public sector should be highlighted here. Peter Katzenstein argues that the welfare state should be viewed as a mechanism for "domestic compensation"—a way of compensating the losers in global competition, financed from the collective gains from trade.[4] The public provision of social welfare, in other words, is an important political lubricant, facilitating social acceptance of economic changes produced by global competition and rapid technological advances.

Clearly, the relationship between social protection and economic growth is far more complex than policymakers in Singapore have generally assumed. The relationship between more social protection and economic growth or efficiency probably has more to do with the *design* of specific social programmes than with aggregate levels of spending. Accordingly, policymakers should approach these issues in a pragmatic, evidence-based way, all the while asking whether the growth-enhancing effects or the growth-inhibiting effects of increased social protection prevail, and constantly examining how social protection programmes can be designed to maximise their social benefits and minimise adverse incentive effects.

## Conclusion

The current social compact served Singapore well for the first 40 years of its nationhood. It ensured growth with equity, and delivered good education, a fiscally sustainable social security system, good basic healthcare, housing for all, and an excellent infrastructure. Nothing in this paper is meant to diminish the achievements of the Singapore government in building the current social compact.

At the same time, the social compact as it is currently conceived is not adequately equipped to deal with the forces unleashed by globalisation, technological change, and Singapore's own policies. The sociopolitical and economic contexts are also changing, and strains are already showing in our social and political fabric.

These trends suggest that the Singapore state needs to reinvent and expand the current social compact. At the same time, many elements of the old compact should be present in the new. These include the long-standing emphasis on work, the goal of achieving fairness and inclusion rather than equality of outcomes, and a pragmatic balance between the state and the market. But the new social compact should also incorporate a number of new elements: broader measures of citizen well-being (including how fairly incomes are distributed), sturdier social safety nets that make intelligent use of social insurance, a more realistic appraisal of the benefits of home price appreciation, expanded health insurance, and the recognition that educational outcomes are affected by the socioeconomic background of the child and a willingness to correct for that.

In reinventing the social compact, Singapore should be informed by the rethinking in economics that is currently underway after the great US financial crisis, as well as by the examples of fiscally sustainable and well-designed social programmes elsewhere. The main obstacle to this is neither the dearth of workable policy alternatives nor that current social policies do not serve their intended purposes and need to be overhauled completely or jettisoned entirely. On the contrary, most of our policies are well-designed and implemented; they provide a strong foundation for Singapore to meet the challenges that globalisation and rapid technological change pose to society. Rather, the main obstacle lies in a *mindset* that often does not recognise the need to make important, and sometimes radical, systemic changes as the operating context changes. Creeping market fundamentalism and the belief in the virtues of small government and low taxes are relatively recent developments in our policy history. They need to be reconsidered in light of the post-crisis re-appraisal of economics and governance.

Similarly, the policymaker's reflexive belief that an expansion of social security will erode our work ethic and reduce national competitiveness may have been appropriate for a previous era. These widely held beliefs and assumptions are not entirely unjustified; they were probably necessary and largely correct for an earlier context. But these may now be precisely the things that hold the government back from thinking creatively and comprehensively about today's inequality and how it should be addressed over the long-term. What is needed therefore is a *return* to the innovative, integrated, pragmatic and adaptive approach that characterised the Singapore government when it first formulated the current social compact and built institutions like public housing and the CPF.

More than anything else, this mindset change among policymakers is necessary to help contain the negative effects of the divisive forces inherent in modern globalisation, and shift Singapore decisively back towards a fairer, more inclusive pattern of growth given our inescapable destiny as a highly globalised city-state.

## Notes

1. This essay is based on longer background paper that was prepared for the Institute of Policy Studies' Singapore Perspectives 2012 Conference on inequality. The paper, "Inequality and the

Need for a New Social Compact," was jointly authored with Manu Bhaskaran, Yeoh Lam Keong, Tan Kim Song, Sudhir Thomas Vadaketh and Ho Seng Chee, and is available at http://www.spp.nus.edu.sg/ips/docs/events/p2012/SP2012_Bkgd%20Pa.pdf.

2. This section draws heavily on Jonas Pontusson, *Inequality and Prosperity: Social Europe vs. Liberal America* (Ithaca: Cornell University Press, 2005), 162–71.

3. George Akerlof and Janet Yellen, "The Fair Wage Effort Hypothesis and Unemployment," *Quarterly Journal of Economics* 105, no.2 (1990): 225–83.

4. Peter Katzenstein, *Small States in World Markets* (Ithaca: Cornell University Press, 1985).

# PART 3

# GOVERNANCE AND DEMOCRACY: PAST, PRESENT & FUTURE

# 11

# THE OLD NORMAL IS THE NEW NORMAL

*Thum Ping Tjin*

Between 1955 (Singapore's first election for partial self-government) and 1963 (Singapore's independence from Britain), Singaporeans went to the polls an average of once a year: three general elections, four by-elections, one City Council election, and one National Referendum. Through these intensely contested, open, and fair elections, the people held the government accountable. Competing parties presented different ideas about how Singapore should be run, and the people of Singapore evidently made wise choices, for Singapore went on to enjoy unparalleled growth and development over the next few decades. Out of this period came the widely admired policies that underpinned Singapore's prosperity for the next 40 years: housing, education, social security, and infrastructure. The Central Provident Fund (CPF) was created in 1955; David Marshall introduced Meet-the-People sessions in 1955; a flexible and open trilingual system of education came out of an All-Party Report on Education in 1956; Nanyang University—the first popularly funded university in Southeast Asia—was proposed in 1953, commenced classes in 1956, and officially opened in 1958; the Housing and Development Board (HDB) succeeded the Singapore Improvement Trust (SIT) in 1959; the Winsemius survey that led to Singapore's industrialisation was done in 1960; the Economic Development Board (EDB) followed in 1961.

Singapore's success is derived from democracy, diversity, and dissent. But this lesson is missing in the official government narrative of history. Instead, the 1950s and 60s are characterised as a turbulent and unstable time.[1] Through the People's Action Party's (PAP) continuous rule since 1959, it has been able to shape Singaporean history to present a specific and purposeful viewpoint.[2] In portraying this period as being a time that was dangerous, rife with subversion, and when Singapore teetered on the brink of communism, it links the liberal ideas of justice and democracy with chaos and instability. The period thus serves as an instructive contrast to the relative peace and stability created by the illiberalism of successor governments.

This perspective imposed by the PAP helped to justify its hold on power, meet the imperatives of nation-building, and satisfy the political realities of the Cold War. Its perspective on history is also dominated by stark political categories and is written to edify and instruct, or as apologia for the post-1965 regime. This subjective account of history, narrow and partial—and by definition incomplete—is today seen as authoritative and complete. But it leads us to incomplete and erroneous conclusions about Singapore's past, makes us forget the lessons of Singapore's history, and makes us lose sight of the basis of Singapore's success.

When we misapprehend the basis of Singapore's success, we limit our understanding of the present and unnecessarily constrain our choices for the future. A careful reading of history based on the British archives and contemporary vernacular sources, however, presents a different view of Singapore's history and demonstrates the limitations of the PAP narrative, especially cherished myths on which its principles of governance are based on—in particular, myths surrounding Singapore's development, authoritarianism, and vulnerability.

## Inequality and Discrimination

By 1930, Singapore was the richest country in Asia, "outwardly one of the most prosperous cities in the British Empire."[3] It was famous then for many of the same things it remains famous for today: tall, glittering, modern buildings; massive department stores; cutting edge technology; cosmopolitanism; its multiethnic community; trade; prosperity. Jean Cocteau, stopping off on his voyage around the world, was struck by Singapore's cleanliness, the "elegant modernity", and how its jungles had been domesticated into neat parks, playing fields, and golf courses.[4] He marvelled at the tall neoclassical buildings surrounding the Padang, luxuriated in the Raffles and Adelphi Hotel, wandered through Raffles Place and the offices and shopping centres around it.[5] Another traveller, Bruce Lockhart, was struck not just by the modernity but also by the diversity. "It's like Liverpool," he remarked, "except that Liverpool has more Chinese."[6]

The Japanese Occupation interrupted this period of success, but could not stop the indomitable spirit of the island's occupants. Singapore quickly shrugged off the economic effects of the Occupation. By 1950, it was largely back to where it had been in 1939, once again the glittering economic capital of Southeast Asia, one of the most prosperous cities in the British Empire.[7]

But Singapore's colonial government was not accountable to its people. It was responsible to London and to the demands of international capital. As a result, it created an incredibly wealthy Singapore, but also a colony that was extremely exploitative and discriminatory.

For the European and local elite, Singapore was the most important commercial, transportation, and communications centre in the Far East, a temple to commerce and technology, the biggest market in the world for natural rubber and tin, a specialised commodities futures market, and a major world oil distribution centre.[8] This rich, wealthy metropolis had a per capita income of about $1,200, higher than any other country in Asia, second only to metropolitan Tokyo.[9] It was conspicuously wealthy and "almost certainly the only place in Asia where there is really a substantial middle class". It had 30 people per private motorcar; the Federation had 70, and no other country in Asia had fewer than 120.[10] Travellers from all over the world marvelled at the clean and orderly city, experiencing exotic tropical Asia while living in the luxury and partaking of all the comforts of civilisation.

Most remarkable was the sheer breadth of its cosmopolitanism. More than New York, London, or Calcutta, it was the twentieth century's first truly global city, "a city of infinite ethnic fractions".[11] The world came to Singapore for trade and for pleasure. The thriving cultural and entertainment scene catered to all tastes, no matter how high or low. It was the centre of Southeast Asian filmmaking, art, music, and literature, exporting its cultural products across the archipelago. With good reason, Singapore was compared with the legendary Italian renaissance port cities of Venice and Florence.[12]

Yet this incredible growth also produced extremely sharp divisions. The city depended heavily on cheap labour to keep Singapore's wheels turning. These people were the chauffeurs, houseboys, guards, gardeners, and maids upon whom the Europeans depended. They were also the dockworkers, bus drivers, shopkeepers, trishaw riders and taxi drivers, factory workers, street cleaners, night soil removers, and hawkers who kept Singapore running. By far the largest employer on the island, the government was able to establish the main criteria for employment. By refusing to employ anyone who did not have an English-language education (regardless of their ability to speak and write English), it condemned most of them to manual labour.

Just as the jungle was pushed to the periphery and hidden away, so too were the labourers upon whom the city's prosperity was built. Over 20,000 families (over 100,000 people, a tenth of the island's population) lived in squatter colonies surrounding the municipal area, crowded into "huts made from attap, old boxes, rusty corrugated iron etc. with no sanitation, water, or any of the elementary health requirements."[13] They were the lucky ones, who had managed to find space on the outskirts of the city to build their own homes. In the city, many workers lived where they worked. Lightermen lived on boats, coolies in godowns, labourers in factories. Some even lived under bridges.[14] Yet even these, with space to breathe and cool ocean breezes, were preferable to the cubicles that most people were confined to. Within the municipal area, multiple families crammed into spaces in subdivided houses measuring only a few feet across, taking turns to rest and work.[15] Two-fifths of municipal residents lived in houses of 21 inhabitants or more, and the average number of inhabitants in each house was 34.[16] In 1957, there were still over 313,000 people—a third of the island's population—crammed into subdivided houses.[17] They lived in squalor, stalked by tuberculosis, rickets, typhoid, and beriberi, suffering from malnutrition, diarrhoea, and tropical sores.[18]

These people were very poor. In 1957, 19 per cent of Singapore households and 25 per cent of individuals (over 360,000 people) were officially defined as living in poverty. For a family of four, the poverty line was $101.85 per month. Yet the modal (most common) wage of male workers in regular employment was about $100–$120 per month, as compared to Singapore's mean (average) wage of $1,200 per month.[19]

This difference reflected a deep structural wage inequality. A 1953 *Sin Chew Jit Poh* (SCJP) study comparing Singapore with Britain found that while wages of senior civil servants in Britain were, on average, three times the wages of dock workers, in Singapore they earned six times more. The SCJP calculated that if the British wage structure was transposed onto Singapore, anyone earning above $800 a month would have their salaries cut in half while wages of low income groups would be doubled.[20] Furthermore, as the official Benham Report on Malaya's GDP noted, "the cost of living was appreciably higher in Malaya" than in the United Kingdom after adjusting for purchasing power parity.[21] Overall, it was estimated, the real income of Malayan blue collar workers relative to purchasing power parity was a tenth of British workers'.[22] Yet British workers still felt unfairly treated and went on strike about as often as their Singapore counterparts, resulting in one-ninth of each working day lost per worker.[23]

The level of direct taxation was significantly higher in Britain, but in return British workers enjoyed free healthcare, pensions, and paid vacations, in addition to having twice the real wages of their Singapore counterparts. Singapore lacked any significant social welfare provisions. It had no minimum wage, little regulation of working hours or conditions. Some shop assistants received wages of only $15 to $28 per month; others worked fifteen-hour days.[24]

With regard to wider legislation enforcing humane conditions for workers, the official government position was that local conditions made it difficult to enforce a uniform standard.[25] Apart from this, labour legislation by the government either recognised principles that workers had already won via their own industrial action, updated previous legislation without changing fundamental principles.[26], or was designed to further control and limit strikes[27]

In fact, widespread unemployment meant that even a wage, however meagre, was beyond the reach of many. Official statistics estimated unemployment at 5 per cent, but this was achieved by considering anyone who averaged just 15 hours of work per week as being "economically active".[28] This included many temporary workers who were hired based on demand, including construction and dock workers. It also included those subsisting as hawkers, trishaw riders, small traders, and nominal employees of small shops, trading concerns, and eateries, who were considered "self-employed".[29]

Their livelihood was tied to global trade cycles of boom and bust, creating a precarious existence. Unemployment was also driven by a massive population increase, "the highest in the world."[30] It was 3.3 per cent between 1931 and 1947, and 4.4 per cent between 1947 and 1957. From 1949, there was an end to the pre-World War II "safety valve" of immigrants returning to their country of origin if sufficiently remunerative employment could not be found in Singapore.[31] All these people scratched out a desperate existence, living just one or two miles from the gleaming colonial city, yet all but invisible to the island's elites.

Housing and employment were the most pressing issues that caused widespread unhappiness, but they were not the only ones. The government refused to recognise any language but English in most of its official dealings, although they were happy to be multilingual when it suited them. For example, law enforcement was multilingual. Preferential treatment was accorded to Europeans, who could quickly receive citizenship after just two years' residence, while tax-paying Asians who had lived in and contributed to Singapore for 30 or 40 years were denied citizenship.[32] The roads and transport system were designed for the cars of the wealthy, while public transport in the city was extremely crowded and expensive, due primarily to a monopoly granted to the British-owned Singapore Traction Company. In general, there was systemic discrimination against the non-English-educated, non-European peoples of Singapore, and this was most clearly reflected in the arrogance and contempt of many in the European community towards the rest of the population.

In these circumstances, frustration and unhappiness grew. But how could Singapore's workers resist? They lacked any ability to influence government policy. For example, in the realm of labour rights, they had no representation. Trade unions were kept under tight control through a mixture of threats, inducements, and government legislation.[33] Under this regime, the colonial government and employers cooperated to render unions ineffective. With the full force of the law behind them, employers easily broke strikes by simply calling in the police, hiring new workers, imposing lock-outs at will, intimidating union officials, and transferring disputes to the Labour Department, which would inevitably rule in favour of employers.[34]

As a result, attempts by unions to negotiate for fairer wages and rights followed a predictable pattern. Employers made desultory and insulting offers while using the legally required 14-day strike notice to hire replacement workers, thus ensuring no disruption to the business.

Within the government, people who understood how the working class of Singapore lived were a tiny minority. Singapore's civil service was dominated by elitist Europeans, who regarded academic background as predictive of the quality of person.[35] The Legislative Council was dominated by pro-British, pro-business voices. Barely anyone on the Council could speak the languages of Singapore's working class, let alone comprehend a life spent in an attap hut or Chinatown cubicle. The government was responsible not to a local electorate, but to ministers in London and global capitalism.

## Political Change

But change arrived rapidly. In the context of their broader British aim to withdraw from their colonies, the British introduced a new constitution giving Singapore partially representative self-government in 1955. They anticipated that the pro-British and pro-business Progressive Party, stimulated by a small radical opposition, would guide Singapore to a peaceful and gradual transition to internal self-government, leaving economic and defence interests undisturbed.[36] Instead, despite a restricted electorate, a pro-labour coalition headed by David Marshall won a convincing victory in the 1955 general election, followed by the left-wing People's Action Party. It was a shock to no one but the British.[37]

Marshall fought for Singapore's people. He implemented the CPF, initiated Meet-the-People sessions, and implemented a Labour Ordinance, to widespread acclaim. To deal with discrimination against non-English education, Marshall convened an All-Party Committee on education. The government's focus on issues of multilingualism, the cost of living, and equitable solutions for labour and education issues, were all highly praised.[38] But equally significant was what he did not do. He refused to call in police to break up legitimate strikes but instead attempted to honestly arbitrate and compromise. He fought against the systemic discrimination that plagued Singapore.

The massive increase in strikes in 1955 reflected the new opportunities to fight against widespread discrimination. Employers tried to keep to the old way of doing business, and repeatedly tried to break strikes and renege on agreements. However, they could not hold out without the government to back them up and without the police to break up strikes. Through industrial action, Singapore's workers won fairer and more equitable working conditions, and new labour legislation enshrining basic workers' rights was passed into law.

The successes of Singapore's first partially-elected government demonstrated how electoral democracy could produce a government that was responsive to the people, and produced sensible policies that empowered Singapore's people to promote growth and prosperity. Critical to this was the widespread realisation that only active political participation could produce positive change. The mid-1950s also saw a massive increase in civil society organisations, trade unions, cultural societies, and other forms of organisations meant to protect and promote the rights and interests of its members. The economy also grew rapidly in 1955–56. Trade, in particular, grew 29.4 per cent, from $4.505 billion in 1954 to $5.831 billion in 1956.[39] This economic performance occurred even as average weekly wages rose from $33.10 in 1954 to $36.80 in 1955, and $37.12 in 1956, while average weekly hours worked fell from 50.5 in 1954 to 50.0 in 1955, and 48.4 in 1956 as new labour legislation took effect.[40] Overall, unemployment fell.[41] In particular, employment of manual labourers increased from 119,400 in March 1955 to 124,600 in March 1956.[42]

Marshall's legacy is thus more than mere legislation. As the first chief minister, he was free of precedent. This allowed him to define the position of government leader and chart new forms of practice, demonstrating that the empowerment of Singapore's people went hand in hand with economic prosperity. His embodiment of democratic and liberal praxis would entrench those patterns into Singapore's political system for years to come.[43] Likewise, Lee Kuan Yew, as leader of the opposition, demonstrated the importance of a loyal and dissenting opposition. His incisive and constructive criticism of government policy kept the government honest, and presented important new perspectives to the debates. His party attacked government repression and authoritarianism, the use of communism and other scare tactics to cow the populace, and the elitism of the system. At the same time, they used their time in opposition to prepare themselves for government. Before he became Prime Minister in 1959, Lee never held any position in government.

The public crammed themselves into the gallery in the Legislative Assembly to listen to the intense debates between Marshall and Lee. Their intelligent and informed verbal sparring was a clear sign to the world that the maturing Singaporean democracy was vibrant and productive.

In 1956, to widespread sadness, Marshall resigned on principle for failing to win self-government for Singapore. However, he won many significant concessions for Singapore, including a universal franchise and a path to citizenship for Singapore's long-term residents. Singapore subsequently won full internal self-government in 1957. Lim Yew Hock succeeded Marshall and introduced some new and successful policies, including establishing the HDB in 1959. However, his government otherwise performed poorly and was marked by veniality and corruption. In the 1959 elections for Singapore's first fully representative government, Singapore again demonstrated its capacity for democracy by kicking out the poorly performing government and taking a chance on the opposition: the PAP.

The PAP, in turn introduced sensible plans and policies. It expanded the CPF and HDB and further extended workers' rights, introducing new legislation for labour arbitration and reorganising the labour movement. It implemented the All-Party Report on Education by guaranteeing equality of language in education and expanded educational opportunities for Singaporeans. The Singapore education system became a major engine of social mobility, taking the sons and daughters of poor working-class Singaporeans and setting them on paths to material success. Many of Singapore's "second generation" leaders emerged from this background, the most prominent being Goh Chok Tong,[44] who eventually became the prime minister in 1990.

The PAP also invited the United Nations (UN) to send a survey team to Singapore. Led by Dutch economist Albert Winsemius, the subsequent Winsemius Report became the blueprint for Singapore's industrialisation programme. It also introduced long-term plans to deal with crime, corruption, and government inefficiency.

## Social, Cultural, and Technological Change

These political changes were enabled by new social, cultural, and technological changes that were sweeping Singapore.

In the 1920s and 30s, new ideas of nationalism and self-determination arrived in Singapore from China, Ireland, Mexico, Russia, Turkey, and above all from elsewhere in Southeast Asia: Indonesia, the Philippines, and Thailand. Nationalists and radicals fleeing counter-revolutionary action in China, Indonesia, and elsewhere sought refuge in the intellectually intoxicating atmosphere of Singapore. Into this world were born all of Singapore's nationalist politicians of the 1950s. These young men and women imbibed of the new ideas: Wilson's Fourteen Points, Gandhi's non-violent civil disobedience, and China's May Fourth and New Culture Movement. This gave birth to an incipient movement for self-determination which would find its ultimate expression in the 1950s.

The Japanese Occupation interrupted but did not disrupt the growth of these new forms of thought and organisation. On the contrary, it catalysed many of these changes by killing or discrediting much of the traditional conservative leadership of Singapore society.

Demographic changes also fuelled increasing interest in participation in local affairs. Where the pre-war population had comprised largely foreign-born illiterate working-age men living alone, the median post-war Singaporean resident was 18, Malayan-born, had never been outside the Malay archipelago, could read and write, and lived in a settled family unit.[45] By 1957, over two-thirds of the population was under 30 years old.[46] They eagerly embraced new ideas and new technologies.

The tremendous post-war growth in communication media created new spaces for debate and discussion. Advances in communications technology meant that news from far-flung places in the world arrived in Singapore within the day, and was reprinted in newspapers, broadcast on radio and Rediffusion, and from 1961, shown on television. With independence inevitable, Singapore hosted robust, lively debates on independent Malayan identity and culture, and how the post-independence Malayan economy should be organised.

The back pages of newspapers were the scene of lively arguments about local politics and events—the social media of their day. These newspapers were widely read. For example, the *Straits Times'* internal studies in the late 1950s showed that each copy of the *Straits Times* was read by an average of three and a half readers, but every copy of the *Nanyang Siang Pao* and the *Sin Chew Jit Poh* had six or seven readers.[47] Even illiterate Chinese would gather by the Singapore River in the evenings to listen to storytellers who would read out the news of the day for a fee, and to argue over the news and events of the day.[48]

Similarly, new ideas were reconfiguring the way people looked at the world. These would have powerful implications for Singapore in the 1960s and 70s. In particular, the triumph of democracy over fascism sent a powerful message that the strength of democratic consensus is a more powerful force than authoritarian dictatorship. Keynesian economics argued that high unemployment was not the product of unreasonable demands by wage labour in a free market, but the result of structural inadequacies in the free market system. It was therefore necessary for the government to step in and put under-utilised savings to work through government spending. Democratic socialism argued for the gradual legislative reform of capitalism in order to make it more equitable and humane, allowing collective benefit from economic production, rather than it accruing to a select few. These ideas suggested that growth and prosperity was underpinned by collective action and empowerment of all people in society, not authoritarianism and laissez-faire economic policy.

The PAP's platform epitomised these ideas. It pledged a fair deal for the working population, greater strength for unions, and government-led restructuring of the economy, including the expansion of industrialisation. This would "transform a feudalistic and conservative outlook to a progressive and socialistic outlook" and "prepare the way for a future socialist society."[49] It condemned the Preservation of Public Security Ordinance (the predecessor to the Internal Security Act) as "fascist and totalitarian" and declared itself for "the higher human values of personal liberty, freedom, and human tolerance."[50]

As Lee Kuan Yew wrote, "A competitive, winner-takes-all society, like colonial Hong Kong, would not be acceptable in Singapore. A colonial government did not have to face elections every five years; the Singapore government did. To even out the results of free market competition, we had to redistribute the GDP through subsidies on things that improved the earning power of citizens, such as education. Housing and public health were also desirable."[51]

## The Shutting Down of Dissent

At the same time, the PAP began to undermine the competitive democratic system that had enabled its own success. From the very beginning of their time in power, the PAP leadership displayed an intolerance of dissent, an authoritarian streak, and an arrogance that its leaders knew best. The intolerance of intra-party dissent nearly tore the party apart. In 1960, Ong Eng Guan was expelled by the party, and two other Assemblymen left with him to form the United People's Party. In 1961, the PAP further expelled 13 Assemblymen, and around two-thirds of the party left with them to form the Barisan Sosialis. In 1963, Toh Chin Chye barely held the party together as it threatened to fracture a third time, this time over the issue of merger with the Federation of Malaya. In all cases, British officials worried about the PAP leadership's "tendencies to party dictatorship"[52] that hampered effective governance, ministers who were "impatient of criticism", writing "sickeningly smug" memoranda[53], taking actions "which smacked of authoritarianism,"[54] and "a Government who feel they know all the answers themselves and do not welcome suggestions."[55] British Commissioner Lord Selkirk lamented that the PAP, "has chiefly fallen down ... over their complete failure to understand the mechanics of successful democratic government."[56]

Seeking to defeat their domestic political opponents, the PAP sought to achieve the widely popular goal of merger.[57] To convince the Federation of Malaya, it promoted the narrative of vulnerability.

Only merger, argued the PAP's leaders, would enable Singapore to survive and allow the Federation to defeat any communist subversion. More importantly for the PAP, it would enable the PAP to go to the 1963 elections on the back of the successful execution of merger. This narrative, combined with the outbreak of the Brunei Rebellion in December 1962, convinced the Federation and the British to agree. The narrative also excused the arrest of 113 members of Singapore's opposition politicians, trade unionists, and activists on 2 February 1963. This was known as Operation Coldstore.

The success of this line of argument probably encouraged its further use, and the PAP subsequently conducted one or more rounds of arrests every year from 1963 to 1979, with further rounds in 1987 and 1988. Contested political spaces were systematically closed down, removing the diversity and dissent that had generated many of Singapore's successful policies. The myth of vulnerability also became self-reinforcing: to prevent subversion, arrests were needed; the need for arrests proved the continued danger of subversion.

In the ensuing decades, control transitioned from a tool of governance to a goal of governance. It was initially desirable in order to implement the sensible policies formulated in the 1955–63 period speedily and efficiently. These included the rapid reform and reconfiguration of labour and economic policy to meet the challenges of industrialisation; slum clearance, forced resettlement, and the speedy building of housing; and the rapid passage of laws to deal with crime and other social issues.

However, as the policies became less enlightened, force was used to push them through without debate. From the 1970s, the PAP imposed a series of policies that, while ostensibly sensible, were implemented without the external review and oversight that a vibrant democracy and vigorous dissent would have provided. Many of the policies failed and had to be retracted eventually. For instance, as the PAP attempted to move Singapore's economy out of low wage, labour-intensive manufacturing to capital intensive, value-added manufacturing, it launched what was termed the "Second Industrial Revolution" from 1979 to 1985. It mandated wage increases and provided incentives for high-technology industrial capital. To ensure the transformation of Singapore's economy, it intensified its control over labour, the media, education, and the parliamentary process. This included the outcomes of the *Goh Keng Swee Report on the Ministry of Education 1978*, which was designed to extract "the maximum potential from a scare resource" and "to fill up the education gap in manpower requirements before Singapore can successfully join the ranks of brain and technology-intensive nations."[58] The Report was designed to maximise the productivity of Singapore's population by focusing resources on its elite, but at the same time undermined meritocracy and possibly social mobility in Singapore's education system (*see* below).

The failure of the Revolution became starkly obvious by 1985, with hardly any technological upgrading, a 40 per cent decline in investment, and a fall in demand for manufactured products. From 1984 to 1985, real GDP growth fell 10 per cent, from 8.2 per cent in 1984 to −1.8 per cent in 1985.[59] The PAP was forced to recognise that technological innovation and economic upgrading could not be imposed by fiat, and that Singapore's position in the global economy could not be unilaterally altered.

At the same time, housing policy underwent radical change. Through the Land Acquisition Act of 1964, the Planning Act of 1970, and various HDB legislations, state ownership of Singapore's land grew from 26.1 per cent in 1968 to 75 per cent in 1985.[60] This reduced private alternatives to the HDB flats and ensured that the working class had no genuine choice of housing. By 1976, the HDB housed the entire working class and much of the middle class, an estimated 76 per cent of the population.[61] This gave the PAP tremendous leverage over its population.

Having stabilised housing conditions, the PAP moved to cut government expenditure, slashing the state grant to the HDB by more than half, from $68.5 million in 1977–78 to $32.9 million in 1979–80. The cost of a HDB flat rose rapidly, with a 38 per cent increase in 1981 alone.[62] CPF withdrawals sharply rose to meet this cost, with 28 per cent of CPF contributions for 1983 being withdrawn for this purpose.

Public unhappiness was reflected in the by-election victory of J. B. Jeyaretnam in 1981; Singapore's first opposition MP since 1968. This shocked the PAP, and among other changes, it quickly increased funding to the HDB. However, the surge in HDB construction, combined with the sharp economic recession in 1984, then led to oversupply and a decline in home values, leading to increased displeasure. Against this backdrop, Jeyartnam reclaimed his seat and a second opposition MP, Chiam See Tong, was elected in 1984.

A third example of government failures during this period was the poorly implemented reversal of the PAP's family planning policy, which from 1969 had imposed harsh financial penalties, lower priority for housing and schooling, and incentives for sterilisation. When births fell below replacement level, the government reversed course. The Graduate Mothers Scheme, which incentivised well-educated, higher-class women to have children, was introduced in 1984. But faced with widespread unhappiness—not least from the better educated women, the target audience of these incentives—and combined with the election results of 1984, the PAP government was forced to withdraw or "soften" many of its pro-natal policies aimed at graduate women in 1986.

These were among the major, but by no means only, policy failures that undermined the PAP's legitimacy in the 1980s. The election of two opposition MPs in 1984 reflected Singaporeans' desire for greater dialogue and debate in policymaking.

To overcome this crisis of legitimacy, the PAP sought to re-establish control through issues like the provision of welfare, including the maintenance and upgrading of HDB blocks, which were tied to electoral support for the government. The introduction of Town Councils from 1986 was the mechanism by which this was enforced. HDB sale and resale regulations were introduced from 1989 to break up racial voting blocks. The building of new executive-class flats was dispersed to prevent a concentration of upper middle class professionals, who were seen as being more willing to vote against the PAP.[63]

Group Representation Constituencies (GRCs), in which a slate of MPs is elected rather than individuals, were initially justified as enabling the creation of Town Councils, but in practice it raised the bar for small opposition parties already struggling to recruit and support candidates. When the GRCs came under fierce criticism for its punitive implications for the opposition, the government switched tack and argued that the GRCs were for ensuring minority race representation in Parliament.[64]

The colonial practice of nominated and non-constituency MPs (NMPs/NCMPs) was reintroduced. As with colonial Singapore, these MPs were supposed to contribute diverse non-partisan voices into the legislative process. In the colonial era, these non-elected MPs in practice gave multiple votes to both the colonial officials (one vote via appointed officials, and more via their nominated members) and to the conservative business elite (one vote from their elected representative, and others from the nominated Chambers of Commerce representatives). In independent Singapore, the NMPs/NCMPs were introduced to meet the public's increasing demand for alternative voices, but risked making the opposition redundant. NMPs and NCMPs also cannot vote on key issues, including supply bills, constitutional amendments, and votes of confidence.

The elected Presidency was introduced as a safety net in the event of a "freak" election loss. In particular, the President was bestowed with powers that ensured a final say over all major financial and personnel matters, but eligibility for the Presidency was severely limited by strict requirements and screened by a Presidential Elections Committee. This increase of control over Parliament was accompanied by the simultaneous marketing of the supremacy of Parliament in Singapore's policymaking process and its role as a forum of genuine political contest.[65]

New laws were also introduced to specifically deal with increasing dissent. In particular, criticism of government policies by the Law Society and the Catholic Church was met with arrests under the Internal Security Act against lawyers and Catholic social workers. This was known as Operation Spectrum.[66] Legislation was introduced to curtail their independence and ability to participate in politics, including the Legal Profession (Amendment) Bill in 1986 and the Maintenance of Religious Harmony Act in 1991.

## Homogeneity of Thought

The suppression of external dissent was accompanied by the homogenisation of the internal PAP elite. After the purges and departures of 1960–62, the PAP had to recruit a new group of talent to their ranks to replace lost talent. Previously, this talent came from a wide diversity of educational, linguistic, and professional backgrounds. In 1959, the PAP had proudly marketed itself as representing ordinary Singaporeans. Its candidates included academics, doctors, ex-civil servants, lawyers, accountants, trade unionists, farmers, barbers, carpenters, and a seamstress. Diversity bred disagreement and dissent, allowing multiple perspectives to be represented within the party and forcing the leadership to respond to the concerns of a wide variety of constituents. The success of the first generation of PAP leadership is testament to how political talent can be found from all backgrounds and the importance of having multiple conflicting views represented.

To implement their policies, replace lost talent, and silence the dissent that had nearly torn the party apart in the 1960s, the PAP leadership increasingly turned to people they could trust: talented friends, colleagues, and relatives. Power became increasingly concentrated in the hands of a narrow few. This elite group also reflected increasing homogeneity of values, thought, and experience. Over time, their definition of "talent" accordingly became increasingly limited and reflective of their own qualities and values. The elimination of the dissent became self-reinforcing.

This was further reinforced via the codification of this definition of success into the education system. The creation of junior colleges in 1970, the introduction of streaming from primary three onwards in 1978, and the further stratification via the Gifted Education Programme (GEP) in 1984, the 1987 Excellence in Schools Report, and the 2002 Report of the Junior College/Upper Secondary Review Committee led to the construction of a stratified education system, with special schools, special classes, special programmes, special teachers, and extra funding for the "best and the brightest".[67] The goal was to identify talent early on to construct a new elite; but instead these policies had the opposite effect of identifying the children of the existing elite as talented.

Various studies of the system have noted several predominant characteristics of Singapore's elite. First, the personal connections with one of the inner circle of PAP leadership. This is the strongest characteristic, persisting even after the pattern of elite recruitment reached a substantial degree of sophistication and had apparently begun moving away from the highly personal recruitment patterns of the 1950s–70s.[68] The elite are overwhelmingly male, ethnic Chinese, from the higher socioeconomic classes, drawn from a narrow range of schools, and have actively served in the military as scholar-officers.

Second, this group enjoys financial and social advantages stemming from their success in the birth lottery. They are identified at a young age; institutional doors are opened to them, and pathways into university, the military, the civil service, and politics are mapped out. There is intense competition *within* this group, leading many to assume that their success was the product of a meritocratic process, a dangerous line of thought since they may think that they do not owe the state or society any favours, having honestly earned their privileged position entirely from their own talent and hard work. Singapore's meritocracy is real, but only among a pre-selected group.[69]

None of this is underhanded or corrupt. Elites everywhere seek to replicate themselves. However, in a system that barely tolerates diversity and dissent, homogeneity is the inevitable product. In the PAP's quest to eliminate dissent on which Singapore's prosperity has been based, it has not only removed dissenters but also created a system to remove diversity of thought within the elite.

## Vulnerability and Invulnerability

A key tenet of government policy—especially foreign policy—has been Singapore's vulnerability.[70] Two historical events are central to this myth of vulnerability.

The first is the Japanese Occupation, which the government often cites as a massive shock and evidence of Singapore's vulnerability. Churchill himself described it as "the worst disaster and largest capitulation in British history." Yet Singapore's fall was such a shock precisely because Singapore was not considered vulnerable. Instead, established as the impregnable and fortified linchpin of British military force in Southeast Asia, it was the least vulnerable of Britain's possessions. It took the massive Japanese war machine—which destroyed Pearl Harbour, and conquered large swathes of China and Southeast Asia; defeated the British, French, and Dutch colonial forces; and fought the Americans to a stalemate for six months—considerable effort and resources to conquer Singapore. Indeed, whether General Percival had to surrender Singapore, or whether he was merely deceived into thinking Singapore was inevitably lost, is still a subject of much historical dispute today.[71] In that context, it can only be argued that Singapore was no more or less vulnerable than the rest of Southeast and East Asia.

The second is the Malayan Emergency and the subsequent communist subversion in Singapore. After the declaration of the Emergency in Singapore in June 1948, the government was empowered to detain individuals without trial, ban publications, take possession of any building or vehicle, control all road movements, disperse any meeting, impose curfews, arrest individuals without a warrant, impose the death penalty for possession of arms, punish anyone suspected of disseminating false information, confiscate businesses suspected of aiding the Malayan Communist Party (MCP), detain anyone suspected of aiding or consorting with the MCP, use all force necessary to arrest persons carrying firearms or suspected of consorting with people who did, and evict persons occupying state land.

The MCP was proscribed along with other nationalist parties and organisations. Newspapers were closed and editors imprisoned. Thousands of political activists and trade unionists were deported or imprisoned. Those not born in Malaya were banished back to their land of birth. Throughout Malaya, over 30,000 people were detained between 1948 and 1952.[72] It was later estimated that in Singapore alone 90,000 people underwent the detention screening process and 20,000 were voluntarily or forcibly deported over the course of the Emergency (1948–60).[73] Intense political repression suspended all forms of left-wing politics in Singapore, legitimate or otherwise.

In the Federation, MCP members fled to the jungles to wage a guerrilla war against the colonial regime. However, the MCP never managed a significant presence in Singapore. Its size and urbanisation made it easier to control. Singapore became a police state, with compulsory registration and police checks. Over 1,000 people were searched daily at roadblocks, with "not a single hour going by" without someone being searched for weapons or having their papers checked.[74] Constantly hounded and lacking manpower and material resources, the MCP's Singapore Town Committee floundered through the Emergency. They were unable to carry out their plans effectively and had little control over their cadres. Indiscriminate attacks were carried out on factories and businesses, both European and locally-owned, without knowledge or authority from the MCP Town Committee; these were blamed on the MCP.[75] This alienated the population and drained any remaining sympathy for the MCP.

In 1950, the entire Singapore Town Committee was arrested. Many MCP cadres were withdrawn to the Federation. Some arrested cadres, including Guo Ren Huey, one of the two leaders of the Singapore Town Committee, joined the Special Branch and enthusiastically helped capture their former comrades.[76] By 1952, the government declared the Emergency had undergone a "complete change in its character" as the MCP declared a cessation of hostilities in Singapore. Attacks all but disappeared and the distribution of MCP propaganda dwindled.

Recognising that armed resistance was futile, the MCP issued new resolutions in October 1951 ordering its cadres to cease violent struggle. Its new goal was to aid any party, no matter its ideology, who was working for independence for Malaya. From then on, the MCP in Singapore worked towards peaceful constitutional decolonisation, seeking to ally itself with the most promising local parties in order to promote independence.[77]

Thus, while the authorities continued to blame the MCP for outbreaks of violence, in fact the MCP was worried about labour and student militancy derailing its plans and urged workers and students to show restraint and use constitutional and non-violent methods. This point was also repeatedly made in its publications and reinforced at underground cell meetings.[78] The MCP, however, was by this time largely toothless and had no ability to influence or coerce workers.[79] Despite repeated investigations by Singapore's Special Branch, no evidence of a widespread communist conspiracy in Singapore has ever been found.[80] Rather, all evidence points to a few scattered individuals, clinging to ideology, ignored by the vast majority of Singaporeans as irrelevant in a fast changing world.

Throughout this period and long after independence, Singapore's security continued to be underwritten by Britain, Australia, and New Zealand. Their combined forces fought the Malayan Emergency and the Confrontation, keeping over 63,000 servicemen, two aircraft carriers, 80 warships, and 20 squadrons of aircraft in Singapore during this time.[81] The British remained in Singapore until 1971. On their departure, they handed all the military bases and facilities on the island over to Singapore, and inaugurated the Five Power Defence Arrangements to continue to secure Singapore's safety. At the same time, the increasing American involvement in Vietnam saw an export boom to South Vietnam. The Americans stayed in Southeast Asia long afterward, acting as a bulwark against communism; today, they continue to operate ships out of Singapore.

Just as significantly, the Singapore Armed Forces (SAF) has military capability far beyond Singapore's small size. Analysts have called it "the militarily most proficient, even powerful state, in Southeast Asia" and "the most sophisticated in Southeast Asia", while noting that neighbours Malaysia and Indonesia perceive the SAF as a threat, not as deterrent.[82]

Externally, Singapore has been protected by Western powers; internally, the ease of controlling a small, urban area has been repeatedly demonstrated. Despite this—as well as the government's pride in the safety of Singapore's streets, the efficiency of the police force, and the advanced capability and power of Singapore's military—the PAP has continued to declare Singapore's vulnerability over the years.

## Then and Now

This synoptic sketch of Singapore's history illustrates the striking parallels between then (the 1950s and 1960s) and now. Singaporeans were open, globalised, more connected, more educated, and more equipped to deal with change. New forms of communication and technology enabled Singaporeans to be more engaged and responsive, helping to foster a change in their relationship to their government. They responded to the challenges of a fast-paced world by debating the important issues of the day, considering the competing plans put forward to them by different political parties, and electing them on the basis of their platforms and values. The frequency of elections gave Singaporeans ample opportunity to pass judgment on the government. The issues that motivated Singapore's peoples and the policies they approved of demonstrated their commitment to sensible, moderate, and competent government.

Then, as now, Singapore was in the midst of a profound economic and sociopolitical transition. It was driven by a number of global and domestic forces converging to create quite a different political and policy landscape in Singapore. These forces changed the nature of governance and policymaking in Singapore in quite profound ways. Decolonisation and the rise of new economic ideologies shaped and influenced policymaking in a Singapore that was very open to global trade, ideas, and immigration. The emergence of a number of large, newly decolonised economies around the world at the very time when Singapore was leaving Malaysia also raised questions of how the city-state could stay relevant in a world dominated by economic giants.

Meanwhile, the economy experienced many external shocks and slowdowns. The Korean and Vietnam Wars caused both economic bust and boom. The invention of artificial rubber, and the rapid growth of its use, threatened to take away one of Singapore's largest exports—Malaya's global market share dropped from 40 per cent in 1941 to about 20 per cent in 1957. A similar trend towards substitution affected Malayan tin exports. Decolonisation and nationalism threatened to close down borders and create boundaries. All this was due to Singapore's increased connectedness with the global economy, to volatile and fickle capital flows, and to technological changes that shortened business cycles.

On the political front, advances in telecommunications dramatically altered state-society relations in Singapore and challenged the long-standing notion that establishment elites in the country knew best. These advances provided highly accessible (and widely accessed) platforms on which citizens could question, scrutinise, and criticise those in power and hold them to account.

These economic and political trends interacted with social forces—high inequality, the exploitation of wage labour, systematic discrimination—to create significant stresses on social cohesion; growing demands for voice, democratic accountability, and representation; and expectations for a more redistributive state.

In this environment, the British colonialists bemoaned the passing of an era in which their rule went largely unquestioned and they were largely insulated from popular criticism. They feared the dangers of populism and the spectres of communism and communalism, especially if Singaporeans could not forge a consensus on the critical challenges confronting the country.

But Singaporeans rose to the challenge. The pages of the newspapers—especially the vernacular press—attest to the vigour of the debate about Singapore's future, its identity, and the policies needed to create a prosperous and more equitable economy. They were given plenty of opportunity to express their democratic preferences. Through open and fair elections, they listened as competing parties debated different ideas about how Singapore should be run. Out of these debates came many of the widely admired policies that under-pinned Singapore's prosperity and equity for the next 30 years: housing, education, social security, transport, and infrastructure.

Singapore's history demonstrates, firstly, the centrality of open debate, resistance, and dissent to its success. These allowed for an open contest of ideas, throwing up not just great policies but great people who would help lay the foundation for Singapore's prosperous future. These ideas came from a great diversity of sources—from outside and inside Singapore, from academia and the popular press, from the English- and Chinese-educated, from the left and right wing. The Labour Front and PAP government continued successful policies from previous governments and adapted ideas from outside their parties. The PAP also used its time in opposition to prepare for successful governance. Its dissent was an essential part of its learning process.

Yet, to its own detriment, the PAP also began to undermine the essential characteristics of Singaporean democracy that enabled it to be successful. The PAP's old guard promoted these myths (of development, authoritar-ianism, and vulnerability) in order to justify its control of Singapore. This allowed it to implement its widely-admired solutions to Singapore's most pressing issues, but in the process the PAP also closed down the vibrant space that had thrown up so many of these policies to begin with. Succeeding generations of PAP leaders, not understanding this, have made control of politics an end in and of itself. Where control was previously adopted to serve policy implementation, increasingly the policies were reconfigured to promote control.[83]

Singapore's democratic moment in the 1950s and 1960s threw up great ideas and a gifted first generation of leaders, leading to the creation of successful reforms and policies. Likewise, the closing down of democratic Singapore has slowly led to less successful policies and increasingly short-sighted reforms. This process began in the late 1960s and was accelerated by the retirement of the first generation of leaders in the 1980s. Subsequent generations of PAP leadership, through their lack of tolerance for dissent, diversity, and democracy, have gradually dismantled the basis for Singapore's success.

Secondly, the PAP's legacy is not, as popularly assumed, from devel-oping Singapore. Singapore was highly developed and rich long before the PAP was formed. Rather, the PAP's deserved reputation of good governance stems from it tackling the great inequalities and the vast poverty that existed alongside the wealth. It empowered its citizens by creating a system of social justice and opportunity, protecting and preserving citizens' rights, and allowing citizens to share in the gains of economic growth, earn fair wages, and attain a livelihood commensurate with the effort they put into building Singapore.

Finally, history also demonstrates that the myth of Singapore being exceptionally vulnerable to external threat is also deeply flawed.

Today, Singapore has returned to many of the same problems that plagued colonial Singapore: inequality, discrimination, and the high cost of living, housing, and transport. The lesson of history is clear: only democracy, dissent, and diversity can offer the leaders and ideas required to meet Singapore's challenges.

## Notes

1. *See*, for example, John Drysdale, Singapore: *Struggle For Success* (London: Allen and Unwin, 1984); Dennis Bloodworth, *The Tiger and the Trojan Horse* (Singapore: Times Books International, 1986); Lee Kuan Yew, *The Singapore Story: Memoirs of Lee Kuan Yew* (Singapore: Times Edition, 1998).

2. Albert Lau, "The National Past and the Writing of the History of Singapore," in *Imagining Singapore*, ed. Ban Kah Choon, Anne Pakir, and Tong Chee Kiong (Singapore: Times Academic Press, 1992); C J W-L Wee, "The Vanquished: Lim Chin Siong and a Progressivist National Narrative," in *Lee's Lieutenants*, ed. Lam Peng Er and Kevin Y. L. Tan (Singapore: Allen & Unwin, 1999); Hong Lysa, "Making the History of Singapore: S Rajaratnam and C.V. Devan Nair," in *Lee's Lieutenants*, ed. Lam Peng Er and Kevin Y. L. Tan (Singapore: Allen & Unwin, 1999), "The Lee Kuan Yew Story as Singapore's History," *Journal of Southeast Asian Studies* 33, no. 3 (Oct. 2002); Loh Kah Seng, "Within The Singapore Story: The Use and Narrative of History in Singapore," *Crossroads* 12, no. 2 (1998).

3. Christopher Bayly and Tim Harper, *Forgotten Armies: Britain's Asian Empire and the War with Japan* (London: Penguin, 2005), 50.

4. Jean Cocteau, *Around the World Again in 80 Days* [*Mon premier voyage*] (Routledge: London, 1936).

5. Ibid.

6. R. H. Bruce Lockhart, *Return to Malaya* (London: Putnam, 1936), 80.

7. *Colony of Singapore, Annual Report 1950*, 140; J. W. F. Rowe, *Primary Commodities and International Trade* (Cambridge: Cambridge University Press, 1965), 47.

8. Ibid.

9. Frederic Benham, *The National Income of Singapore 1956* (Oxford: Oxford University Press, 1959)1–9; W. G. Huff, *The Economic Growth of Singapore: Trade and Development in the Twentieth Century* (Cambridge: Cambridge University Press, 1994), 1–2, 32–3.

10. T. H. Silcock, *The Commonwealth Economy in Southeast Asia* (Durham: Duke University Press, 1959), 43, 158.

11. Bayly and Harper, *Forgotten Armies*, 51.

12. *Sin Chew Jit Poh (SCJP)*, 8 Dec 1959; Ursula K. Hicks, "The Finance of the City State," *Malayan Economic Review* 5, no. 2 (1960): 1–9; John Hicks, *A Theory of Economic History* (Oxford: Oxford University Press, 1969), 42–59.

13. Colony of Singapore, "Report of the Housing Committee," (1947), 1.

14. James Dobbs, *The Singapore River: A Social History 1819–2002* (Singapore: Singapore University Press, 2003): 84–5.

15. For a detailed analysis of one of these communities, *see* Barrington Kaye, *Upper Nankin Street Singapore: A Sociological Study of Chinese Households Living in a Densely Populated Area*, 1st ed. (Singapore: University of Malaya Press, 1960), 26–85.

16. M. V. Del Tufo, *Malaya: A Report of the 1947 Census of Population* (London: Crown Agents for the Colonies, 1949), 129.

17. S. C. Chua, *Report on the Census of Population 1957* (Singapore: Singapore Government Printer, 1964), 93.

18. For a detailed description of Singapore's poverty, *see* James Francis Warren, *Rickshaw Coolie: A People's History of Singapore, 1880–1940* (Singapore: Oxford University Press, 1986), 194–215.

19. Singapore, "Report of the Committee on Minimum Standards of Livelihood," (Singapore Legislative Assembly sessional paper, Cmd. 5 of 1957), 13–26.

20. *SCJP,* 8 March 1955.

21. Frederic Benham, The National Income of Malaya, 1947–49 (Singapore: Government Printing Office, 1951).

22. *SCJP,* 1 May 1957; *Chung Shing Jit Poh (CSJP)*, 1 May 1957.

23. *Colony of Singapore, Annual Report* 1953, 32; *SCJP,* 16 Dec 1953.

24. *Nanyang Siang Pao (NYSP)*, 24 July 1953; *SCJP,* 25 July 1953; *Nanfang Evening Post (NEP)*, 7 Nov 1953.

25. *NYSP,* 18 July 1953.

26. The Contributory Negligence and Personal Injuries Ordinance 1953 and Workman's Compensation Ordinance 1954. See *NEP,* 21 July 1953.

27. The Arbitration Ordinance 1953 and the Wages Council Ordinance 1953.

28. Chua, 1957 Census, 10; Goh Keng Swee, "Urban Incomes & Housing: A Report on the Social Survey of Singapore, 1953–54," ed. Department of Social Welfare (Government Printing Office, Singapore, 1956), 125.

29. Singapore, "Report of the Committee on Minimum Standards of Livelihood," 3; *International Labour Office*, "Report to the government of Singapore on social security measures," (Cmd. 56 of 1957), 9, 47.

30. State of Singapore, "Development Plan 1961–64," (Singapore 1961), 1.

31. Huff, *Economic Growth of Singapore*, 33.

32. David Marshall made it a priority to address this, declaring that "perpetrating an injustice cannot bring about justice." *See* David Marshall, Interview with Lily Tan, 24 Sep. 1984, Accession 156, Singapore National Archives Oral History Centre; *NEP* 7 July 1955; *NYSP, SCJP, NEP, CSJP* 8 July 1955; *SCJP* 5 Aug 1955. His work laid the foundation for the 1957 Citizenship Ordinance. *See* Thum Ping Tjin, "'Living Buddha': Chinese Perspectives on David Marshall and his Government, 1955–56," *Indonesia and the Malay World* 39, no. 114 (2011): 258–62.

33. Yeo Kim Wah, *Political Development in Singapore, 1945–55* (Singapore: Singapore University Press, 1973), 229–31.

34. Ibid., 233–6.

35. J. de Vere Allen, "Malayan Civil Service 1874–1941," *Comparative Studies in Society and History* 12, no. 2 (April 1970): 149–178.

36. 'Singapore: Memorandum by the Secretary of State for the Colonies,' 23.3.56, *CAB* 129/80, CP (56) 85, The National Archives, UK (TNA); *See also* C. M. Turnbull, *A History of Modern Singapore, 1819–2005* (Singapore: NUS Press, 2009), 260–62.

37. Thum, "'Living Buddha': Chinese Perspectives on David Marshall and his Government, 1955–56," 251.

38. Ibid.

39. Colony of Singapore, Department of Commerce and Industry Annual Report 1955, 1–176; Colony of Singapore, Department of Commerce and Industry Annual Report 1956, 1–167.

40. Colony of Singapore, Department of Labour Annual Report 1954, 6; Colony of Singapore, Department of Labour Annual Report 1955, 3, 6; Colony of Singapore, Department of Labour Annual Report 1956, 3, 7.

41. Colony of Singapore, Annual Report 1956, 32–6, 79–80; Colony of Singapore, Annual Report 1959, 128, 133–6, 161–3.

42. Colony of Singapore, Department of Labour Annual Report 1955, 3; Colony of Singapore, Department of Labour Annual Report 1956, 3.

43. For more on Marshall's short but highly influential term of office, *see* Thum, "'Living Buddha': Chinese Perspectives on David Marshall and his Government, 1955–56".

44. Michael Barr, *The Ruling Elite of Singapore: Networks of Power and Influence* (London: I. B. Tauris, 2013), 74.

45. Chua Beng Huat, *Communitarian Ideology and Democracy in Singapore*, Routledge Politics in Asia Series (London: Routledge, 1995), 43–53, 72–75.

46. Chua, 1957 Census, 50.

47. Chin Kah Cheong, interviewer unknown, Singapore National Archives, Oral History Accession 2954, undated.

48. Dobbs, *The Singapore River: A Social History 1819–2002*, 92–93.

49. *Straits Times* (*ST*), 30 May 1959.

50. *ST*, 26 May 1959.

51. Lee Kuan Yew, *From Third World to First: the Singapore Story, 1965–2000* (Singapore: Times Edition, 2000), 116.

52. Extract from Letter from Bourdillon (Singapore) to CO dated 3/12/59, CO 1030/1148, TNA.

53. From Wallace (CO) to Smith (CRO), 14 Mar. 1960, CO 1030/1157, TNA.

54. Letter from Shattock (UK Delegation to NATO) to Petrie (FO) dated 17 Feb. 1960, CO 1030/1148, TNA.

55. Report from Selkirk to MacLeod (SoS Colonies) dated 20 May 1960, CO 1030/1148, TNA.

56. "Singapore: Political Developments," Selkirk to CO, dated 4 Aug 1961, CO 1030/1150, TNA.

57. Every single political party in 1955 and 1959 supported the reunification of Singapore and the Federation as part of its platform. For more, *see* Thum Ping Tjin, "'Flesh and Bone Reunite As One Body': Singapore's Chinese-speaking and their Perspectives on Merger," *Chinese Southern Disapora Studies* 5, no. 5 (2011–12): 29–56.

58. Seah Chee Meow and Linda Seah, "Education Reform and National Integration," in *Singapore Development Policies and Trends*, ed. Peter S. J. Chen (Singapore: Oxford University Press, 1983), 248–49.

59. Lim Chong Yah, "From High Growth Rates to Recession," in *Management of Success: The Moulding of Modern Singapore*, ed. K. S. Sandhu and Paul Wheatley (Singapore: Institute of Southeast Asian Studies, 1989), 208.

60. Linda Lim, "Social Welfare," in *Management of Success: The Moulding of Modern Singapore*, ed. K. S. Sandhu and Paul Wheatley (Singapore: Institute of Southeast Asian Studies, 1989), 185; Aline K Wong and Ooi Giok Ling, "Spatial Reorganisation," in *Management of Success: The Moulding of Modern Singapore*, ed. K. S. Sandhu and Paul Wheatley (Singapore: Institute of Southeast Asian Studies, 1989), 791.

61. Chan Heng Chee, *The Dynamics of One Party Dominance: The P.A.P. at the Grass-Roots* (Singapore: Singapore University Press, 1976), 34.

62. Cedric Pugh, "The Political Economy of Public Housing," in *Management of Success: The Moulding of Modern Singapore,* ed. K. S. Sandhu and Paul Wheatley (Singapore: Institute of Southeast Asian Studies, 1989), 849.

63. Linda Low and Toh Mun Heng, *The Elected Presidency as a Safeguard for Official Reserves: What is at Stake?* (Singapore: Institute of Policy Studies, 1989), 183.

64. Christopher Tremewan, *The Political Economy of Social Control in Singapore* (London: Macmillan, 1994), 167.

65. Ibid., 162.

66. Jothie Rajah, *Authoritarian Rule of Law: Legislation, Discourse, and Legitimacy in Singapore* (Cambridge: Cambridge University Press, 2012), 161–258.

67. Barr, *Ruling Elite of Singapore*, 74.

68. Ibid., 49.

69. For more, *see* ibid., 19–49; Tremewan, *The Political Economy of Social Control in Singapore*, 74–151; Michael Barr and Zlatko Skrbis, *Constructing Singapore: Elitism, Ethnicity, and the Nation-Building Project* (Copenhagen: NIAS Press, 2008); Jason Tan, "Education in Singapore: Sorting Them Out?", in *Management of Success: Singapore Revisited*, ed. Terence Chong (Singapore: Institute of Southeast Asian Studies, 2010), 288–308.

70. *See*, for example, Michael Leifer, *Singapore's Foreign Policy: Coping with Vulnerability* (London: Routledge, 2000).

71. *See*, for example, Kevin Blackburn and Karl Hack, *Did Singapore Have to Fall?: Churchill and the Impregnable Fortress* (London: Routledge, 2003).

72. Federation of Malaya, "Detention and Deportation during the Emergency in the Federation of Malaya," Command Paper No. 24 of 1953; No. 456, Nicoll to CO, 23 July 1952, CO 1022/132, TNA.

73. Alex Josey, *Singapore: Its Past, Present and Future* (London: Andre Deutsch, 1980), 189.

74. Colony of Singapore, Annual Report 1948, 114.

75. Guo Ren Huey, interview by author, 5 Nov 2007.

76. Fang Chuan Pi, "*The Plen": The Memoirs of Fang Chuan Pi* (Selangor: Strategic Information and Research Development Centre, 2007), 105–6; C. C. Chin, ed. *Dreams on Waves: Eu Chooi Yip's Idealistic Life* (Selangor: Strategic Information and Research Development Centre, 2006), 30–3; Karl Hack, *Defence and Decolonisation in Southeast Asia: Britain, Malaya and Singapore, 1941–68* (Richmond: Curzon Press, 2001), 126.

77. "The Security Situation in Singapore as on the 1st August 1961," *ISC* (61) (S) 5, dated 10 Aug. 1961, CO 1030/1162, TNA.

78. *Freedom News*, No. 64 (Aug. 1955), No. 65 (Sept. 1955); Lee Ting Hui, *The Open United Front: The Communist Struggle in Singapore 1954–1966* (Singapore: South Seas Society, 1996), 87, 112 n. 1; Dennis Bloodworth, *The Tiger and the Trojan Horse*, 170–1.

79. Lee Yew Seng, interviewer unknown, date unknown, accession 73, Singapore National Archives Oral History Centre.

80. Marshall, *LAD*, 29 June 1955, C340–41; *NYSP*, 25 June 1955; Lee Ting Hui, *The Open United Front*, 86.

81. Lee Kuan Yew, *The Singapore Story*, 20.

82. Andrew Tan, "Force Modernisation Trends in Southeast Asia," *Institute of Defence and Strategic Studies Working Paper Series*, no. 59 (Jan. 2004), 7, 10, 17.

83. *See* Jothie Rajah, *Authoritarian Rule of Law: Legislation, Discourse, and Legitimacy in Singapore* (Cambridge: Cambridge University Press, 2012); Tremewan, *The Political Economy of Social Control in Singapore*.

# 12

# WHAT WENT WRONG FOR THE PAP IN 2011?

*Donald Low*

With a 75.3 per cent vote, the People's Action Party (PAP) won a landslide victory at the 2001 General Election (GE 2011). Held soon after the September 11 terrorist attacks and the collapse of the US tech bubble, it showed that in times of crisis, Singaporeans turn instinctively to the trusted hands of the PAP.[1]

At GE 2011, the PAP won just 60.1 per cent of the popular vote, down by 15 percentage points compared with just ten years before. What went wrong for the PAP in 2011? What does the report card for the PAP government look like today? Why has Singaporeans' trust in the PAP government—perhaps the most important commodity in the country's system of elite governance—diminished? Do Singaporeans still accept the PAP's basic ideologies of vulnerability, elite governance, and performance legitimacy? In the wake of GE 2011 and the

Prime Minister's calls for the PAP to remake and reinvent itself, these questions must lie at the heart of any serious attempt to analyse the PAP government's performance and its prospects for self-reinvention.

About the fairest assessment that one can make about the PAP government's performance in the last ten years is that while GDP growth has been quite respectable, the decade has also been characterised by a number of policy missteps and mistakes. Segments of the Singaporean population wonder why headline GDP figures do not translate into increasing levels of happiness. Despite all the economic advances made in the past decade, the country's trajectory in terms of people's satisfaction levels and their confidence in the future seems flat, if not negative. So what has gone wrong?

The purpose of this essay is to identify the underlying causes of why the PAP government persisted in pursuing the policies that caused increasing public unhappiness and disaffection. In the immediate aftermath of the election, the emerging consensus was that the PAP did badly in GE 2011 because it was out of touch with the ground, and that it has become arrogant and deaf to increasing unhappiness over issues such as congestion, rising home prices, and the excessive reliance on foreign workers. The corrective to this, the narrative goes, is that the PAP government needs to make a conscious effort to listen more, consult and engage more, and communicate its essentially sound policies with greater empathy.

This narrative, although not entirely incorrect, is grossly incomplete. It does not explain why the PAP lost touch with the ground, why it ignored public unhappiness and resentment for so long, and why the government pursued the policies it did despite more than sufficient evidence that they were flawed and deeply unpopular. This essay hopes to shed light on these questions.

My basic contention is that over the last ten years, the economic policies aimed at maintaining GDP growth were mostly successful but came with an unusually high number of negative externalities. The unintended consequences of growth-enhancing policies were largely ignored at the time when these policies were introduced. Consequently, the policies aimed at sustaining growth were not sufficiently accompanied by policies that sought to ensure an even distribution of the fruits of growth, with policies that sought to ameliorate citizen unhappiness, or compensate them for their sacrifices and reductions in well-being.

I will also try to explain why these policy missteps and mistakes took place at all. I do not accept the argument—often peddled by the reflexive cynics on anti-establishment websites—that the PAP regime is a self-serving one that seeks only personal gain (high ministerial salaries are usually cited as the main evidence that this is indeed so). My 14-year experience in government has led me to the conclusion that the senior levels of government are mostly staffed by well-meaning, highly qualified, intelligent and publicly-minded individuals—both among civil servants and ministers.

## Cognitive Biases in Government

The mistakes of the government in the last decade are less the result of bad intentions, ignorance, or incompetence than the result of deeply-held ideological assumptions and mental models of decision-makers in power. Like ordinary folk, policymakers too are fallible; they suffer from cognitive biases and blinkers. These include confirmation bias, which is the tendency for people to only seek evidence that supports their pet theories while refusing to subject opposing views to serious consideration. People are also affected by the availability bias, the propensity to pay a lot more attention to events or risks that are more recent, more salient, or more easily recallable even if they are not representative statistically. Lastly, the status quo bias occurs when people anchor on the status quo as the reference state from which changes are often viewed with great aversion.

The strength of these cognitive biases, and the grip they have over our leaders, is increased by the fact that the PAP has been successful in government for such a long time. PAP ministers are therefore less likely to subject their assumptions and worldviews to serious scrutiny. These biases, which impact decision-making, are accumulated from past experiences. While past experience may work well as a basis for decision-making in an environment of relative predictability, it is often found wanting when dealing with complex problems in which multi-disciplinary or exponential thinking is required, or in novel situations where the past offers little guidance for the future. In such cases, these cognitive biases and blinkers can lead to fundamental misdiagnoses and stifle the innovative thinking that is required to tackle them.

## Interactive Complexity in Policymaking

Policymaking in Singapore has become far more complex, uncertain, and unpredictable for at least two reasons. First, much of the low-hanging fruit in terms of economic growth have already been plucked. Singapore's growth in the first 40 years was partly the result of economic catch-up—employing the ideas and technologies of more advanced economies to narrow the development gap. Most of the opportunities for convergence with the developed world probably dried up at the start of this century. Beyond the catch-up phase, rapid economic growth will increasingly come with risks that need to be managed. Take for instance Singapore's reliance on cheap foreign labour. As the economy matures, taking in more foreign workers increases economic growth, but only at the expense of depressing the wages of local low-skilled workers. Pursuing growth may mean increasing our intake of foreign workers, but this has to be balanced against the reduction in the subjective well-being of citizens; if not, they will have to be compensated for the inconveniences they suffer due to liberal foreign worker policies.

The mistake of Singapore's policymakers was not that they pursued growth, but that they did so in the belief that it was a necessary and sufficient condition for the well-being of citizens. This growth fetishism, in turn, is partly explained by the cognitive bias of extrapolating the future from our past experiences. Because Singapore has done well in the past by following the adage "grow first, worry about distribution later", and because Singapore's economic growth in the past has benefitted most segments of society, it was quite natural for our policymakers to assume that pursuing economic growth was sufficient. Other concerns were, at best, secondary considerations.

However, if one accepts that growth no longer translates into an equitable distribution of income or to benefits for large segments of the population, then policymakers must seriously question the validity of their growth fetish. Instead of denying that it merits policy attention, they will need to address rising inequality as a policy or structural problem in its own right. At the very least, they have to consider how their growth-enhancing policies should be accompanied by redistributive policies that spread the fruits of growth widely and evenly.

This interdependence—between economic policies to increase growth and social policies to redistribute the fruits of growth—increases the interactive complexity of policymaking in Singapore, and creates new demands on policymakers. That the PAP government has been quite slow in combining aggressive growth policies with aggressive redistribution policies suggests that, intellectually and cognitively, our policymakers have not yet accepted the fact that the economic realities that Singapore faces today are rather different from those from 15 or 20 years ago. Singapore's policymakers also subscribe to deep ideological and cognitive biases on inequality (*see* chapter 1, "The Four Myths of Inequality in Singapore"), in a way that prevents them from thinking creatively about the problem.

## A More Demanding, Less Accommodating Citizenry

Second, policymaking has become more complex because our policy problems have become more interconnected at a time when our citizens have become less accommodating and forgiving of government mistakes. Increased macroeconomic volatility in the past decade has also made it extremely difficult for microeconomic planners in the areas of housing, public transport, and foreign workers to get their projections and policies right. This point is often lost in the frenzied bashing of government on these issues.

The experience in public housing is especially instructive. The Housing and Development Board's (HDB) experience of boom-and-bust in the decade after the Asian financial crisis is a good example of how macroeconomic volatility has made the job of microeconomic planners a far more unpredictable one. In response to rising demand for public housing in the mid-1990s, the HDB ramped up its public housing construction program. The rise in demand was in turn the result of strong economic growth, the liberalisation of CPF rules for housing, and the growing perception that house prices would rise inexorably. The collapse of the housing bubble—induced by a combination of cooling measures and the onset of the Asian financial crisis—left the HDB with a huge excess supply of flats. It took the HDB nearly seven years—a period in which it almost stopped building new flats—to clear its stock of unsold flats.

This experience left a permanent scar in the psyche of housing planners in government, making the HDB extremely wary of stepping up construction in response to an anticipated increase in demand. The time lags between the decision to build more flats and the time in which the flats are completed make HDB's wariness understandable, even justifiable. Although the HDB now relies on actual orders (under the Build-to-Order scheme) instead of queue length to determine the pace of its building programme, the former creates its own rigidities and delays as well.

The same analysis applies to our transport policies as well and in particular, the development of new MRT lines. In the early 2000s, development of the MRT network slowed significantly. This decision was made on the basis of the government's experience with the Northeast Line (NEL). The government had approved the NEL on the premise that there would be new, large public housing estates in Punggol and Sengkang. These projections were made during the fast growth years before the Asian crisis. But the late 1990s and early 2000s turned out to be much more economically sluggish than planners had expected. The formation of new households slowed, and the new estates of Punggol and Sengkang failed to take off as the government had originally anticipated, making the NEL less viable commercially. This experience led the government to take a far more cautious approach to subsequent proposals to develop new train lines. The benefit of hindsight reveals that this was an overreaction.

Like public housing, the construction of subway lines involves long, and often uncertain, time lags. Thus, when the Singapore economy finally picked up momentum after 2006, transport planners found themselves woefully behind in the construction of new train lines. This problem was compounded by the fact that throughout the early 2000s, the Ministry of Finance (MOF) had pursued a policy of lowering car ownership taxes (to reduce the tax burden on Singaporeans) and relying instead on congestion charges (Electronic Road Pricing, or ERP) to manage road traffic. The combination of these two policies led to many more cars on Singapore's roads, with the inevitable consequence of congestion. Meanwhile, raising congestion charges turned out to be much more difficult than policymakers had imagined. While reductions in car ownership taxes are easy to implement, it is also quickly forgotten by the beneficiaries. On the other hand, increases in ERP cause more angst because people are loss averse (i.e., people tend to pay more attention to losses than commensurate savings or gains). Furthermore, tax reductions are passive and people only notice it when they buy a car, an infrequent occurrence. ERP deductions, however, are experienced on an almost daily basis.

In this more complex, unpredictable, and uncertain environment, the government clearly needs greater agility and adaptability. But the paradox of governance today is that at a time when the government needs more room for manoeuvre, the population is also becoming less tolerant of mistakes, less likely to trust government by default, less ready to give it the benefit of the doubt, and less willing to cut it some slack. It is also more demanding of transparency and instant accountability.

High ministerial salaries do not help and lead many Singaporeans to set an impossible benchmark for what they consider good governance: perfection. Any mistake made by the government—real or perceived—is held up against ministerial salaries and used as evidence that government is incompetent relative to how well it pays its ministers and senior officials. This poisons the political discourse and is not conducive to mature, reasoned public debate of our policy problems.

In this constrained space, policymakers have less room for experimentation and innovation. They are also more likely to resort to tried-and-tested solutions that worked in the past. After all, they will not be blamed for sticking with the status quo, but they will be pilloried for failed experiments.

## Two Conclusions

My experiences in the Singapore government have led me to two broad conclusions. The first is that our traditional approach to governance—which can be described as the "machine model" or the social engineering approach—has reached the limits of its usefulness. For too long now, the PAP government has viewed the economy and society as machines, each governed by stable and predictable causal relations. This engineering worldview results in a certain linearity in thinking:

to achieve X, find the immediate cause for X and yank on that lever until the predictable result occurs.

Ironically, as an economist, I found that perspectives offered by standard economics (much of which is premised on the predictability of rational agents) to be limited in many areas and to have led to quite perverse policy outcomes in a few. One of those perspectives is the economist's belief that incentives are the primary lever to shape people's decisions and actions: if one is offered sufficient monetary inducements, he or she will predictably do what is required. This naïve faith in the power of incentives has wrought some highly unusual and negative consequences in Singapore, for example, the use of material incentives to encourage child-bearing and the reliance on high salaries of ministers to ensure talented people are attracted to government work.

The insights of cognitive and social psychology in the last 30 years in particular are profoundly important and should broaden, if not reshape, the way we think about policy, economics, governance, and even life in general. For example, psychologists have found that what really motivates workers whose work requires cognitive effort—beyond material rewards—is their ability to achieve "autonomy, mastery and purpose."[2] Social psychologists have also emphasised the importance of social norms as a determinant of individual behaviour. If the psychologists are right, the implications for governments, and the Singapore government especially, are wide-ranging and profound.

Meanwhile, complexity theorists have found that complex systems are not characterised by stable, predictable, and linear causal relations. Instead, they often exhibit emergence, non-linearity, network effects, path dependency, and constant change. To deal with many of the complex social and economic problems that Singapore faces, the government itself has to become a complex adaptive system. This means drawing on diverse and dissenting viewpoints. Policies should also be put under constant stress-testing. The essential insight of complex adaptive systems is that systems that are subject to frequent shocks and minor failures are far more resilient than those that try to avoid them altogether. The latter tends to exhibit long periods of stability, creating a false sense of security, but when they eventually fail, it is usually catastrophic and fatal.

The second conclusion is that given the PAP government's long stranglehold on power, it is critical for it to acknowledge the cognitive biases and ideological assumptions that have developed over time, and to take conscious steps to correct for them. There is a real risk that as a result of its long and successful tenure, the PAP government has begun to elevate its operating assumptions—which served Singapore well in the past—to the level of ideology. There is growing concern that these assumptions are now held dogmatically and hinder creative thinking on the problems Singapore faces.

More often than not, when the government says it has to pursue a certain course of action—say to cut income taxes, increase the Goods and Services Tax (GST), or avoid welfare spending—because of certain "imperatives" such as global competition or globalisation, it is more a reflection of its biases, values, and beliefs rather than any iron law of economics. For instance, when the government says that if Singapore want to grow economically residents will have no choice but to accept greater inequality, there is in fact very little empirical basis to show this has been the experience internationally.

Also, the rhetoric in the Singapore government far too often is that because we are small and vulnerable, we have few viable alternatives. This stifles and limits the imagination of our policymakers. We lock ourselves into certain modes of thinking that we are familiar with and which have delivered success in the past. These paradigms or mental models critically shape and constrain our future choices: our past casts a long shadow on the present and well into the future.

The PAP government is also not as rational or pragmatic as it claims. Instead of subjecting new arguments or evidence to critical analysis, it often reverts to a few unspoken but deeply held ideological biases (e.g., an aversion to welfare, elite governance, the primacy of growth, Singapore's inherent vulnerabilities etc.). These ideological assumptions and biases are frequently relied on to deflect policy proposals that decision-makers are instinctively uncomfortable with. They represent a security blanket that policymakers take refuge in whenever our policies are subject to serious criticism; they hinder genuine out-of-the-box thinking in dealing with our most pressing problems. They are also aided by the fact that it is often difficult to prove the counter-factual, unless one actually takes the risk of pursuing alternative policy approaches.

Path dependency—the term used to describe how past choices affect current and future choices—is neither good nor bad; it is simply a reflection of reality and of people's (and organisations') bounded rationality. Individuals and organisations do certain things not because they are logically the right thing to do, but because they are what we have always done. But path dependency is also a reminder to Singapore's policymakers not to take their boasts of rational pragmatism too seriously. What appears to to be an eminently sensible course of action is often the manifestation of subjective preferences, dispositions and biases accumulated over several years, rather than the result of a rational weighing of costs and benefits, or a careful assessment of risks and opportunities.

This is the essence of the groupthink critique that is sometimes directed at the PAP government. Decision-makers share the same mental paradigms and orientations and then apply these to policy ideas. Policy approaches that are successful elsewhere but that do not fit neatly into the paradigms of policymakers are rejected instinctively because they pose too great a challenge to the policymakers' worldviews. This cognitive dissonance means that alternative approaches are ruled out right from the outset, even before they are subject to proper debate and empirical study.

By framing policy problems and Singapore's challenges in terms that are broader and different from the way the PAP state has tended to portray them, one arrives at quite different conclusions. Consequently, the choices that Singapore faces are also less stark and less binary than the government often makes them out to be. Hopefully, such a reframing of issues invites Singaporeans to think more widely about our problems, and encourages us to be less constrained by the prevailing wisdoms and biases of the PAP.

## Notes

1. This piece was written soon after Singapore's general election on 8 May 2011. It has been slightly modified for this compilation of essays.

2. Daniel H. Pink, *Drive: The Surprising Truth About What Motivates Us* (New York: Riverhead Books, 2009).

# 13

# GOVERNING IN THE NEW NORMAL

*Donald Low*

The two elections of 2011 herald a significant shift in the political values, attitudes and aspirations of Singaporeans. While the People's Action Party (PAP) and its preferred candidate for the presidency were returned to power, it would be a mistake for the PAP Government to assume that it can return to the business of governance along the technocratic lines it is used to.[1]

The Singapore polity has changed profoundly, perhaps irrevocably. President Tony Tan hinted at this when he said at the start of his election campaign that politics in Singapore can be described as a "new normal". Prime Minister Lee Hsien Loong too recognised this when he warned of the dangers of polarisation and populism; he also argued that to get our policies right, we must first get the politics right.

For more than 40 years, the PAP Government "got politics right" by containing and minimising it. Apart from parliamentary elections, the PAP drove out many forms of democratic politics from public life. It saw governance as a rational pursuit that should be only minimally subject to democratic contest and political competition. Governance, government leaders believed, should be undertaken by an enlightened elite insulated from political pressures, which they believed would lead to extremism, demagoguery, and populism.

Democracy "Singapore-style" allowed for a system of technocratic governance dominated by elites to emerge. To the extent that there was politics and a contest of policy ideas, it was kept largely *within* the establishment, a state of affairs described by Professor Chan Heng Chee in the 1970s as the "politics of an administrative state".[2] For their part, citizens mostly accepted this state of affairs, trading away many of the liberties found in democratic societies for a government that delivered the goods.

In the aftermath of the 2011 elections, the government can no longer take citizens' general acquiescence for granted. Competitive politics has returned to Singapore; the government can expect a political landscape that is far more contested, contentious, and vexed. Can good governance be sustained in the new normal? How should the system of technocratic governance adapt?

My contention is that good governance is possible in the new normal, but it requires the government to accommodate and adapt to the new sociopolitical and economic realities of Singapore. In particular, I believe the Singapore government needs to rethink its current model of governance in at least three ways.

## Policy Reforms: Rethinking the Social Compact

The reforms at the policy or technocratic level are probably the most straightforward—not because the issues are easy to address, but because they are mostly not dependent on the government achieving more fundamental political or ideological change. On the vexed issues of affordability of public housing, congestion on our transport system, and the excessive reliance on foreign workers, the government has already taken a few steps to address public unhappiness. In public housing and transport for instance, the government has stepped up infrastructure development to meet rising demand, while on foreign workers it has committed to tighten immigration and permanent residency requirements.

A more challenging set of policy issues lies in the realm of social security reform and the social compact. For genuine change to occur here, the PAP government must first abandon some long-held assumptions on the relationship between growth and equity, the impact of more social protection on economic competitiveness, and the appropriate balance between individual responsibility and state provision.

The current social compact was appropriate for an era characterised by youthful demographics, rising incomes across-the-board, and the need to achieve exceptional rates of GDP growth. In such a context, policies that emphasised individual responsibility, high national savings, relatively weak social safety nets, and public housing as the de facto instrument of redistribution were successful in ensuring growth with equity. This created a relatively benign political environment that gave the government the room to pursue long-term, growth-oriented policies with minimal political constraints and social demands.

This is now changing: our population is ageing, social mobility is slowing, economic growth is more erratic, and the fruits of growth are distributed far more unevenly than before. These forces are largely external, but have made it much harder for Singapore to achieve the equitable growth that it achieved before the turn of the century. Adapting the social compact for this new context requires the government to expand social protection significantly and redistribute far more aggressively than it has done.

A conservative sceptic might argue that the measures suggested in this volume of essays would invariably reduce economic competitiveness and erode our growth prospects. This need not be so. To begin with, the effect of more social protection on economic performance is an empirical rather than an ideological question. What is more important than the level of spending on social protection is the way the programmes are designed, and the incentive effects they create.

Among developed countries for instance, it is not the low welfare spending countries of southern Europe that are the most prosperous or competitive, but the high welfare spenders of Germany and the Nordic countries. This is not to suggest that more welfare spending leads to more competitive economies and higher growth, but simply to point out that the relationship between social protection and economic prosperity is a complex one that defies simple, reductionist arguments. Policymakers should therefore approach these issues with an open mind, subject their existing biases and assumptions to critical scrutiny, and be prepared to consider previously unthinkable solutions.

Even if we find that at some point, we have to make a trade-off between more redistribution and economic growth, it is not immediately obvious that we should always choose the latter. Economic growth is not something that societies should pursue in an unfettered, unquestioning way. To the extent that higher growth comes with distributional, environmental, or other social costs, it has to be tempered, moderated and balanced with the other things citizens care about.

Psychologists have also found that people care not just about their absolute levels of income, but their relative position as well. In short, people have a strong equity bias: in repeated experiments of the ultimatum game for instance, participants consistently demonstrated a high regard for what they perceive to be fair outcomes, to a point that seems irrational to conventional economists.[3] The upshot of all this is that what policymakers should aim to maximise is not economic growth per se, but citizen well-being, a concept that also takes into account the distribution of resources.

## Political Reforms: Rethinking the Basis of Legitimacy

A second area of reform lies in the political realm. Here, the first order of business must be to address public unhappiness over high ministerial salaries. From a narrow economic viewpoint, high ministerial salaries are efficient. They help to attract and retain good people in public office, and they reward good performance. But as psychologists have found, we need to pay people enough just to take the issue of money off the table. Beyond that, further increases in pay may actually reduce performance, both individually and organisationally. At the individual level, excessive pay increases stress and induces risk aversion. Why should I challenge the status quo if doing so might cause me to lose my lucrative job? At the organisational level, large wage disparities heighten status differentials and de-motivate workers lower on the organisation's pecking order. Why should I work hard if those above me are paid several times more, and I see no chance of rising to their stratospheric pay levels?

The unintended but negative impacts of high ministerial salaries on the body politic are also worth highlighting here. By raising public expectations of ministers and senior civil servants to impossibly high levels, high ministerial salaries narrow the space for reasoned policy dialogue. They make Singaporeans demand the impossible (i.e., perfection!) and intolerant of any mistakes—even if they are understandable under ordinary circumstances. High ministerial salaries may also erode the norms that are essential in a functioning democracy: trust in our political institutions and the moral authority of political leaders. They raise the suspicion that people pursuing political office are doing it for less than noble reasons. Over time, citizens lose trust in the government and develop cynical and corrosive attitudes about their national leaders. Excessively high ministerial salaries may also replace the social norms of service and sacrifice in government service with market norms of pay-for-performance and incentives.

More specifically, the current policy of pegging ministerial salaries to the pay of senior executives in the private sector is a flawed one. As the financial crisis has demonstrated, markets can get some things—like how senior executives in the financial industry are paid—terribly wrong. In the financial industry, pay has very little correlation with the company's long-term performance or with individual productivity. With the benefit of hindsight, we now know that the policy of pegging ministerial salaries to market benchmarks, which included the pay of bankers, was a mistake.

Second, the government also needs to reform the parts of the political system that are clearly unfair in the minds of Singaporeans. That the electoral process is skewed in favour of the ruling party is widely known but seldom discussed. The constant redrawing of electoral boundaries (some of which admittedly are justified) and expansion of Group Representation Constituencies (GRCs) over the years (until the recent election) conferred significant advantages to the incumbents. As analysts such as Cherian George have argued, these changes have tilted the playing field in a way that causes voters to apply a form of electoral "affirmative action" in favour of the opposition. Mistakes by the opposition are ignored or discounted, while those by the ruling party are seized upon, amplified and exaggerated.[4] This cannot be healthy, not only for the PAP, but also for Singapore. It stunts the development of a fair-minded, sensible, and mature electorate. But until we have a fairer electoral system, the PAP should not be surprised if voters correct for this at the polls.

For more than 40 years, the PAP regime secured broad-based support on the basis of superior performance. This is now changing. Increasingly, Singaporeans care also about the fairness of our political system and about having checks and balances on government. Trust in government can no longer be assumed. Instead, it has to be earned through transparent and fair processes.

One reason the Workers' Party did well in the 2011 General Election was that its calls for a first-world Parliament that can provide a check on the government struck a chord with the electorate. The response of many Singaporeans to the spat between the Workers' Party and the People's Association (PA) over the use of community spaces in 2011, and the subsequent debate over who should be appointed as advisers to grassroots organisations, are also indicative of the newfound appetite for fairness.

So a third area of political reform is to depoliticise our grassroots organisations and keep our civil society as non-partisan as possible. One of the paradoxes of political life in Singapore is that the grassroots organisations that were established to foster cohesion and community relationships have, over time, become a source of political division. Singaporeans increasingly associate them, and the PA that they are formed under, with the PAP. Whether this outcome was intended or not, the grassroots organisations are now perceived as partisan. That they are disconnected from the elected MPs if these happen to be opposition MPs is not only unfair, it is also unnecessarily divisive and polarising.

If the current grassroots organisations are seen to be extensions of the PAP, opposition parties will have little choice but to organise and develop their own local community organisations. Civil society organisations may also start to align themselves with the opposition to provide a balance to the pro-PAP grassroots organisations (the union movement can be included as well). While some may think that such competition for the affections of residents is a good thing, these dubious benefits have to be weighed against the costs of political polarisation.

In a socially depleted polity where most social groupings are highly politicised and politically charged, people will begin to form their identities around their narrow political ideologies: they have little else to latch on to. In such an environment, reasoned policy discourse becomes increasingly difficult as everything is tainted by narrow political partisanship. Politics becomes tribal, social relationships are less dense and rich, and society is more fragile.[5]

This scenario of a divided polity was inconceivable in an age of (largely) unchallenged PAP supremacy but is now a real possibility. It is also an outcome that a responsible government can preempt through sensible reforms of Singapore's political system—reforms that will also encourage the ruling party to rely less on the "crutches" of the past 20 years: gerrymandering, mega-GRCs, and the PA and its network of grassroots organisations.

## Ideological Transformation: Rethinking Elite Governance

The third pillar of a comprehensive reform agenda for the government is ideological transformation. The PAP's underlying ideologies of elite governance, the primacy of economic growth, and Singapore's inherent vulnerabilities are less inspiring and increasingly dissonant for many Singaporeans. Whatever the usefulness of these ideological assumptions (or "hard truths") in preventing Singaporeans from becoming soft, the PAP government needs to expand its repertoire of narratives if it is to connect with the increasingly large number of educated Singaporeans bred on the non-hierarchical, egalitarian ethos of the internet.

This commitment to fairness is critical—not just economic fairness, but also political fairness. Indeed, fairness is one of the most important foundations of a good society. Fairness also means that the PAP must move beyond its reliance on performance legitimacy—that the government's mandate is gained primarily through good performance and *not* through fair political processes—to embrace procedural or systemic legitimacy.

The PAP government also needs to rethink the narratives and practices of elite governance. The review of ministerial salaries is important in this regard but is not sufficient. The starting point of this reappraisal of elite governance must be that Singapore's educated elite has become more fragmented, more diverse and heterogeneous, and less cohesive ideologically and politically. The constant drumbeat on how vulnerable Singapore is, and how important it is for the country to be led by a carefully selected elite, will only alienate more and more Singaporeans.

The first step may well be for the PAP ministers to take a (big) step back, open up the space for policy and political dialogue, and see their role as that of a facilitator, convenor and aggregator (of ideas and diverse views). It means moving away from the model of elite governance centred on leaders sitting atop a vast government hierarchy to one of collective governance built on a distributed, non-partisan network of community activists, policy researchers, members of parliament, social workers, and, of course, civil servants. It means tapping on the collective wisdom of citizens, and leveraging the tools of social innovation, co-creation, and crowd-sourcing.

This model of distributed and networked governance not only places new demands on the government, which now has to develop stronger network management capabilities, but also requires citizens to step up to the plate. To contribute meaningfully to the policy and political discourse, Singaporeans have to be informed and educated about such matters. They should also be realistic about the limits of democratic participation: not everyone will get heard, and even fewer will have their views taken on board. Ignorance and misguided idealism will only turn into cynicism when citizens' hopes for participation in the way they conceived it are not fulfilled. In short, the process of democratic engagement needs to be properly sequenced and managed, not just widened.

To nudge the process along, the government must liberalise its hitherto restrictive policies on data sharing and information dissemination. For Singaporeans to be engaged in the trade-offs and dilemmas of governance, they must first be aware of those trade-offs. This requires that Singaporeans have access to the policy considerations and data that are presently accessible only to policymakers. An open and inclusive democratic polity needs a more transparent information environment.

Finally, the government needs to find a new narrative that

resonates with younger Singaporeans. At our level of prosperity, a narrative founded mainly on the country's vulnerabilities (as important as that may be given our geopolitical constraints) is unlikely to inspire many Singaporeans. More than ever, the national narrative has to shift to what makes a good society: fairness, opportunity, equality, and resilience.

## Towards a Model Democracy

I began the previous essay by asking what went wrong for the PAP government in the last decade. My main argument is that the policy mistakes and missteps of the past decade were largely the result of cognitive failures and biases on the part of decision-makers in government. These in turn were the result of the PAP's ideologies of vulnerability, elite governance, and performance legitimacy. Over time, these ideologies bred hubris and created the illusions of invulnerability and indispensability; invulnerability as in the belief that "we cannot be wrong", and indispensability as in the belief that "only we know how to govern Singapore well".

All this sets the stage for the perceptions of government arrogance and imperiousness that many analysts have identified as one of the main causes of the PAP's declining vote share. Knowing this, the PAP leadership has little choice but to rethink many of its assumptions and systems. This process of reflection and reform has just begun, but already it is quite clear that humility should be the new watchword of the PAP. I hope this humility is not just confined to leadership style, but also extends to the acknowledgement that what we do not know is much greater than what we know.

My hope for Singapore is that we become a model democracy that is characterised by fairness. There is also no necessary reason why politics in Singapore should become polarised or paralysing. We also should not conclude that the only way to ensure good governance is to deny Singaporeans their newfound political energies, in the vain hope that politics can return to what it was before the elections of 2011.

The forces revealed by the elections of 2011 make it incumbent on the PAP government to pursue bold policy and political reforms. These reforms, founded on the virtues of fairness, equality, and resilience will not only make us a more "normal" democracy, but will also help to sustain good governance in the new normal.

## Notes

1. An abbreviated version of this essay was published in the *Straits Times*'s Opinion pages on 10 Sept. 2011 under the same title.

2. Chan Heng Chee, "Politics in an Administrative State: Where has the Politics Gone?", in *Trends in Singapore*, ed. S. C. Meow (Singapore: Institute of Southeast Asia Studies, 1975), 51–58.

3. The ultimatum game is a game played in economic experiments to establish whether and to what extent people care about equity. In the game, Player A is told that he would be given a sum of money if and only if Player B accepts his proposal on how that money is to be divided between the two of them. If Player B accepts the offer, the money is split according to the proposal and both players are better off. If Player B rejects the offer, neither player gets anything and they are both worse off. Rationally speaking, Player B should accept whatever offer Player A makes, no matter how small. In reality though, because of people's equity bias, offers that are deemed too low are rejected. The game is played only once so that issues of reciprocity do not arise.

4. Cherian George, "Towards a Democratic Society", text of a talk given at a post-election forum organised by Maruah and *Online Citizen* on 15 May 2011, http://www.airconditionednation.com/2011/05/15/ge2011-aftermath/.

5. David Brooks, *The Social Animal: The Hidden Sources of Love, Character and Achievement* (New York: Random House, 2011).

# 14

# THE FUTURE OF DEMOCRACY IN SINGAPORE

*Sudhir Thomas Vadaketh*

The essays in this book have offered several reasons why greater democratisation will benefit Singapore. First, more established channels of dialogue, including the media and civil society institutions, will allow the political elite to bridge what Singaporean author Catherine Lim called in the mid-1990s the "great affective divide" between ordinary Singaporeans and the PAP (People's Action Party). This divide has arguably worsened over the past two decades, at least partly due to the greater income disparity between Singapore's highest-paid politicians and the median worker.

The second argument is economic. Singapore's model of benevolent developmental authoritarianism may have been suited to the country's early stages of development but is ill-equipped to serve as the basis of a knowledge economy, which requires the freedom of thought and expression only a democracy can guarantee. This partly relates to the greater need for free information flows given the increasing complexity of policymaking and economic development. In a modern, knowledge economy in an open, globalised world, information and knowledge exists in disparate pockets everywhere. More transparent informational flows, perhaps buttressed by a Freedom of Information Act, will, by allowing a diversity of ideas to emerge, lead to more optimal economic, political and social outcomes.

Finally, there is the reasoning grounded in the resilience of ecological systems—outlined in the next essay—about the need for Singapore's political structure to become a more complex, adaptive system. While an authoritarian state may have been necessary for fast decision-making, resource mobilisation, and nation building in the 1960s to the 1980s, Singapore's future success will depend on its ability to adapt and respond to a multitude of complex new challenges. This adaptability is best fostered by a properly functioning democracy that, by its very nature, promotes diversity and the competition of ideas.

Even though a growing number of Singaporeans share this liberal view of democracy's imperative, there are many others in the country who at best, are unconvinced, and at worst, believe democratic liberalisation will spell the end of the Singapore fairy tale. The contestation between these groups will determine the future of Singapore's democracy.

## Democracy in Singapore

Nominally, Singapore is a parliamentary democracy in the British Westminster tradition. It holds free and fair elections every five years. The majority party or coalition gets to choose the prime minister, who then selects his cabinet of ministers. The other executive leader is the president, who is elected separately for a six-year term. The role is largely ceremonial but has limited powers over, among other things, the use of Singapore's reserves. The prime minister nominates judges to the Supreme Court, which leads the judiciary, an independent body in theory.

In practice, however, Singapore has been governed as an authoritarian state. One party, the PAP, dominates parliament. Since independence it has controlled more than two-thirds of the legislature, allowing it to make constitutional amendments as it chooses.

The PAP's dominance is so complete that it has transcended mere legislative and political control, forging strong emotional and psychological bonds with the polity. Singaporeans have long equated the ruling party with the country. In other words, if you are loyal to the PAP, you are loyal to Singapore. On the other hand, if you are not loyal to the PAP, you are not loyal to Singapore. If you vote for the opposition, you are somehow being un-Singaporean. Many Singaporeans have this marriage between party and country firmly planted in their minds, hence the fear of voting for the opposition. Moreover, numerous hurdles—including a government-controlled media that is muzzled—have long crippled opposition parties' ability to grow.

Thus Singapore is, in practice, an imperfect or illiberal democracy. Some of Singapore's establishment commentators justify Singapore's approach to democracy as the best one by citing "Asian values", or by contrasting it with the supposed chaos and paralysis one occasionally finds in Western liberal democracies.

This essay will steer clear of arguments grounded in cultural relativism because many of the characteristics of a thriving democracy, such as freedom of expression and thought, are basic civil liberties that humans anywhere should enjoy.

Some might say there is a normative democratic argument for, say, the need to control the press in order to protect society from potentially inflammatory commentary. However, this essay argues that the conditions that may have applied to newly-independent Singapore in the 1960s to 1980s but have long since lost their relevance. It is important, therefore, to analyse Singapore against traditional notions of democracy—not the alternative visions that Asian cultural relativists proffer.

With that in mind, an interesting analytical comparison for Singapore is Hong Kong. There are numerous economic and sociological similarities between the two: they are city-states, former British colonies, extremely open economies, and have majority Chinese populations with high per capita GDP. However, they have prospered with very different forms of democracy. Consider how Hong Kong and Singapore fare in terms of Robert Dahl's checklist of "The Institutions of Polyarchy". Dahl writes that "the institutions of polyarchy are necessary to democracy on a large scale, particularly the scale of the modern national state."[1]

Dahl proposes seven institutions whose existence distinguishes a political order as polyarchy:

1. **Elected officials:** Control over government decisions about policy is constitutionally vested in elected officials.

2. **Free and fair elections:** Elected officials are chosen in frequent and fairly conducted elections in which coercion is comparatively uncommon.

3. **Right to run for office:** Practically all adults have the right to run for elective offices in the government, though age limits may be higher for holding office than for suffrage.

4. **Inclusive suffrage:** Practically all adults have the right to vote in the election of officials.

5. **Freedom of expression:** Citizens have a right to express themselves without the danger of severe punishment on political matters broadly defined, including criticism of officials, the government, the regime, the socioeconomic order, and the prevailing ideology.

6. **Alternative information:** Citizens have a right to seek out alternative sources of information. Moreover, alternative sources of information exist and are protected by laws.

7. **Associational autonomy:** To achieve their various rights, including those listed above, citizens also have a right to form relatively independent associations or organizations, including independent political parties and interest groups.

It is striking that Hong Kong and Singapore appear to possess complementary institutions, yet neither has the entire gamut of institutions normally found in a thriving, full-fledged democracy (*see* table on next page). Also interesting is that while Hong Kong lacks effective representation in government, it boasts strong grassroots democratic institutions and protects individual freedoms. In Singapore, the inverse is true.

An immediately obvious advantage for both governments in these

|  | Hong Kong | Singapore |
|---|---|---|
| Elected officials[2] | N | Y |
| Free and fair elections[3] | N | Y |
| Right to run for office | N | Y |
| Inclusive suffrage | Y | Y |
| Freedom of expression | Y | N |
| Alternative information | Y | N |
| Associational autonomy | Y | N |
| (Note: The Ys and Ns do not mean that the particular institution is completely present nor wholly absent, respectively. Rather, they denote a *relative* presence or absence, in comparison to institutions of polyarchy in other democracies.) | | |

countries is that they rarely have to fear for their positions of power. In Hong Kong, this insulation between the people and their supposed representatives has existed since the beginning of British colonial rule, and is perhaps a reason why successive governors and now the chief executive have been tolerant of the robust grassroots democratic institutions highlighted above.

The last governor of Hong Kong Chris Patten writes, "So a free society lived and breathed—up to that boundary line beyond which a governing class wrestled with the arduous choices of politics. There was freedom of a substantial sort: but there was no freedom to choose those who would be wholly responsible for even the most mundane of public services."

Unlike the Hong Kong Government, which has never had to fear its popular removal, the PAP in Singapore has. It is theoretically possible that it loses an election, and hence its vice-like grip on power. Therefore, in order to severely undermine the opposition's chances, the PAP has had to maintain hegemony over many spheres of democratic life. It has restricted freedom of expression lest anti-government messages of subversion are spread. It has moulded the media into a governmental mouthpiece that rarely questions Singapore's overall direction and priorities. Its controls on associational life have resulted in an insipid civil society that has effectively detached the electorate from political life.

The PAP has also meticulously and relentlessly tweaked the rules of the political game to an extent that it rarely has to worry about its opponents, both inside and outside the political arena. Perry, Kong, and Yeoh comment on this effect, "The net result has been to give the state considerable freedom of action. Major infrastructure projects, for example, necessitating the removal and relocation of large numbers of urban residents, have not been constrained by the demands of sectoral lobbyists, community advocates or other interest groups as they have in other major cities of Southeast Asia. Similarly, it has been comparatively easy to reverse policy decisions, even where this requires abandoning once firmly held positions, as in the case of population policies."[4]

Using a different, more contemporary democratic analysis, Singapore does not score well either. Consider the Democracy Index published by the Economist Intelligence Unit (EIU), which ranks countries based on five categories: "Electoral process and pluralism", "Functioning of government", "Political participation", "Political culture", and "Civil liberties".

After scoring the Index, the EIU then divides the countries into four segments to denote their level of democratic development: "Full democracies", "Flawed democracies", "Hybrid regimes", and "Authoritarian regimes".

In the 2012 Index, Singapore ranked 81st, well below "Full democracies" such as Norway (1st), South Korea (20th) and Costa Rica (22nd), but also below "Flawed democracies" such as Botswana (30th), Indonesia (53rd), Hong Kong (63rd) and Malaysia (64th). The EIU reckons that Singapore is a "Hybrid regime", alongside Guatemala and Tanzania (all joint 81st) and just above Bangladesh (84th).

Singapore scores particularly poorly for "Electoral process and pluralism" and "Political participation". For the former, Singapore's poor showing reflects a lack of pluralism, given the opposition parties' relatively weak positions vis-à-vis the PAP. For the latter, Singapore is marked down for everything from female representation in parliament to citizens' political engagement.

## Forces for Change

It is clear that Singapore's democracy still faces broad deficits in terms of "Freedom of expression", "Alternative information" and "Associational autonomy", in reference to Dahl's framework, as well as "Electoral process and pluralism" and "Political participation", to use the EIU's Democracy Index.

However, it is also apparent that over the past decade several different forces that increase demand for those democratic institutions have emerged. Perhaps the most important underlying drivers are perceived policy missteps and state failures. This includes everything from the PAP's broader socioeconomic management, such as population policies, to more specific incidents, such as suspected terrorist Mas Selamat's escape from detention in 2008.

These have caused a growing number of Singaporeans to question what they long took for granted: the efficiency of the single-party state, if not of the PAP itself. That impulse, in turn, has led to a desire for greater freedoms of expression, more alternative news sources and a wider diversity of non-governmental organisations in society. The polity's growing democratic aspirations have necessarily meant that the PAP has slowly lost control of an ever-expanding civic, intellectual and political arena.

The second force for change, then, is the increasing number of credible political and non-political actors that have emerged to contest this space. This includes alternative news sites such as *The Online Citizen* (TOC) as well as civil society groups such as Transient Workers Count Too (TWC2). Whereas the PAP and other establishment vehicles dominated this nominally democratic space for most of Singapore's history, today there is a proliferation of non-establishment power sources vying for mindshare.

Undergirding these two forces is a third: technological change. As in many other democratisation processes around the world, in Singapore, the internet has provided the base for flourishing new channels of communication between non-establishment actors and citizens. Contributing to their efficacy are Singapore's high rates of computer and mobile phone penetration.

Finally, a fourth force for change, arguably, comprises the progressives and reformists within the PAP itself. Although the party on the whole appears to remain highly sceptical of traditional democratic ideals, it does not want to come across as ignoring shifts in societal attitudes either. For instance, in April 2013, Tharman Shanmugaratnam, Singapore's deputy prime minister, stressed the importance of alternative and diverse viewpoints in Singapore, "I believe we [PAP] can play a dominant role, retain a dominant position without wanting to completely dominate." [5]

Some might sneer and say that this is mere window dressing. But even if there is an underlying political motive, such comments—which represent a marked departure from the "PAP knows best" attitude of yesteryear—inevitably broaden the horizons of Singapore's polity and provide more space for democratic ideas and processes.

## What will Democratic Change Look Like?

Political forecasting is always fraught with difficulties, more so given Singapore's current position on the journey from authoritarianism to real democracy. Other Asian political liberalisations, from Japan to Malaysia, have shown that when a long-standing, dominant political party loses the electorate's faith, the rate of change can be non-linear, surprising even the most seasoned of political observers.

For instance, in Singapore's last electoral contest, a by-election in Punggol in January 2013, not even the most starry-eyed opposition supporter could have foreseen the more than 10 percentage-point swing away from the PAP towards the Worker's Party (WP). It was an unprecedented blowout that handed the WP its seventh elected parliamentary seat.

Bearing in mind these forecasting challenges, let us consider how different aspects of Singapore's democracy might evolve over the next one or two election cycles.

### *Freedom of Expression*

It is by no means certain that Singaporeans will enjoy greater freedoms of expression anytime soon. On the one hand, an energetic, liberal grassroots movement, intent on pushing the boundaries of socially acceptable expression, has arisen. On the other hand, a fierce resistance, comprised of conservative politicians and risk-averse segments of the broader population, seems to have formed.

Two recent incidents shed light on this tension. First, in January 2013, Lynn Lee, a documentary film-maker, published video interviews with two former bus drivers who had been part of a large industrial strike by Mainland Chinese bus drivers in Singapore in 2012. In the video, the two men make allegations of police brutality during the post-strike interrogations. After the videos were published, Singapore's Ministry of Home Affairs ordered an investigation into the allegations, partly for the sake of "public confidence and trust in the integrity of the SPF" (Singapore Police Force).

Bizarrely, however, Ms Lee herself then appeared to become the subject of a police investigation. Over the course of two days, the police asked Ms Lee more than 150 questions, many of which had absolutely nothing to do with the drivers' allegations of assault. "I started wondering seriously if I, rather than the alleged perpetrators, was the one being investigated," wrote Ms Lee on her blog.[6] "Were they trying to establish if I had somehow manufactured the allegations?"

However, while Ms Lee's harrowing experience might have been forgotten in the Singapore of yesteryear, in today's world, a restless, technology-empowered society did not let the police and government rest. Ms Lee's friends used Facebook and Twitter to provide live updates of her status. Upon release, she immediately blogged about her experience, informing her fellow Singaporeans about the police's use of draconian methods. One of the few non-PAP members of parliament later asked a parliamentary question about the police treatment of Ms Lee.

The second incident, in April 2013, concerns the arrest of Leslie Chew, an online cartoonist, for publishing allegedly seditious cartoons. He appears to have been targeted for asking, through his cartoons, a very pertinent question: is there institutionalised discrimination against Malays in Singapore?

Although many in the artistic community were up in arms over the arrest, some Singaporeans complained about how Mr Chew framed the discussion, including the use of the phrase "Damn racist government!" Perhaps most worrying is the fact that some Singaporeans believe that Mr Chew should not even be considered an artist and that the government should be the one to determine what constitutes "art". In keeping with conservative Singapore practice, this attitude represents a desire to radically rethink certain basic, fundamental human conditions—art, creativity, and freedom—and shoehorn them into some Singaporean utopia.

However, just like with Ms Lee, the internet provided a platform not only for Mr Chew to communicate with his followers through cartoons, but also for ordinary citizens to protest against the government's perceived heavy-handedness.

In both these stories there are vestiges of the old Singapore and elements of the new. When it comes to creative freedoms, the government seems as intent as ever on reminding society of certain out-of-bound (OB) markers. It continues to be deliberately vague about what people can and cannot say or express, feeding an environment of excessive self-censorship. Mr Chew's case is instructive, as he practises his art form only online, a space that many believed to be sacrosanct. To be sure, there are many Singaporeans who seem to agree with the government's enforcement of these seemingly archaic OB markers. Therefore, it is unlikely that change will come from the top as long as the PAP remains the dominant political party.

There is, of course, a chance that the PAP may realise—as the ruling Barisan Nasional (BN) did in Malaysia—that beyond a certain point, stifling freedoms of expression becomes counter-productive. First, it engenders ill-feeling among the electorate. Second, it consumes valuable time and political capital that is in increasingly short supply. Third, because of the internet, censorship serves only to boost the supposed offender's popularity—Mr Chew was a virtual unknown before the police arrested him.

Nevertheless, it is more likely that change may be forced upon the PAP from below. As both Ms Lee's and Mr Chew's incidents show, Singapore's social climate is changing rapidly—ordinary people are seeking out more alternative, non-establishment viewpoints, and are increasingly unwilling to tolerate any perceived attempts at suppressing them.

## Alternative Information

How might Singapore's media landscape evolve? Malaysia's experience might provide some guidance, as its alternative news sector is several years ahead of Singapore's.

At the end of the 1990s, most Malaysians were still faithfully reading national newspapers, including *The New Straits Times* and *The Star*. Nevertheless, many Malaysians had, by that point, gotten weary of the media's pro-government stance. *Malaysiakini*, a website launched in 1999, precipitated a gradual shift towards alternative news sources. Today, Malaysia's media has bifurcated dramatically. On the one side there are the mainstream media outlets that broadly support the BN and are followed mostly by BN supporters. On the other side there is the non-establishment bloc, comprised of a hodgepodge of actors, including opposition parties and civil society groups, who converse mostly through the internet or via SMS text broadcasts. (This bifurcation is, of course, a crude simplification of a diverse media and society.)

Malaysians now have access to a whole range of credible and very readable online blogs and news sites, including *Malaysiakini* and the *Malaysian Insider*. Many Malaysians have altogether stopped listening to the mainstream media.

Could the same happen in Singapore? Just a few years ago, it might have seemed impossible, partly because many more people were seemingly satisfied with the government media channels, despite their well-known pro-PAP bias.

However, over the past few years, and particularly leading up to GE 2011, many Singaporeans, particularly the younger generations, started shifting away from the pro-government mainstream media towards the independent online news sources. Some of the country's best political analysis can also be found online. This includes personal blogs, such as Alex Au's *Yawning Bread*, as well as online news portals and discussion forums, such as *The Online Citizen*.

These online sources tend to start off with an anti-establishment, liberal bent, but then over time move more to the centre. Their emergence has partly forced mainstream outlets such as *The Straits Times* (ST) to become more balanced in their reporting, as seen during GE 2011, when opposition parties were offered some genuine real estate in our main national paper.

In other words, both the mainstream media and the alternative online media have slowly started to embrace opinions outside their usual remit. Nevertheless, just like in Malaysia, an unhealthy bifurcation has emerged: pro-establishment reportage in the mainstream media, and mostly non-establishment opinion on the internet. This has polarised many. Followers of Singapore's mainstream media tend to be older and/or more conservative. They are more likely to be PAP-supporters. Conversely, followers of Singapore's alternative media tend to be younger and/or more liberal. They are relatively more likely to support the opposition.

GE 2011 only served to sharpen the divide. By the next election, which must be held by 2016, few will be surprised if Singapore is even more polarised than today; the camps will be the mainstream media/ PAP and the alternative media/opposition. At worst, opponents of the national media believe it is in cahoots with a narrow elite, whose interests they protect. Meanwhile, opponents of the alternative media believe it is anti-government and anti-Singapore. Both mediums face very different challenges.

First, it remains to be seen whether the national media channels can reinvent themselves sufficiently to win back support from disenchanted citizens. In order to do so, they will surely have to ditch their old biased, sycophantic ways and embrace a more diverse brand of journalism that is tolerant of non-establishment views.

Meanwhile, Singapore's online news sites are still relatively immature, particularly in comparison to Malaysia's, which are much more developed (i.e., with wider readerships, more sustainable business models, and clearer editorial direction). The reason is partly size: Singapore's tiny market may be too small to support numerous advertisement-based internet sites. It is therefore uncertain if Singapore will ever have an internet newspaper akin to *Malaysiakini* or if the alternative media will remain in its current state, an ocean of small, independent news sites and blogs that publish good analysis and opinion, albeit inconsistently.

As with OB markers, change is unlikely to come from the top despite the benefits of media liberalisation. A generation of Singaporean leaders has grown up believing that a state-controlled media is essential for stability and prosperity. Disabusing them of this notion will be tough. "Reporters have to be careful in their coverage of local news, as Singapore's leaders will likely come down hard on anyone who reports negative stories about the government or its leadership," a Singaporean journalist told the US Ambassador in 2009, according to a WikiLeaks report released in 2011. "The government exerts significant pressure on ST editors to ensure that published articles follow the government's line. In the past, the editors had to contend only with the opinions of former Prime Minister Lee Kuan Yew and former deputy Prime Minister Goh Chok Tong. However, a younger generation of government ministers is now vying for future leadership positions and one way for them to burnish their credentials with the old guard is to show they can be tough with the media."

Not only does the establishment fear mainstream media liberalisation, it also seems intent on bringing internet journalists in line with its larger media ideals. On 1 June 2013, the government began efforts to regulate the online media through a new online licensing scheme. "I think it is important for us to ensure that they [ordinary Singaporeans] read the right thing," Yaacob Ibrahim, the Minister of Communications and Information, told the BBC.[7] That remarkably candid statement confirms the government's conservative media stance while also reasserting its belief in the need for enlightened elites to guide and lead the undiscerning masses.

Nevertheless, regardless of exactly how Singapore's media landscape changes, citizens today now have access to scores of alternative news and information sources. This trend has undoubtedly enriched the country's democracy.

## Associational Autonomy

After years of operating in the shadow of a dominant government, civil society organisations (CSOs) are today developing rapidly, in tandem with the civic and political awakening of many Singaporeans. The influx of foreigners and foreign organisations such as Habitat for Humanity has also contributed to the sector's growth, partly by importing into Singapore organisational best practices and standards but also, at a more philosophical level, generating a general enthusiasm for civil society participation.

Today there are CSOs representing a plethora of causes, from animal rights and the arts to foreign workers and the elderly. The internet has, unsurprisingly, allowed them to organise their constituents far more effectively than they ever could in Singapore.

"Today, civil society is sexy and attractive," Braema Mathi, president of Maruah, an ASEAN-focussed human rights organisation in Singapore, wrote in 2008.[8] "Individuals are keen to be part of it. Government wants to engage it, to consult and solicit its views; and to also show that they too are becoming open and democratic. The private sector is keen to partner civil society to show its own commitment to people's well-being as part of its corporate social responsibility. Everybody wants in."

However, as with other aspects of democracy, it appears as if civil society change is being forced from below, while many in the establishment remain deeply sceptical about democratic liberalisation. Singapore's government has always tried to draw a very sharp distinction between civil and political society in Singapore. The traditional role of CSOs in Singapore is as a provider of certain specific services, nothing more.

"Essentially some commentators define civil society as groups and associations in between the state and family that are non-partisan," James Gomez, an opposition politician, wrote in 1999 when he was a researcher at the Friedrich Naumann Foundation Singapore.[9] "They work with the government to provide direct services and bring about improvements in public policy. While on the other hand, political society is defined as the realm where political parties contest for dominance over government."

Perhaps this position might have been justified in Singapore's early development, when the state was more dominant and ordinary citizens more homogenous in terms of their sociopolitical beliefs. But it appears clear that the government is intent on keeping CSOs firmly in their place. It controls them in two ways. The first is by monitoring and regulating them through the Registry of Societies (ROS). According to the Ministry of Home Affairs, any club, company, partnership or association of more than ten people should register itself with the ROS.

More pernicious, perhaps, is the government's willingness to gazette as a "political organisation" any CSO that it believes is intruding into the sacred political space. Gazetting seriously throttles an organisation's activities, making it harder for it to, among other things, raise money. The most alarming recent instance of gazetting was of *TOC*, the alternative news site, just a few months before GE 2011. In other words, for more than three years now, one of Singapore's leading online news sites has been officially considered a "political organisation". TOC is not a traditional CSO, but there are many others, including Maruah, that have also been gazetted.

"In recent years, we have witnessed the demise of civil society think tank groups, like Sintercom and Roundtable, as a result of their work being seen to be political or because the groups felt restricted in their self-expression," wrote Ms Mathi.

In addition to gazetting, the government puts pressure on CSOs if it believes they are straying too far from their regular mandate. This can sometimes involve individual character assassination. For instance, in May 2013, Nizam Ismail resigned from his position on the board of the Association of Muslim Professionals (AMP), claiming that the government had threatened to cut AMP's funding because of speeches he had made at a WP youth forum and a protest at Hong Lim Park.[10] (The government denied the allegation.) The Ministry of Culture, Community and Youth then issued a statement accusing Mr Ismail of using AMP to promote "race-based politics".[11] (Mr Nizam denied the allegation.) It would appear that Mr Nizam's main mistake was to be a prominent CSO leader while maintaining certain public views in opposition to government policies. This would, of course, have been acceptable in any other developed democracy.

The most significant civil society evolution that we will observe in Singapore over the next decade is the gradual blurring of lines between civil and political society. Spurred on by their ever-more vocal constituents, CSOs will necessarily have to engage with the government and the private sector on all manner of policy issues that will, inevitably, stray into the broad space considered "politics".

Members of the establishment are trying to resist this shift, but ultimately they may realise the futility of doing so. First, the Singapore public is growing increasingly intolerant of any perceived attempts to stifle the nascent democracy. Hence the scope for selective gazetting of organisations is narrowing, partly because it might be counter-productive (e.g., TOC's readership spiked after it was gazetted).

Second, rather than resisting the intrusion of civil society into "politics", it may soon become politically expedient for the PAP to allow CSOs that are broadly aligned to its national development goals to organise freely. Otherwise, it runs the risk of stifling friendly CSOs while constantly fending off more daring non-aligned CSOs.

This shift will bring Singapore's CSOs even closer to those in other developed democracies. "Commentators, by separating civil and political society in such a clinical manner, also fail to acknowledge the role of civil society in the political process," noted Mr Gomez. "Civil society, in addition to its role as a service provider for the community, is often looked upon to contribute to the democratisation process. In addition to political party actors, civil society groups and their members are seen as another set of actors coming together to urge reforms in the constitution to ensure that democratic governance is in place."

To conclude, when considering "freedom of expression", "alternative information" and "associational autonomy" in Singapore, it is clear that there is a growing, broad-based grassroots desire for liberalisation, particularly since GE 2011. Just as certain, though, appears the PAP's resolve to resist any sort of significant change.

The government's toolkit will allow it to better control "freedom of expression" and "alternative information"—for instance, through public assembly and newspaper licensing laws respectively. However, it will find it increasingly difficult to rein in CSOs. "Associational autonomy" in Singapore's democracy will, therefore, probably strengthen faster.

## Political Candidates and Parties

Political pluralism has been on the rise, as Singapore's main opposition parties, particularly the WP, have become stronger dramatically in the past few years. They have started to recruit more credible candidates and their support base is growing fast. The main impetus for their development has been Singaporeans' desire for a stronger opposition voice in parliament. Therefore, it seems likely that no matter what the PAP does in the short-term, it is likely to lose more votes and seats in the next one or two elections. Barring some major disaster or error by the opposition, there are many Singaporeans, even those who still want the PAP to form the government, who will vote for the opposition almost regardless of who stands for election.

This trend will probably continue until Singapore reaches a new PAP-opposition equilibrium in parliament. Estimates put this at between 20–30 opposition MPs of the 87. If the opposition wins 30 seats, it will deny the PAP the two-thirds majority it needs to make constitutional changes.

Part of the underlying assumption here is that many Singaporeans want to grow the alternative to the PAP to the point that it is strong enough to possibly take over government in the event of a serious failure within the PAP. Of course, in a multi-party democracy, there will not be any one alternative, but several permutations of possible coalitions. After that happens—perhaps by the next general election—Singaporeans will probably start to pay much closer attention to individual candidates, party manifestos, and policy recommendations. This will all be part of the growing maturity of the electorate.

Beneath that broad outlook, there are several different political trends that are worth examining:

### Two-party or multi-party democracy?

After GE 2011, the WP established itself as the main opposition party. It is the only one with elected MPs, and the first to wrest a Group Representation Constituency (GRC) from the PAP. Early indications are that it is only going to get stronger, particularly in the east of Singapore. Among other things, WP is famed for its community outreach and grassroots organisation.

If WP further consolidates its position in GE 2016, this could suggest the beginnings of a two-party democracy. Some of its critics deride the WP's lack of substantive, original policy ideas, calling it "PAP-lite". It is entirely possible, however, that the WP is playing a long game, seeking to win the trust of risk-averse Singaporeans before pushing for more significant policy changes. That said, given their apparent ideological closeness, it is not difficult to envision an electoral scenario, possibly even within two election cycles, where the PAP secures fewer than half the parliamentary seats, and is forced into an alliance with the WP to form Singapore's government.

If Singaporeans desire greater policy changes in the short-term, then they might actually veer towards one of the other opposition parties, particularly the Singapore Democratic Party (SDP), which has over the past two years suggested fairly radical reworking of Singapore's healthcare and public housing systems. The likelihood of this is low though, not least because of the SDP's relative inexperience in grassroots organisation.

The most likely ten-year scenario, then, is for the WP to remain the PAP's primary opponent, with the more radical, original policy ideas coming from one or two other opposition parties, including the SDP.

### Will the PAP split?

Some analysts wonder if the PAP will one day see a split between the supposed conservatives and the supposed reformers. Lee Kuan Yew's passing, when it comes, will apparently raise the likelihood of that happening. But there are two reasons why this may not happen soon. The first is that between the PAP and WP in their current forms, it is difficult to see what niche a new political party might try to exploit. If anything, the PAP's best defence against the WP is to convince Singaporeans that it does indeed represent a fairly broad spectrum of views, rather than simply being a party of like-minded elites, a charge that has undermined it of late. A split, then, would weaken both sides within the PAP.

On a related note, it does appear that the PAP is harking back to its socialist roots in order to win back votes from liberals and progressives who may have strayed. Deputy Prime Minister Tharman Shanmugaratnam's comment that the party is now "left-of-centre" was the clearest indication of this. In the longer term, it may become increasingly difficult for the PAP to appeal to many different segments of the political spectrum. But over the next decade, this electoral strategy should work.

### Politicians: Fewer Elites

It seems almost certain that the traditional Singapore preference for selecting bureaucratic and military elites for political office is ending. Two forces are driving this. First, many voters are increasingly disenchanted with elite governance and are keen to elect candidates who may more closely resemble the common person. This is both because they may perceive such candidates as more personable, but also because of a desire for greater experiential diversity in parliament. Although there were other factors at play, the election of the WP's Lee

Li Lian over the academically better-qualified Koh Poh Koon of the PAP in the 2013 Punggol by-election is evidence of this shift.

Second, it is becoming harder to attract the traditional elites to politics. The shift away from one-party rule has meant more intense rivalry and politicking. Meanwhile, the electorate's growing interest in politics—coupled with the proliferation of technological tools—has translated into greater public scrutiny of politicians. All this has turned off some of the traditional elites, many of whom are blessed with numerous alternative career options.

### PAP's entrenched grassroots linkages will weaken

For much of Singapore's history, grassroots community activity has been politicised in some way or the other. Government critics frequently lament the close ties between the PAP and the People's Association (PA), a statutory board that, among other things, organises community events and provides services such as free legal advice. However, these ties are weakening in the face of a strengthening opposition and growing public disgruntlement over the apparent use of community structures, roles, and funds for long-term political gain.

## Conclusion

Democracy advocates around the world often assume that authoritarian states will naturally become more democratic as their citizens' incomes grow and they read, travel, and just generally experience more of the outside world.

Going by the Singapore example, it does seem like citizens are clamouring for some aspects of democracy, such as a more active civil society and greater political participation. But it is not at all certain that people want to eschew the one-party state model for a multi-party democracy. An effective political monopoly that governed with nary any opposition or civil society has made Singapore into a developed economy. Perhaps the next stage of political evolution will involve one majority party in government, which is kept on its toes by an active opposition and vocal citizenry.

With more than half the seats in parliament, the PAP can continue to legislate and run Singapore efficiently, avoiding the gridlock that undermines policy implementation in some other countries. But it will have to listen more attentively and sincerely to the alternative opinions and views of the opposition and ordinary citizens, who will together contribute to and improve policymaking.

It seems as if a broad swathe of the electorate, including many current opposition voters, desire this political scenario. But in order for that to happen, the PAP will have to change. It will have to recruit politicians who are representative of the increasing diversity of political views that Singaporeans hold, instead of continuing as a grouping of like-minded elites. On a related note, the party will have to become much more consultative and open to alternative viewpoints.

If the PAP can do all that, it might very well go down as one of the most successful parties anywhere in the world. However, given the available evidence so far—including the PAP's apparent unwillingness to embrace real change, as well as the difficulty the party has had in recruiting candidates quite different from those it has attracted in its recent past—it seems more likely that Singapore's democracy is going to evolve on a trajectory similar to other former authoritarian Asian states. The PAP then will be remembered simply as a highly competent, efficient and ruthless machine—a dramatic experiment that worked in a unique place and at a very specific point in history.

## Notes

1. Robert Dahl, *Democracy and its Critics* (Yale University Press, 1989), 221–22.

2. Less than half of Hong Kong's legislature is elected by popular vote; more than half are appointed under heavy Chinese influence.

3. Singapore's elections are ostensibly free and fair, although there is significant gerrymandering and pre-election fear-mongering.

4. Perry, Kong, Yeoh. *Singapore: A Developmental City State* (Chichester: John Wiley & Sons, 1997), 61–62.

5. *ST*, "PAP: To remain dominant without being dominating," 19 Apr. 2013.

6. Lianain Films, www.lianainfilms.com.

7. *BBC*, "New regulations hit Singapore's online press," 31 May 2013.

8. Braema Mathi, "Growing civil society in Singapore," Social Space 2008, Lien Centre for Social Innovation.

9. James Gomez, "Civil and political society in Singapore and Southeast Asia: Emerging Trends and Definitions," *Singapore Window*, 1999.

10. "The politics of being dominant and dominating," fikir, 24 Apr. 2013.

11. "No to exploiting NGOs, VWOs for political ends," Ministry of Culture, Community and Youth, 29 Apr. 2013.

# 15

# LIBERAL IDEAS IN THE NEW NORMAL

*Donald Low*

Right after the 2011 General Election (GE 2011), it was probably fair to say most liberals and progressives in Singapore believed that the policy and institutional changes that they wished to see would be best advanced by the incumbent PAP government. Most, I think, subscribed to the view that it was preferable for these changes to be driven from within, rather than forced on the government from without. Substantive reforms in a liberal direction, initiated and driven by a secure, confident and still dominant PAP government were (in the minds of liberals and progressives at least) more desirable than politically calculated half measures pursued by a weakened, demoralised regime seeking short-term political advantage.

Almost three years after GE 2011, there are indeed quite a few signs that the government is moving in the right direction. It has made concerted efforts to address the various grievances that had led to the results of GE 2011 and to the other political setbacks that the PAP has suffered since. These include measures to moderate the price of new HDB flats, increase capacity and government subsidies in public healthcare, expand the public transport network to ease over-crowding, and reform the education system to ensure fair opportunities for those with lesser means. Even on foreign worker and immigration policy, still a source of great public unhappiness as the reactions to the Population White Paper attest, an objective assessor would conclude that the government has moved to reduce the country's intake of low-skilled foreign labour—even if it has not moved as quickly or as far as some would like to see.

These reforms should be commended. They are important for restoring public trust in a government that has, in recent years, appeared quite fallible and even incompetent at times. Deputy Prime Minister Tharman Shanmugaratnam's comment in an interview with *Straits Times* in April 2013 that the centre of gravity in the PAP government has shifted to the "left-of-centre" is also noteworthy in this context.[1] It was the first time a senior PAP minister has explicitly signalled a desire by the government to turn left. It also marks an implicit acknowledgement that the growth-promoting policies of the PAP government of the last decade may have come at the expense of social equity and citizen well-being, exposed citizens to risks that should have been socialised, and resulted in outcomes that were less than fair. Such acknowledgement is welcome as any substantive reform programme must first begin with an acknowledgement of the government's recent failings.

## Falling Short

Yet despite the wide range of policy changes that have been undertaken in the last two years, there remains a palpable sense among many Singaporeans of a liberal bent that the pace and scope of reform that the PAP government is willing to pursue falls well short of their expectations. This perception stems partly from the fact that in a number of areas, the results of policy change will take at least a few years to bear fruit. This is especially so with respect to infrastructure investments with a long gestation period. The perception is also partly the result of the PAP's own conservative rhetoric and its constant reminders that Singapore must avoid drastic or destabilising change. In the 2012 PAP conference for instance, Prime Minister Lee Hsien Loong reminded Singaporeans "that we have to be very careful not to go overboard as we recalibrate left a bit, right a bit, don't flip-flop, flip-flop, and turn upside down."[2] This "under-selling" of the government's reforms—already seen by many as modest and limited to begin with—reinforces the impression that this government has not been sufficiently bold or reformist in the last three years.

But more important than the widely held perception that the PAP does not favour radical change is the fact that, compared with how quickly and profoundly Singapore's context is changing, the PAP's appetite for change—in terms of reforming Singapore's growth model, overhauling its population policies, expanding social protection, and liberalising the political system—is considerably smaller than what many deem necessary. This is especially so with respect to two key areas.

The first area is that of inequality. While the government acknowledges that inequality in Singapore has risen in the last decade and that it merits (some) policy action, this has *not* been accompanied by a more fundamental reappraisal of some deeply-held beliefs in government. These include meritocracy, the primacy of economic growth, the belief that prosperity is created by the rich and talented (and so policy must focus on helping them succeed), and the idea that increased welfare spending (which has to be financed by higher taxes) will undermine economic competitiveness. These beliefs continue to be held despite the fact that there is very little empirical evidence to show that countries with lower levels of inequality or more aggressive redistribution pay a large economic price. Indeed, there is some evidence to suggest that the opposite is true.

Still saddled with the belief that trickle-down economics works, the PAP government remains ideologically committed to low income taxes, relatively thin social safety nets, and limited fiscal redistribution. Consequently, even after taking into account government taxes and transfers, inequality continues its relentless march upwards.

The second area where the pace of reform has been slow lies in the realm of political liberalisation and measures to strengthen the democratic rights and liberties of citizens. This compilation of essays has focussed mostly on policy and governance debates. But these debates do not take place in a vacuum: they reflect the wider political context and the political constraints that the participants of the debate must contend with. And the political context in Singapore has been one in which the PAP has achieved its current position of dominance not just through superior performance and results, but also partly through coercive means and suppression of political alternatives.

Since GE 2011, there remains a widespread perception that little has changed with respect to the PAP's readiness to resort to the repressive instruments of the state. These include the Internal Security Act and Sedition Act, its controls on the media and on free speech, the threat of legal action and defamation suits against political opponents, and a wide array of informal but deeply entrenched tools of (soft) coercion that have developed over 50 years of PAP rule. In the months since GE 2011, there have also been enough instances of political coercion and hardball tactics to suggest that when it comes to democratic reforms, change has been even slower than it has been on the technocratic or policy front. To the extent that the PAP regime has "softened" its approach towards critics and dissidents, this is more a function of realpolitik calculations—of what it believes it can or cannot get away with in the new normal—rather than any deeply held belief in the virtues of an open and competitive democracy.

The political analyst and journalism scholar Cherian George has enumerated a list of democratic and institutional reforms that the PAP government still has to undertake to win him (and I suspect, other liberals in Singapore as well) over.[3] These include a requirement for the PAP "not just to tolerate alternative views on a case-by-case basis, but also to protect with passion the space for dissent." Specific institutional reforms George suggests include the establishment of an Ombudsman's office, introducing open government reforms such as the right to information, and taking a stand against the politics of fear by giving up the use of defamation suits to settle political debates, and declaring a moratorium on the use of detention without trial against peaceful political opponents. George would also like to see a truly independent election commission such that the determination of electoral boundaries would be insulated from the executive branch. Meanwhile, mainstream media should be explicitly required to be impartial in its coverage of politics. George contends that such a political system—which embraces political competition and the contest of ideas on a level playing field—might lead to the PAP winning fewer seats, but this disadvantage will be more than offset by the extra legitimacy it would gain from winning those seats fairly. I believe liberals in Singapore will find it hard to disagree with any of the reforms George proposes.

## A Liberal Agenda for the New Normal

The PAP's relative inertia in these areas of inequality and democratic reform are especially worth highlighting because equality and liberty are the ideals closest to the hearts of liberals. Classical liberalism, which finds its origins in Locke, Smith, and Hume, opposes any undue curtailment of an individual's economic or personal freedoms. This explains why liberals generally believe in market economies—not because free markets advance growth, but rather because they enable economic freedom. Liberals thus support political arrangements that make possible the utmost freedom for individuals to pursue their own conceptions of the good life. Governments should remove income and wealth from individuals only when they have excellent reasons to do so.

But liberals also recognise occasions that demand state intervention and regulation. Market failures—of monopoly power, externalities, asymmetric information between buyers and sellers, collective action problems—are familiar to students of economics as a justification for some forms of government action. (Whether governments intervene intelligently or not is another story altogether.) Among liberals, a second justification for government intervention is reducing income and wealth inequalities in a way that does not curb individual freedoms excessively, and in a way consistent with people's preferences for a just and fair society.

In the rest of this essay, I shall try to sketch out what a new, liberal agenda for policy and governance reforms in Singapore might look like.

### A Just City, Not (Just) a Global City

First, liberals have to come to terms with Singapore's inescapable destiny as a city-state. The choice for Singaporeans is not one between Singapore as a city and Singapore as a nation-state. This dichotomy is not particularly helpful. The reality is that Singapore is both: we are both a city and a state. We do not get to choose between the two. The real question is what kind of city-state should we aspire to be? How do we reconcile the demands of Singapore as a city and a land of economic opportunity with those of Singapore as a nation in which questions of identity and citizenship are unavoidable?

Since Singapore's first foreign minister S Rajaratnam gave articulation to it, the idea of Singapore as a global city has animated the PAP's vision for Singapore. But although the idea has been around since 1973, it was only in the 2000s that it was revived by the PAP leadership to frame its ambitions for Singapore in the context of rapid globalisation, the rise of large emerging economies such as China and India, and more searching questions about Singapore's role in an increasingly globalised economy.

Paradoxically, the vision of a global city reflects both the success and failure of the PAP. It is a success because in a short span of under 50 years, the PAP government has come close to realising a vision that its founding fathers articulated, and which at the time of conception, seemed unachievable. But at the same time, the repeated references to Singapore as a global city represent a certain failure. It is a failure in that the PAP government does not seem to recognise the inherent limits, tensions, and contradictions of its global city vision.

The limits of the global city idea became particularly salient in the years just before GE 2011 as Singapore's population surged on the back of very liberal immigration and foreign worker policies, inequality rose from levels that were already much higher than other developed countries, congestion and overcrowding began to undermine citizens' trust in government, and citizens began expressing greater unease about competition from foreigners and the wage stagnation caused by cheap foreign labour. Yet despite ample evidence that citizens no longer automatically accepted the policies motivated by the state's global city ambitions, there has been little change to the PAP's rhetoric in this regard. The reaction of many (if not most) Singaporeans to the Population White Paper—which in many ways, represents a continuation of the global city vision—should give the government pause to reflect on the very real possibility that the global city idea has probably reached the end of its useful lifespan, that it no longer resonates with or inspires Singaporeans, and that it should probably be retired as a vision for the country. As the director of the Institute of Policy Studies, Janadas Devan, asked in January 2013, "Is it possible that we may have reached the limit of Rajaratnam's vision? Is it possible that we have to readjust our relationship with globalisation in order to remain Singapore?"[4]

So what should liberals in Singapore look to as an alternative narrative to the global city idea? The "just city" perspective suggested by Harvard University's Susan Fainstein provides a useful starting point.[5] Fainstein defines a "just city" as having three essential attributes: equity, diversity, and democracy. Rather than view the city only or primarily through the lens of economic growth or competitiveness, Fainstein's framework encourages us to analyse the city through the lens of urban and social justice. Global cities such as London and New York score well on the diversity and democracy dimensions, but they are also much less equal than other rich cities. Others such as Amsterdam and Copenhagen do very well on equity and democracy, but find it hard to absorb and integrate their ethnic minorities.

How does Singapore fare as a just city? At one level, the state's aggressive involvement in urban redevelopment and in providing public housing has helped to foster a sense of community and equity. In the first 40 years of independent Singapore, state and society also forged an egalitarian ethos that frowned on extreme inequality and conspicuous displays of wealth. But our recent experience of high and rising income inequality, coupled with the fact that Singapore has been "importing the world's inequality" (the city attracts extremely well-paid foreign talents and very lowly-paid foreign workers), the city has become much more unequal—and visibly so—in the last decade.

Furthermore, although the city has become more cosmopolitan in recent years, one might also argue that this diversity has been of quite a superficial kind, with well-heeled foreigners ensconced in private estates and gated communities and foreign workers hidden away in their worksites and dormitories. The Little India riot on 8 December 2013 has highlighted the fact that for all our claims to being a diverse, multiracial society, our current conception of diversity does not extend beyond Singaporeans and permanent residents. Foreign workers—there are currently around 1.5 million of them in Singapore, increasing to around 2.5 million by 2030—are seldom viewed as part of the Singaporean community by the government and society at large. Meanwhile, on democracy, it would be a stretch to say that the citizens of Singapore feel that they have significantly more voice and enjoy more democratic rights today than they did a decade ago.

Embracing the idea of a just city would suggest far-reaching, structural reforms in a wide range of public policies and institutions. For instance, taking the diversity and equity objectives seriously would entail a major overhaul of current policies on Singapore's large contingent of guest workers. For a start, it would mean paying them the same wages as Singaporean workers doing the same job. That this is probably not acceptable to many Singaporeans is an indication of how unequal we have become. In highly unequal societies, people tend to view the world in zero-sum terms: what is good for others not like me must be against my interests. They also guard what they have jealously and resist efforts to extend the benefits and privileges they enjoy to other social groups. This is the essence of the inequality trap discussed earlier (*see* chapter 9, "Beware the Inequality Trap"): persistent inequality breeds distrust, suspicion and resistance to measures aimed at improving access to opportunity and resources by marginalised groups, further entrenching inequality.

To ensure that measures that guarantee fairer, more ethical treatment of our guest workers are widely accepted, they have to be complemented by at least two other sets of policy reforms. The first would be to set much tighter immigration and foreign worker policies than what Singapore has allowed in the last decade. This will sharpen incentives for employers to increase productivity and raise wages, especially at the lower-end of the labour market—for Singaporean and foreigners alike. Second, we need to develop a stronger welfare state that gives lower-educated, lower-skilled Singaporeans not just adequate social protection (especially in education, healthcare, retirement funding, and unemployment support), but also stronger incentives to remain employed (for instance, via a significantly enhanced Workfare Income Supplement). Such measures would "compensate" Singaporeans for accepting the economic restructuring that is likely to raise costs, facilitating and securing public support for the process.

A just city perspective also helps liberals to see that the Singapore economy no longer delivers the inclusion and cohesion it did in the past, even if it continues to achieve decent macroeconomic growth rates. Not only has inequality increased significantly in the last decade, but this has also been accompanied by real wages that have been quite stagnant for about a third of the workforce in the past decade or so. The relative decline in wages of those at the lower reaches of the labour market—especially when contrasted with the opportunities available to those at the top and the many sources of advantage they can draw on—represents one of the most significant challenges to the idea of Singapore as a land of opportunity and an inclusive society. Economic growth, on its own, no longer creates the just society that liberals seek.

## Primacy of Well-Being

This leads to a second set of policy and institutional reforms that liberals should strive for, and that is for the state to prioritise citizen and social well-being. In an earlier context—when the Singaporean population was young, wages across-the-board were rising, and economic growth benefitted virtually all segments of society—the emphasis on economic growth was quite sensible. In that context, a social contract that emphasised individual responsibility, low social protection, and minimal redistribution (save for state investments in education and public housing) was appropriate, and probably "fit for purpose". But in an era of an ageing population, a maturing economy, stagnating wages for about a third of the workforce, and growth that no longer lifts all boats, a stubborn insistence on the primacy of growth is hardly desirable or sustainable. This new context calls for new social compact.

Alongside the evolution of a new social compact, we will also need to develop new metrics to measure society's well-being. Growth of per capita GDP is a highly imperfect proxy of individual and social well-being at best. At worst, it distorts society's allocation of resources, erodes the social norms and values that hold societies together, and increases economic instability and fragility.

The higher a country's per capita income, the more perverse the consequences of an unthinking emphasis on economic growth. The Easterlin Paradox, for instance, says that beyond a certain level of income per capita (of around US$15,000 in average income—Singapore is well past that level), further increases in that country's level of income no longer raise the level of happiness reported by citizens. The Easterlin Paradox is a paradox because at the individual level, higher incomes are associated with higher levels of reported happiness. The weak relationship between income per capita and happiness once a country passes a certain threshold of prosperity has been borne out by a number of surveys measuring life satisfaction levels across different countries. At higher levels of income, what matters more as determinants of people's well-being are attributes such as income stability (rather than growth), social trust and equality.

In recent years, some governments have begun to embrace and incorporate the well-being perspective into their national reporting systems. The British government, for instance, began to measure its citizens' life satisfaction levels in 2012.[6] Among cognitive and social psychologists, well-being (or life satisfaction) has also emerged as a major area of research. To summarise a fast-growing field of research, people "thrive" when they have a sense of autonomy and purpose in their lives, security and optimism about the future, rich social relationships, and when they live in high trust societies that foster cooperation.

The Commission on the Measurement of Economic Performance and Social Progress, established by former French president Nicolas Sarkozy in 2009 and led by prominent economists Joseph Stiglitz, Amartya Sen, and Jean-Paul Fitoussi, suggested that instead of focussing on production or GDP growth, countries should focus on measuring and enhancing the well-being of their people. They should also take into account objective and subjective dimensions of well-being or quality of life. Finally, countries should measure and monitor sustainability and environmental pressures.

In prioritising individual and social well-being, measures to foster greater equality are especially important. Equity is positively correlated with social mobility, trust, and many other things that social scientists believe to be necessary for healthy societies. Psychologists have also found that at the individual level, humans have a deep neurological preference for equity. This fairness bias is also found in many other mammals. In a well-known study, capuchin monkeys were found to reject unequal rewards even though they were happy to perform the tasks when there was no differentiation in the rewards.[7]

Social trust in particular has been under-emphasised in Singapore. As argued in the Introduction to this volume, the vulnerability narrative—Singaporeans are taught that only a strong government, a Leviathan, stands between them and racial conflict because of permanent and immutable fault lines—hinders the growth of social trust.

It can also be argued that Singapore state's long-standing emphasis on individual responsibility and on using economic incentives to shape individuals' behaviours has eroded trust. While the use of economic incentives in various domains—transport, housing, healthcare to name but a few—has produced efficient (and mostly desirable) consequences, it may also have produced a number of unintended and undesirable consequences. For instance, the emphasis on economic incentives may have dulled and undermined norms of trust and cooperation. The negative reactions of some Singaporeans to the government's proposals to build eldercare facilities in their neighbourhoods[8] suggest that the government's constant drumbeat on individual responsibility and asset enhancement may have run counter to a sense of commonality and identity. It may also have produced a highly individualistic and atomised society—one in which people see only the "me" rather than the "we"—and eroded norms of trust and inclusion.

Seen in this context, it is hardly surprising that Singapore scores poorly in international comparisons of social trust. Social trust is usually measured by asking the respondents in a country whether "most people can be trusted" or "you need to be very careful in dealing with most people". In the high trust societies of the Nordic countries, Netherlands, and Switzerland, between 50 and nearly 80 per cent of each country's respondents believed that most people can be trusted. The level of social trust in Singapore was just 14.7 per cent in 2002, comparable to the levels recorded in other low trust countries such as Romania, Russia, South Africa, Argentina, and Mexico, and considerably lower than the 35–40 per cent levels reported in United States, Britain, and Germany.[9]

A related consideration for liberals to bear in mind is how the state can foster norms of inclusion and fairness. The work of social psychologists and behavioural economists on how people respond not only to economic incentives (as economists mostly believe), but also to social norms and values, is particularly instructive here. Consider first what the state should do to ameliorate inequality. The standard economic response to rising inequality is to increase taxes on the rich and increase social transfers to the poor. While these measures are clearly necessary in an era of rising income inequality, liberals should also consider how public policies and institutions might strengthen society's norms of inclusion and fairness. The Workfare Income Supplement (WIS) in Singapore—a wage supplement for low wage workers—is an example of a policy that creates the right incentives and supports desirable social norms. As a negative income tax, it aims to "make work pay" and provides stronger incentives for low wage workers to stay in work. But more than that, it also supports norms of inclusion and fairness. A job is not just an income-generating activity: it also enables people to participate more fully in society. Meanwhile, taxpayers are more likely to see transfer payments as fair—and are more likely to support them—if beneficiaries have to work to receive the supplement. This strengthens the ideas of reciprocity and mutual obligation.

Or consider the state's efforts to raise Singapore's declining fertility rate. The emphasis so far has been on enhancing the financial incentives for new parents. At first glance, this appears similar to what the countries that have succeeded in reversing declining fertility rates—for instance, the Nordic countries—are doing. These countries provide a wide range of financial support for parents, ranging from generous childcare support to paid maternity and paternity leave. But closer inspection leads to a different conclusion. The *manner* in which the financial support is provided and the way it is framed probably matter more than the fact that it is provided. In these countries, the language used is not one of incentives and cash gifts, but that of universal and comprehensive social support. Neither do their societies view the child-related benefits narrowly as monetary *incentives* to boost their fertility rates. Rather, the benefits are part of a wider social protection system that includes unemployment insurance, disability benefits, heavily subsidised healthcare, and publicly-financed pensions, all of which reflect these societies' egalitarian ethos and contribute to a sense of solidarity and cohesion. Norms of gender equity are also an important factor in explaining the Nordic countries' relatively high fertility rates. It is this wider social compact that may explain their relatively high fertility rates, more so than any specific pro-natal "incentives".

The lesson for policymakers in all this is not that economic incentives do not work or produce perverse consequences. Behavioural economists have also highlighted instances where financial incentives complement and work in tandem with intrinsic motivations as well as instances where incentives reinforce valuable social norms. What policymakers should strive for are policy solutions that create the right incentives and reinforce and support desirable social norms, such as those of fairness and inclusion. Policy should not go against the grain of incentives and people's psychology. What matters just as much as the policy itself is its *social context.*

This emphasis on getting not just incentives right, but also getting institutions and norms right, leads to a third perspective that liberals should embrace: viewing society as a complex adaptive system, rather than as a "machine" that can be (socially) engineered.

### Society as a Complex Adaptive System, Not an Engineered One

As elaborated many times in this book, one of the defining characteristics of the PAP regime has been its belief in the inherent and immutable vulnerability of Singapore—a condition that justifies and legitimises "exceptional" policies and institutional arrangements. This belief has very much shaped the PAP's approach to governance and policymaking. It explains the government's prioritisation of political and social stability, suppressing things that pose the slightest risk of offending racial or religious sensibilities and preserving laws, such as the Internal Security Act and Sedition Act, which give the executive wide-ranging powers to suppress conflicts. The Singapore state's "social engineering" approach to governance reflects its belief that Singapore society is fragile; much like Humpty-Dumpty, once it is broken, it cannot be put back together.

The social engineering approach to governance is not always conducive for fostering social or political resilience. To understand why this might be so, consider what gives a biological system, a species, or any complex system resilience. In the same way a muscle becomes stronger by being stretched and stressed, a biological or evolutionary system becomes more resilient by developing responses to a wider array of shocks and stimuli. Ashby's Law of Requisite Variety says that "(only) variety can destroy variety." A system's resilience is dependent on the range of responses it can mobilise relative to the types of disturbances and perturbations it is subject to. The greater the number of shocks or disturbances that a system might be subject to, the larger the variety of responses it must be able to muster. A system that lacks the requisite variety risks collapse if it encounters a sudden shock or disturbance for which it has not developed an appropriate response.

In some respects, Singapore is already quite resilient. Consider the Singapore economy. The government understands that what makes the economy stronger is not insulation from competition and shocks, or the suppression of diversity and variety. It knows that what enables an economy to thrive is its exposure to external forces and influences, and the relentless pressure to compete in and adapt to an uncertain, fast-changing environment. Although the Singapore economy is not without active government interventions to organise and "design" it (e.g., through the use of industrial policies that target particular sectors), there is nonetheless a greater acceptance of the state's limited ability to precisely control its evolution. Markets here are mostly free from heavy-handed government interventions, and although the state pursues activist industrial policies, it has been disciplined enough to ensure that these support, rather than replace or supplant, markets.

In political and social management on the other hand, there is much less willingness to accept the messiness, shocks, uncertainty and unpredictability that arise from the interactions of a dynamic, complex system. Here, the policymaker's instincts are still very much those of social engineering: control, order, stability and the avoidance of shocks or crises. Policymakers tend to think primarily in terms of mitigating and avoiding shocks to a fragile society, rather than in terms of adapting to them or developing greater resilience to deal with them. They also tend to think of the future as a linear and mechanistic extension of the present, as if sociopolitical developments are governed by stable and predictable causal laws.

This desire to engineer social and political outcomes is borne of the state's deeply held vulnerability perspective. Because government leaders view the world essentially through the lens of Singapore's inherent, immutable vulnerabilities—of geography, of the country's lack of natural resources, of our ethnic make-up— they conclude that this island's "natural" state is that of a stagnant backwater. That Singapore is a vibrant metropolis must therefore be the result of superior elite governance and social engineering. And having become a vibrant metropolis, Singapore's political leaders struggle to conceive of how this place can be governed differently. After all, the social engineering approach has worked for a large part of Singapore's history. This success, sustained over several decades, has bred ideology, inertia and incumbency (i.e., the unwillingness or inability to question existing assumptions and worldviews, and to disrupt and challenge these modes of thinking). Success, whether of a country or a company, often sows the seeds of its own destruction.

The corrective to the view of society and politics as systems that can and should be engineered is to understand them as biological systems—complex, highly connected or networked, and frequently unpredictable in how they evolve. This appreciation of society and politics as a complex adaptive system has a number of implications for the liberal state, the most important of which is that it too must become a complex adaptive system. This means that it should eschew simplifying dogmas or truisms in government, such as the idea that people only respond to incentives, or that markets are always efficient, or that welfare erodes competitiveness. Instead, the government ought to rely a lot more on experiments, the use of randomised controlled trials and evidence-based policymaking. For policymakers, this means a greater willingness to question and challenge received wisdoms in the government.

Governance as a complex adaptive system also requires policymakers to embrace debate and dissent, both inside and outside of government.[10] If freedom and equality represent liberalism in substantive terms, protecting and institutionalising debate and dissent represent liberalism in procedural terms. This requires the government to be willing to consider ideas previously deemed taboo, and to actively and deliberately gather outside views that challenge its own. This diversity and contest of ideas is necessary for Singapore's long-term survival in the same way that other biological systems thrive as a result of variety and selection. For the same reason that the market system is resilient—because it promotes variety and selection through competition—so too must a governance system develop the mechanisms to generate diverse ideas and promote a healthy competition of these ideas. A properly functioning democracy, like a functioning free market, is not always optimal or efficient. But like markets, they can be extremely *effective* in generating the requisite variety of policy and institutional responses to our ever more complex problems.

## Conclusion

The PAP's inability to change ideologically or change fast enough resembles, in many ways, Clayton Christensen's story of the innovator's dilemma.[11] Established firms in an industry are naturally resistant to disruptive innovations that threaten their existing capabilities and cannibalise their existing products. A collection of the brightest scholars in Cabinet might at first sight appear to be a means of assembling the capabilities needed to drive and manage change. In practice, it is a means of gathering everyone who has benefited the most from the current system and who therefore struggle to see why change is needed or desirable.

As a liberal, the policy and institutional changes I wish to see are those that would make Singapore a more just city-state, one that prioritises the well-being of its citizens over narrow measures of economic progress. Achieving these require the government of the day to go beyond its old beliefs in the virtues of elite governance, of social engineering and of the primacy of growth—all grounded in the idea of Singapore as an exceptionally vulnerable and fragile state. This constant harping on Singapore's vulnerability has not given way to a more secure, confident, and resilient Singapore. Neither has it made citizens more autonomous and less dependent on the PAP state. Instead, as various essays in this collection have argued, it has produced an economy and society that are less than what Singapore can be. Increasingly, the vulnerability narrative is an albatross around Singapore's neck, a binding constraint and a psychological barrier that limit the potential of this country and its people.

Abandoning ideas and values that we have always held dear is never easy—especially if those ideas and values are seen to be the very reason for our success. But given profound changes in Singapore's context—both domestically and externally—the policy, institutional, and political changes advanced in this series of essays are no longer hard choices confronting Singaporeans: they are also critical for Singapore's continued success.

## *Notes*

1. *Straits Times*, "Cabinet "more left-of-centre now; helping the lower income," 19 Apr. 2013, http://www.straitstimes.com/breaking-news/singapore/story/cabinet-more-left-centre-now-helping-the-lower-income-20130419.

2. Lee Hsien Loong, Speech at PAP's 2012 Party Conference, 2 Dec. 2012, http://maintmp.pap.org.sg/uploads/ap/8435/documents/secgen_party_conference_speech_2012.pdf.

3. Cherian George, "What would make me a fan?," *Air-conditioned Nation*, 27 Dec. 2012, http://www.airconditionednation.com/2012/12/27/the-pap/.

4. Janadas Devan, Opening Remarks at Singapore Perspectives 2013, https://www.youtube.com/watch?v=SDIBbW3rCLs.

5. Susan Fainstein, *The Just City* (Ithaca: Cornell University Press, 2010). For a summary of the ideas in *The Just City, see* Prof Fainstein's lecture at the Centre for Liveable Cities, Singapore on "Principles of a Just City," https://www.youtube.com/watch?v=zIP1kImZwBA.

6. Office for National Statistics, "Measuring National Well-being: Life in the UK, 2012," 20 Nov. 2012, http://www.ons.gov.uk/ons/dcp171766_287415.pdf.

7. *See* for instance, "Capuchin monkeys reject unequal pay," http://www.youtube.com/watch?v=gOtlN4pNArk.

8. In 2012, news reports highlighted a number of Singaporeans voicing their concerns over eldercare facilities being built in their vicinities: for example, some residents of Woodlands, over the proposed construction of a day care centre for the elderly; some residents of Toh Yi estate in Bukit Timah, over plans to build an eldercare facility; and some residents in Bishan, over plans to build a nursing home.

9. Data on countries' social trust can be obtained from the World Values Survey Longitudinal Data File 1981–2008 comprising the waves 1981, 1990, 1995/1998, and 1999/2000, 2005/2008 and the European Values Survey Longitudinal Data File 1981–2008 comprising the waves 1981, 1990, 1999, and 2008. http://www.wvsevsdb.com/wvs/WVSIntegratedEVSWVSinfo.jsp?Idioma=I.

10. For more on why diversity, dissent and debate are necessary, Margaret Heffernan's *Wilful Blindness: Why we Ignore the Obvious at Our Peril* (New York: Walker & Company, 2011) and Tim Harford's *Adapt: Why Success Always Starts with Failure* (London: Little, Brown, 2011) provide excellent overviews of the research by cognitive and social psychologists, evolutionary biologists and complexity theorists.

11. Clayton Christensen, *The Innovator's Dilemma: When New Technologies Cause Great Firms to Fail* (Cambridge: Harvard Business Press, 1997).

# INDEX